Fatherhood and the British W(1865–1914

A pioneering study of Victorian and Edwardian fatherhood, this book investigates what being, and having, a father meant to working-class people. Based on working-class autobiography, the book challenges dominant assumptions about absent or 'feckless' fathers, and reintegrates the paternal figure within the emotional life of families. Locating autobiography within broader social and cultural commentary, Julie-Marie Strange considers material culture, everyday practice, obligation, duty and comedy as sites for the development and expression of complex emotional lives. Emphasising the importance of separating men as husbands from men as fathers, Strange explores how emotional ties were formed between fathers and their children, the models of fatherhood available to working-class men, and the ways in which fathers interacted with children inside and outside the home. She explodes the myth that working-class interiorities are inaccessible or unrecoverable, and locates life stories in the context of other sources, including social surveys, visual culture and popular fiction.

JULIE-MARIE STRANGE is Senior Lecturer in History at the University of Manchester. She is author of *Death, Grief and Poverty, 1870–1914* (Cambridge, 2005).

The working-class family: Alfred Hartley, calico print labourer, and his wife, Sarah, with children, Alfred and Albert, c.1907.

Fatherhood and the British Working Class, 1865–1914

Julie-Marie Strange
University of Manchester

CAMBRIDGE
UNIVERSITY PRESS

University Printing House, Cambridge CB2 8BS, United Kingdom

One Liberty Plaza, 20th Floor, New York, NY 10006, USA

477 Williamstown Road, Port Melbourne, VIC 3207, Australia

314-321, 3rd Floor, Plot 3, Splendor Forum, Jasola District Centre, New Delhi - 110025, India

79 Anson Road, #06-04/06, Singapore 079906

Cambridge University Press is part of the University of Cambridge.

It furthers the University's mission by disseminating knowledge in the pursuit of education, learning and research at the highest international levels of excellence.

www.cambridge.org
Information on this title: www.cambridge.org/9781107446861

© Julie-Marie Strange 2015

This publication is in copyright. Subject to statutory exception and to the provisions of relevant collective licensing agreements, no reproduction of any part may take place without the written permission of Cambridge University Press.

First published 2015
First paperback edition 2018

A catalogue record for this publication is available from the British Library

Library of Congress Cataloging in Publication data
Strange, Julie-Marie, 1973–
Fatherhood and the British working class, 1865–1914 / Julie-Marie Strange.
pages cm
ISBN 978-1-107-08487-2 (Hardback)
1. Fatherhood–Great Britain–History–19th century. 2. Fatherhood–Great Britain–History–20th century. 3. Working class families–Great Britain–History–19th century. 4. Working class families–Great Britain–History–20th century. 5. Working class men–Great Britain–History–19th century. 6. Working class men–Great Britain–History–20th century. 7. Great Britain–Social conditions–19th century. 8. Great Britain–Social conditions–20th century. I. Title.
HQ613.S77 2015
306.874′2094109034–dc23   2014035054

ISBN 978-1-107-08487-2 Hardback
ISBN 978-1-107-44686-1 Paperback

Cambridge University Press has no responsibility for the persistence or accuracy of URLs for external or third-party internet websites referred to in this publication, and does not guarantee that any content on such websites is, or will remain, accurate or appropriate.

For
David William Strange
Who worked hard for his children

Contents

	Acknowledgements	*page* viii
	Introduction: O Father, where art thou?	1
1	Love and toil: fatherhood, providing and attachment	21
2	Love and want: unemployment, failure and the fragile father	49
3	Man and home: the inter-personal dynamics of fathers at home	82
4	Front stage values, back stage lives: family togetherness, respectability and 'real' fathers	111
5	Funny talk: laughter, family and fathering	145
6	The fond father: protection, authority, reconciliation	177
	Conclusion: discovering fatherhood	211
	Bibliography	216
	Index	231

Acknowledgements

The research for this project was generously funded by the ESRC (RES-000-22-2966). I am grateful to the AHRC (Arts and Humanities Research Council (grant ref: AH/I001875/1) for funding time to write up the research. Thank you to Joanna Bourke and David Feldman who were early supporters of the project. The book has been incubating for some time and I appreciate all the colleagues who turned out for conference or seminar papers over the years. I would especially like to thank Helen Rogers who staked a claim for taking fathers seriously with a conference, co-organised with Trev Lynn Broughton, at Liverpool John Moores in 2003. For encouragement, advice and feedback at different stages and in different contexts, many thanks to Andrew Davies, Ginger Frost, Simon Gunn, Laura King, Jon Lawrence, Donna Loftus, Lucie Matthews-Jones, Daniel Miller, Michael Roper, Ellen Ross, Valerie Sanders, Claudia Soares, Carolyn Steedman, John Tosh and David Vincent. Claudia Nelson and Susan Egenolf are the very best of colleagues. I would particularly like to thank Megan Doolittle whose generosity in sharing her considerable expertise on family and fathers I very much appreciate. Thanks to my students at the University of Manchester and to my colleagues, especially the Modern British cohort, Anne-Marie Hughes, sympathetic Heads of Department Hannah Barker and Paul Fouracre, Penny Tinkler and to Mike Sanders and Bertrand Taithe who have listened to a lot of father talk and have been generous with feedback. Eloise Moss and Caroline Yorston undertook much transcription and their input was invaluable: thank you. Lily Rose Matthews took my library of working-class autobiographies in hand, organised them and created a spreadsheet of texts so that I might stop buying multiple copies of the same book. Many thanks to readers at Cambridge University Press and to Michael Watson who is a model of patience.

Steve Humphries of Testimony Films gave me the opportunity to disseminate the findings of the early research through *A Century of Fatherhood* (BBC4 2010). Versions of Chapters 1 and 3 appeared in

Historical Journal, 55:4 (2012), 1007–27 and *Urban History*, 40:2 (2013), 271–86 respectively.

To George Dent and the Dent Collective (not least Pepper, very clever collie dog): big love. Like many of the autobiographers discussed in this book, I am grateful to both my parents, David and Christina, for their parenting and the sacrifices they made to enable me to get to, and through, university. This book is, of course, partly our story too.

Introduction: O Father, where art thou?

'Is the working-class father as black as he is painted?' The question was posed by the district nurse, M. E. Loane, in the first line of a chapter on 'The working-class father' in her collection of short essays, *From their point of view* (1908). As Loane noted, the 'prejudice' that the working-class father was rough, drunken and profane was 'so strong' that even commentary in his defence was apt to be misread or ignored. Why, Loane asked, was he always out of favour? True, he was no paragon of long-term planning and had limited powers to control or direct the future of his offspring. But did this make him 'less affectionate' than the bourgeois paterfamilias? For Loane's part, she admired working men's patience, good humour, pride and 'genuine personal feeling' for offspring. There were 'no bounds' to what a 'mere ordinary' father might do for the sake of his children.[1] Some ninety years later, the historian Lynn Abrams echoed Loane's lament. Despite historians' discovery of Victorian bourgeois men as fathers, the working-class man remained out of favour: he was 'rarely associated with home', 'still less' with his children and located overwhelmingly in work, the pub or club, his allotment or with his pigeons. When historians and contemporaries talked about 'family', they overwhelmingly meant mothers and children. This 'unflattering' portrayal identified working men as 'absent fathers', a prototype of the absent father of tabloid reportage at the end of the twentieth century. As Abrams noted, working-class fathers existed, for sure, but working-class father*hood* remained uncertain.[2]

Loane's essay on the working-class father noted that readers often took it for granted that middle-class fathers were self-sacrificing, solicitous and devoted. Was the working-class father that different? This book seeks to develop Loane's question and address the persistent gap in histories of

---

[1] M. E. Loane, *From their point of view* (London: Edward Arnold, 1908), 144–56.
[2] Lynn Abrams, 'There was Nobody like my Daddy: Fathers, the Family and the Marginalisation of Men in Modern Scotland', *Scottish Historical Review* 78:2 (1999), 219–42.

the working-class family that Abrams identified. It advances a counter-narrative to histories and contemporary commentaries that rely on a 'deficit' model of fatherhood, that is, a focus on the failures, flaws and shortcomings of men.[3] The book acknowledges that feckless, tyrannical or absent fathers existed, to be sure. But, it argues, they do not represent the family experience of most working-class children. This is not to say that working-class fathers were paragons of virtue or sentimental fathers. Rather, it suggests that fathering meant different things, at different times, to different actors: much depended on context.

Engaging with working-class autobiography, this book deviates from most social histories of the working-class family in that it does not dwell on contested contributions to domestic economy, spousal dynamics, differences within and between elements of the working class, specific labour issues or claims to citizenship. Neither does the book trace the development of welfare and social policy on family life during the late Victorian and Edwardian periods. Superb studies addressing these issues exist already. The established scholarship highlights the marginalisation of fathers as parents by labour, state and voluntary organisations in favour of mothers and compounds that marginalisation by focusing, overwhelmingly, on men in family life as women's husbands or, it refracts men's role as fathers through the prism of male claims for suffrage and representation. Rather, this book looks to working-class autobiographers for a research agenda and follows the preoccupations and priorities of authors in producing meaningful and coherent life stories. It interrogates how children and fathers invested meaning in paternal identities and practices. In doing so, it distinguishes men as fathers from men as mothers' husbands. It also alights on unexpected facets of family stories, such as the importance of laughter and comedy. Focusing on authorial literary styles and processes of reflection, the fathers and children under discussion in this book are often multiple characters in one story; their roles and dynamic rarely stayed the same over the life cycle.

*

The standard text on working-class family is Ellen Ross's 1993 monograph, *Love and toil*. An excellent and important book, it is unmistakeably about mothers: the clue is in the subtitle, *Motherhood in outcast London, 1870–1918*.[4] Scholarship that focuses on women's experience and

---

[3] Adrienne Burgess, *The Fatherhood Institute: advocating for involved fatherhood in the UK, 1999–2012* (London: The Fatherhood Institute, 2012).
[4] Ellen Ross, *Love and toil: motherhood in outcast London, 1870–1918* (Oxford: Oxford University Press, 1993).

oppression will inevitably sideline men in family life because they are peripheral to the story being told, or, they are present as the negative embodiment of patriarchy.[5] However brilliant Ross's study of women and children, it does not tell the story of fathers. Yet it is impossible to fully understand child development and women's inequality if we fragment family into opposing interest groups that do not necessarily map onto lived experience.[6] Carolyn Steedman urged in 1986 that history needed to consider how (non-bourgeois) fathers mattered and to interrogate father-child relationships, 'not just a longing that they might be different'.[7] More specifically, classic histories of women and family do not unpack the differences between women's relationships with husbands and children's dynamic with fathers.[8] In interpersonal terms, a husband is not the same as a father. Likewise, histories that chart the negative interventions of some men in some families do not necessarily enable us to understand how, as adults, children explained and understood the micro-workings of family inequalities and everyday unhappiness.[9]

Prescriptive literature and official welfare policy in the nineteenth century increasingly diminished the significance of fathers while motherhood gained increasing ideological importance and responsibility. Claudia Nelson's *Invisible Men: Fatherhood in Victorian Periodicals, 1850–1910* (1995) and, to a lesser extent, John Gillis's, *A World of Their Own Making: Myth, Ritual and the Quest for Family Values* (1996) identified the 'absence of fatherhood' rather than the absent father: men were fundamental to Victorian legal and political definitions of family but, aside from that, they were 'strangers' who hovered on the threshold of

---

[5] Abrams, 'There was Nobody like my Daddy'.
[6] As Burgess stresses, this is not the same as claiming that fathers are 'victims': such an approach risks, equally, forgetting to embed fathers within family life and overlooking the fact that, clearly, 'men are still the ones with the power'. Burgess, *The Fatherhood Institute*, 23; 29–31.
[7] Carolyn Steedman, *Landscape for a good woman* (London: Virago, 1986), 18–19.
[8] Classic examples of the women's history approach to 'family' include: Elizabeth Roberts, *A woman's place: an oral history of working-class women, 1890–1940* (Oxford: Blackwell, 1984); Carl Chinn, *They worked all their lives: women of the urban poor, 1880–1939* (Manchester University Press, 1988); Andrew August, *Poor Women's Lives: Gender, Work and poverty in late-Victorian London* (London and Cranbury: Associated University Presses, 1999); Jane Lewis, *The politics of motherhood: child and maternal welfare in England, 1900–1939* (London: Croom Helm, 1980); Jane Lewis, (ed.), *Labour and love: women's experiences of home and family, 1850–1940* (Oxford: Blackwell, 1986). An exception to the trend is Joanna Bourke's *Working-class cultures in Britain, 1899–1960* (London: Routledge, 1994), 81–95. Bourke conflated husbands with fathers to a degree in examining the power dynamics of domestic space but she at least recognised that men had different roles to perform within family contexts.
[9] For a sociological perspective on everyday unhappiness in families see Carol Smart, *Personal life: new directions in sociological thinking* (Cambridge: Polity Press, 2007), 133–55.

everyday and interpersonal family life.[10] John Tosh's groundbreaking *A Man's Place: Masculinity and the Middle-Class Home in Victorian England* (1999) sought to locate men in family life and correct the stereotype of the Victorian father as merely a disciplinarian who believed children should be seen and not heard. The 'tyrannical' father existed but in a minority; his fathering probably said more about a dysfunctional personality than about fatherhood in general. For Tosh, three other kinds of father were also readily discernible. First, the 'absent' father: men who spent little time with offspring, were aloof, irritated and bewildered by the world of children. Tosh makes the point that this, too, is a common stereotype of the Victorian father, recycled in histories because it foregrounds the late-twentieth-century preoccupation with encouraging fathers to be more 'involved'. Far more common to most bourgeois families' experience, Tosh asserted, were distant or fond fathers.

The distant man was deeply concerned with the responsibility of parenthood but manifested his obligations and responsibilities in anxiety for his children's moral welfare and unease with what seemed the 'feminine' world of affection and play. Tosh's moving study of Edward Benson's hard-hearted fathering in the 1860s and 70s demonstrates the chasm between what his children experienced, a harsh and intimidating man, and what the father imagined, that his adherence to duty gave adequate intimation to the fulsome love he felt towards his children, expressed only in correspondence with his wife. His children realised their father's affection for them after his death when they read their parents' letters. In many ways, this distant father was the most perplexing because he hovered on the periphery of family life, uncertain of his place within it. In stark contrast, the 'intimate' or fond father enjoyed demonstrative and easy familiarity with his offspring: they were playmates and friends with a respect for the authority and protection of fathers.[11] In the preface to the paperback edition of *A man's place* (2007), Tosh wryly commented on the criticism he received for his discussion of 'tender and tolerant' fathers as a 'gratuitous feelgood approach'. Some reviewers were so attached to the negative stereotype of Victorian paterfamilias as the emblem *par excellence* of patriarchy that they were unwilling to counter the possibility that not all fathers quite fit that mould.[12]

---

[10] Claudia Nelson, *Invisible Men: Fatherhood in Victorian Periodicals, 1850–1910* (Athens, Georgia, and London: University of Georgia Press, 1995); John Gillis, *A world of their own making: a history of myth and ritual in family life* (Oxford University Press, 1997).

[11] John Tosh, *A man's place: masculinity and the middle-class home in Victorian England* (New Haven: Yale University Press, [1999] 2007), 91–100.

[12] Tosh, *A man's place*, xi–xii.

Thankfully, studies post-Tosh confirmed the complexity of the bourgeois father.[13] Most recently, Valerie Sanders's *The tragi-comedy of Victorian fatherhood* (2009) traced fathering among the intellectual and cultural elite. Sanders's fathers by turn are affectionate, demanding, suffused with self-recrimination and guilt, cross at the shortcomings of offspring, consumed by grief for dead children, educators and guides, disciplinarians and friends.[14] Despite the inclusive title of the book, Sanders's fathers were a relatively small group of men. The ongoing conflation of 'Victorian' fatherhood with bourgeois men perpetuates assumptions that working-class fathers' experiences are 'other' without interrogating what those experiences might be or, how working-class actors invested meaning in paternal identities and processes. The focus on histories of bourgeois fatherhood since the 1990s is, perhaps, a reflection of the ready availability of sources for middle-class interiority but, also, that middle-class scholars have a preconceived notion of what affect and attachment look like that precludes interrogation of obscure working-class selfhoods. Aside from studies of fatherhood in popular culture and social science in the mid-twentieth century, the interpersonal dimensions of working-class fatherhood remain obscure.[15] Yet, as Steedman noted, we must resist the temptation to gloss working-class lives with the 'patina of stolid emotional sameness'.[16]

Research into working-class men and family remains preoccupied with paternal role and its relation to family economy, citizenship, men and work and the highs and lows of spousal relations.[17] Histories of working-class family life in the late-nineteenth and early-twentieth centuries rely

---

[13] See especially, Eleanor Gordon and Gwyneth Nair, 'Fathers and the Victorian Parental Role', *Women's History Review* 15:4 (2006), 551–9; Valerie Sanders, 'What do you want to know about next? Charles Kingsley's model of educational fatherhood' in Trev Lynn Broughton and Helen Rogers (eds.), *Gender and fatherhood in the nineteenth century* (Basingstoke: Palgrave, 2006), 55–70; Elizabeth Buettner, 'Fatherhood real, imagined, denied: British men in Imperial India' in Broughton and Rogers, *Gender and fatherhood*, 178–189.

[14] Valerie Sanders, *The tragi-comedy of Victorian fatherhood* (Cambridge University Press, 2009).

[15] See especially Tim Fisher, "Fatherhood and the British Fathercraft Movement, 1919–1939', *Gender and History* 17:2 (2005), 441–62; Laura King, *Family men: fatherhood and masculinity, c.1914–1960* (Oxford University Press, 2014).

[16] *Ibid,*, 12.

[17] See for example, Ginger Frost, *Living in sin: co-habiting as husband and wife in the nineteenth century* (Manchester University Press, 2008); Anna Clark, *The struggle for the breeches: gender and the making of the British working class* (London: Rovers Oram, 1995); Matthew McCormack, 'Married men and the fathers of families: fatherhood and franchise reform in Britain' in Broughton and Rogers, *Gender and fatherhood*, 43–54; Andrew Walker, 'Father's pride? Fatherhood in industrialising communities' in Broughton and Rogers, *Gender and fatherhood*, 113–125.

overwhelmingly on official discourse. Inevitably, such methodologies reproduce a contemporary fixation with separate spheres and the increasing social welfare policies targeted at mothers. They focus on the minority of fathers who were drunk, violent or who deserted their families. Even accounts of good husbands tend to place them in a negative context; they did not drink their wages nor did they beat their wives.[18] Likewise, the dominant chronology of social reform skews the research agenda towards legislation and policy initiatives aimed at cementing the 'family wage' and men and women's prescribed roles within it. This closes down potential questions about everyday working-class life and imposes a model on working-class family members that does not necessarily tally with the priorities of individuals seeking to make sense of childhood experience.

At the outset of this project, I also turned to the substantial corpus of social investigation and commentary on working-class family life. The vast majority of these texts discuss men as agents of family decline, through drink, wilful idleness or brutality. Where studies did engage with working or 'respectable' men, it was primarily in the context of the labour question and economics. Little wonder the 'absent' or 'feckless' father is such a perennial figure in histories of the plebeian family; other kinds of fathers are literally 'absent' from the political, welfare or social family story.[19] It is not surprising that despite Abrams's call to take up the cause of 'invisible' fathers, there has been little published scholarship to rectify working-class men's peripheral status in the family story. A notable exception to this trend is Megan Doolittle's incisive mapping of the power dynamics of family life in relation to gender, age and fathers' responsibilities.[20]

In the introduction to their collection of essays on gender and fatherhood in the nineteenth century, Trev Lynn Broughton and Helen Rogers (2007) mapped the key sites in which Victorian fatherhood had

---

[18] Lynn Abrams, 'There was nobody like my daddy'.
[19] This is not to say that these sources cannot be used in others ways. The development of a critical literature on the 'slum imaginary' and analysis of social investigators' motives is one example. See for instance, Seth Koven, *Slumming: sexual and social politics in Victorian London* (University of Princeton Press, 2004) and Ellen Ross (ed.), *Slum travellers: ladies and London poverty, 1860–1920* (Berkeley, London: University of California Press, 2007), 1–39.
[20] Megan Doolittle, 'Missing Fathers: Assembling a History of Fatherhood in Mid-Nineteenth Century England', PhD Thesis, University of Essex, 1996; Megan Doolittle, 'Fatherhood and family shame: masculinity, welfare and the workhouse in late-nineteenth-century England' in Lucy Delap, Ben Griffin and Abigail Wills (eds.), *The politics of domestic authority in Britain since 1800* (London: Palgrave Macmillan, 2009), 84–108; Megan Doolittle, 'Time, space, and memories; the father's chair and grandfather clocks in Victorian working-class domestic lives', *Home Cultures*, 8:3 (2011), 245–264.

typically been the subject of scholarly analysis: the law, industrialisation, demography and fertility and religion.[21] These could only partially account for fatherhood as experience and identity. Rather, they argued, fatherhood needed to be approached as a process whereby men could embrace the multiple dimensions of fathering and family over the life course.[22] This book runs with Broughton and Rogers's model of fatherhood, constituted of multiple components that certainly brought power but also responsibilities, pleasures and anguish, and that were subject to continual contextual change.

*

Walter Citrine was born in Liverpool, 1887. He wrote his autobiography at the age of seventy-seven having spent his adult life engaged in trade union activism and Labour politics. His mother was a hospital nurse before she married Citrine's father, a widower seafarer, in 1881. Citrine had five siblings, including a half-brother from his father's first marriage. Citrine said little of his mother except that he loved her, bore deep gratitude for her self-sacrifice on behalf of her children and that she was a 'kind soul'. His discussion of his father focused overwhelmingly on the ship rigger's working life and identity. Citing neither love nor gratitude, Citrine rehearsed his father's youthful adventures at sea combined with reflections on the sailor's lot, and the impact of his father on home life. A strong and powerful man, Citrine Senior was inclined to fight and drink heavily, sometimes standing drinks for mates instead of handing his wages immediately to his wife.

And there we might leave Citrine and his father: so far, so predictable. Adult children (especially males) were grateful for the sacrifices of their mothers but said little about feelings for their fathers. Although working-class women rarely fit bourgeois or twentieth-century conceptions of the loving mother, their battle to feed, clothe and nurse offspring to better futures was a well-established trope of mother love.[23] The same children were typically more circumspect about fathers. Sure, most worked for their families but these men spent comparatively little time at home (especially the seafarer who left for weeks or months at a time) or engaged in what we commonly recognise as 'nurturing' tasks. The vast majority of working-class adults who grew up at the turn of the twentieth

---

[21] See also Leonore Davidoff, Megan Doolittle, Janet Fink and Katherine Holden, *The family story: blood, contract and intimacy, 1830–1960* (London and New York: Longman, 1999), 135–57.
[22] Trev Lynn Broughton and Helen Rogers, 'Introduction: the empire of the father' in Broughton and Rogers, *Gender and fatherhood*, 1–30.
[23] This is the key argument shaping Ellen Ross's *Love and toil*.

century replicated official bifurcations between women and men, home and work. Although such polarisations reflect a degree of lived experience, scholarship on working-class domestic economy shows that, financially at least, the sexual division of labour was usually muddier than that.[24] The implications of this polarised model, however, mapped onto the affective economy of family, places fathers at the periphery of family life, as Citrine's memoir might initially suggest.

The objective of my book is to complicate this model. Citrine sketched out a familiar dynamic: mother and children formed a unit of togetherness while father made contributions or incursions to that unit. But he, and his peers, rarely left their stories there. Neither should we. This book is interested in adults, like Citrine, and the stories they told about late Victorian and Edwardian fathers. Citrine's account of his father's labour was a story of sacrifice. On a literal level, labouring for his family took a significant toll on the man's body: his hand was crushed, he lost two fingers, his knee smashed, he was shipwrecked three times and each sailing was a dalliance with death. Citrine presented his father's everyday martyrdom as different entirely to that of his mother. Hers was rooted in the domestic interior and readily associated with her children; his father's sacrifice took place outside the home. The older man's courage, 'wonderful stamina' and determination to survive hardships that 'would have killed many men' were in no doubt. More to the point, although situated beyond the domestic, the meaning Citrine invested in his father's experience was grounded firmly within family.

The older man was flawed: he sometimes drank and shouted belligerently about the house. Nevertheless, Citrine did not depict his father in one-dimensional terms as merely feckless or neglectful, for this was not who his father was all the time. He had long periods of sobriety, drank mostly beer (although if he did drink spirits, his temper was foul) and became far steadier as he got older. He often threatened to thrash his offspring but never delivered; he was neither cruel nor inconsiderate; he defended his children against other men's violence; he had a clear intelligence and masterful personality. His father enabled Citrine's occupational future, securing him an apprenticeship on the understanding that his son would forego wages (in other words, the family forfeited wages) for the first six months in lieu of his father paying an apprenticeship premium he could not afford.

As a staunch trade unionist and Labour peer, the adult Citrine's 'labour' angle on his father's life was not surprising. Yet this emphasis hinted at other kinds of interchange too, where a father's strength,

---

[24] This is discussed further in Chapter 1.

courage and work provided a prism through which father and son could communicate. When his father ran a ship around the port to check that all was in working order, he would take the young Citrine with him for a boys' own adventure. Citrine knew so much about his father's work because, when the older man came home, he regaled his family with stories of the sea in all its terrible glory: they 'drank in every word' of his quarrels, escapades and accidents aboard ship. Work remained a mode of 'man-talk' for Citrine and his father as the boy matured into the trade union activist and successful politician. After his father retired, Citrine acted as amanuensis, recording his memories.

Inevitably, politics featured in Citrine's reconstruction of his childhood. As a boy, Citrine had donned a blue rosette and accompanied his Conservative father to political meetings, helping him canvass for local elections. 'What was good enough for my father', Citrine reflected, had been 'good enough for me.' Citrine's mischievous tone made the serious point that parents, and particularly fathers who, after all, were the ones with the vote, were strong formative influences on offspring while hinting at the young boys' admiration for, and pride in, the father that so often gave way in juvenile years to a bid for independence and varying degrees of conflict. That his father became a Labour voter in his older years suggested that father and son continued to talk politics, the Labour child delighting in his Tory pater's defection across the political divide. More importantly, Citrine's autobiography indicated the ways in which relationships that characterised childhood adopted different hues throughout the life cycle. As Citrine noted, people had to develop or they stagnated. The adult Citrine, a proud father of two sons, viewed his father from an entirely different perspective to the boy(s) he had been.[25]

Drawing on the published autobiographies of working-class children born between c.1865 and 1910, this book interrogates, first, the caveats, qualifications and motivations that characterise personal accounts of fathers and, second, the ways in which authors chose to relate stories of fathers. As Citrine's career as a politician, government minister and peer indicates, many authors of published autobiography were exceptional.[26] But what makes them so exceptional is their banal beginnings. If Citrine and authors like him were extraordinary, it is notable that their siblings, cousins and friends were usually markedly more pedestrian. Census returns for 1891, 1901 and 1911 show that three of Citrine's brothers

---

[25] Walter Citrine, *Men and work: an autobiography* (London: Hutchinson, 1964), 11–27; 54–5; 61.
[26] Citrine felt the need to explain at length his peerage: he claimed it as a necessary responsibility to get Labour representation in the House of Lords. *Ibid*, 310–322.

trained as a pupil teacher, a locksmith's apprentice and a sheet metal worker. His sister was a laundry clerk. None of them appears to have been distinguished in public life at local, regional or national level.

A pioneer of reading working-class autobiography as historical source, David Vincent argued that authors with exceptional life outcomes were able to 'project a pencil of light into the darkness of unspoken memories' of others whose 'lives were conditioned by the same social experience'.[27] The life stories considered here were written by political activists, trade unionists, Labour politicians, campaigners for adult literacy, lay ministers, clergymen and evangelists, and agrarian, industrial and domestic workers. Some were written as propaganda, entertainment, self-examination or morality tales; others fell into a 'commemorative' genre, charting a disappearing world. Mostly men composed published autobiography. Vincent pointed to the reasons for this: the exclusion of women from working-class organizations that proved a stimulus and guide to self-expression; the lack of women who attained public position in this period; the subordinate position of women within the family (they were too busy to write and the important task of committing family stories to posterity was left to men); and that they lacked self-confidence.[28] Other scholars have focused on women's reluctance to write about themselves as a form of feminine self-effacement.[29] When women did write, they were typically much more explicit about interpersonal dynamics, family conflicts and men at home. They were also alive to the gendered dynamics of family life. In her study of three working and lower-middle-class women's writing on fathers, Helen Rogers pointed to the particular sensitivity of female authors to paternal nurturing and their acute perception of the uneven separation of work and family in households.[30]

It is notable that, with the over-representation of male autobiography, relatively few authors studied here paid explicit critical attention to the gendered dynamic of family. It is likely that many male authors unthinkingly replicated the inequalities of their parents' relationship in their marriages. Certainly, almost all the male authors cited here subscribed

---

[27] David Vincent, *Bread, knowledge and freedom: a study of nineteenth-century working-class autobiography* (London and New York: Methuen, 1981), 7.

[28] *Ibid*, 8–9.

[29] For discussion of relationship between female self-effacement, autobiography and the camouflage of biography, see Helen Rogers, 'In the name of the father: political biographies by radical daughters' in David Amigoni (ed.). *Life writing and Victorian culture* (Aldershot: Ashgate, 2006), 145–164.

[30] Helen Rogers, 'First in the house: daughters on working-class fathers and fatherhood' in Broughton and Rogers, *Gender and fatherhood*, 126–37.

to the ideology of the 'family wage' and, while articulating sympathy and admiration for the hard labour performed by women as wives and mothers, rarely questioned the sexual division of labour. Relatively few even mentioned the raft of family-centred legislation aimed at reducing infant mortality rates and improving infant health in the Edwardian period, and where they did, it was in the context of mothers. The sympathy male authors typically articulated towards mothers operated as a kind of proxy for acknowledging that they, too, had wives whose identities were grounded in domestic labour and childcare and that, as fathers, they were absent for large chunks of their children's lives. For all the drawbacks of men's overrepresentation in autobiography, the preponderance of male stories does facilitate particular attention to masculine modes of expression concerning family relations. Further, most male authors were fathers by the time they composed memoirs, adding authorial insight into the dynamic between what being and having a father meant.

Most of the female autobiographers represented here were ambitious: a female medical practitioner, activists in adult education and politics and writers. For the most part, they drew sympathetic alignments with fathers, not least from a desire to share in men's freedoms while criticising the structures that limited their mothers' (women's) opportunities and trapped them in domestic servitude. Though sensitive to the gendered assumptions embedded in adult memories of childhood, the book does not aim to rehearse the criticism of, or regret for, those assumptions but, rather, to interrogate how adult men and women gave meaning to sexed parenting practices and identities and, in many cases, how they made those practices meaningful.

Like many of his peers, Citrine professed awkwardness in writing about his life, claiming to have written only in response to requests from friends.[31] He wanted to keep the intimate, 'beautiful' aspects of his life private in favour of focusing on the political. He dedicated a mere fifteen pages to recounting his childhood up to his leaving school. Even then, Citrine's family story was politically charged, in its contemplation of work, economy, hardship and responsibility. His agenda was firmly rooted in a masculine world of Labour/labour, as exemplified by the book's title: *Men and Work*. Most of the life stories featured in this book

---

[31] The majority of the book charted Citrine's career in relation to major (Labour) national and international (Russia, the West Indies and the rise of Nazism) events. Gagnier notes how working-class authors typically began life stories with the discomfort of differentiation. Regenia Gagnier, *Subjectivities: a history of self-representation in Britain. 1832–1920* (Oxford University Press, 1991), 139–50.

were political to an extent, even if only through commentary on everyday inequalities. In telling their stories, class, gender and politics were inseparable from personal life. The inextricability of family stories from wider issues and preoccupations does not diminish their value. If anything, it amplifies the importance of family as the locus, in real time and memory, for challenging (and surviving) inequalities, forming and rehearsing political opinions – that is, politics with a small and capital 'p'.

Inevitably, adult authorial identities shaped the telling of life stories.[32] This is not a weakness of autobiography; it is its great strength. Autobiography is a deliberate composition, with emphasis on particular events and characters, written in a chosen genre with particular stylistic modes and edited for coherence. Accounts of fathers in this context were never accidental. Indeed, this is why I decided to eschew oral history testimonies because they were invariably a dialogue between interviewer and interviewee. Certainly, the oral history collections available for this period are very much a product of a particular moment in social history (the late 1970s and 80s) and reflect contemporary preoccupations (and polarisations) of investigators.[33]

The family offers an interface that highlights how individuals constitute the self as an ideological subject. For some commentators, this has proven a limitation of working-class autobiography: the personal forever treads a fine line with the political.[34] For me, this is a resource. In the Citrine example, his narrative of childhood provided a matrix through which to view the formation of his politics; his politics also provided a lens through which to constitute the personal. When authors told stories about the 'public' components of fatherhood (work, leisure, politics), they were also telling stories about the men they believed their fathers to be, their values and how those men mattered to them (or, in some cases, did not). Similarly, stories of fathers at home or in play often advanced an implicit, sometimes explicit, critique of socioeconomic conditions. Home and family were (and are) places where inequalities were rehearsed and resisted: when autobiographers recreated childhood family characters and plots, they tended to provide blueprints for life on the 'outside', too.

Citrine's introduction made myriad claims for the reliability of his memory. This was a common device in autobiographies that sought to

---

[32] *Ibid*, 138–70.
[33] When I began the research for this, I trawled several large collections of oral histories. I kept a handful of these stories but decided to leave oral histories of family for a different project because the material is so different.
[34] See Gagnier's discussion of the public/personal dimensions of working-class autobiography. Gagnier, *Subjectivities*, 138–50 and Nan Hackett, 'A Different form of self: narrative style in British nineteenth-century working-class autobiography', *Biography* 12:3 (1989), 208–26.

chart a 'public' history and one's place within it. Other life stories, especially those written by authors who achieved success as novelists or journalists, were less strident about authenticity. For writers who made their living from fiction, the dramatization of autobiography was not only inevitable but also desirable. Autobiographical accounts of childhood were often psychological rather than literal accounts.[35] In her recent exploration of the everyday life of the English working class, Carolyn Steedman urged that historians could, and should, practise stylistic analysis of working-class (and other) texts instead of simply mining them for empirical information.[36] This book is not preoccupied by the reliability or 'truth' of memory. Along with some oral historians, the book takes the line that the frailty (or creativity) of memory can be a historical resource.[37] The choices authors made in constructing the stories of their childhoods provide insights into how adults thought fathers 'mattered', in real time and in reflection.

Numerous scholars have identified the inter and post-war periods as key moments when notions of interiority and personality development replaced 'Victorian' models of character and self-control as tools for fashioning identity.[38] Retrospectives on late Victorian and Edwardian families written in this period acquire extra significance in this context. The majority of authors discussed here were alert to psychological models of behaviour and the importance of childhood in personal development. Some, such as Edwin Muir and D.R. Davies, had consulted psychoanalysts and their autobiographies were characterised by introspection and self-analysis. Others inferred that their childhood experiences had shaped their adult selves, whether by acting as a motor to political commitment, in developing personalities or explaining particular life choices and outcomes.[39] Some authors applied mid-twentieth-century popular models of psychology to the character of their fathers in

---

[35] Gagnier, *Subjectivities*, 52.
[36] Carolyn Steedman, *An everyday life of the English working-class: work, self and sociability in the early nineteenth century* (Cambridge University Press, 2013), 13–28.
[37] Alistair Thomson, 'Unreliable Memories? The use and abuse of oral history' in W. Lamont (ed.) *Historical Controversies and Historians* (London: UCL Press 1998); Luisa Passerini, 'Work, Ideology and Consensus under Italian Fascism', *History Workshop Journal*, 8 (1979), 82–108; Penny Summerfield, 'Culture and Composure: creating narratives of the gendered self in oral history interviews', *Cultural and Social History*, 1:1 (2004), 65–93.
[38] See especially Michael Roper, *The secret battle: emotional survival in the Great War* (Manchester University Press, 2011).
[39] Edwin Muir, *An autobiography* (London: The Hogarth Press, 1954) and David Davies, *In search of myself: the autobiography of D. R. Davies* (London: Geoffrey Bles, 1961). For an example of childhood as a motor to adult interest see, George Barber, *From workhouse to Lord Mayor: an autobiography* (Tunstall: The Author, 1937).

a bid to explain men's affective lives. Grace Foakes tried to love her father but he consistently rejected her. Foakes laid complaints about her father's lack of affection at his mother's feet; she had never been demonstrative towards her children.[40] William Bowyer represented his father as deeply disturbed. Bowyer not only mined his father's past to explain the older man's shortcomings, but also used those flaws to explain the imperfections of his adult authorial self.[41] Other authors, such as A.V. Christie, acknowledged popular psychology only to reject its relevance to interpreting their stories.[42]

Whether authors self-consciously embraced new modes of psychology or not, recreating one's past demanded an imaginative leap – authors assigned meanings to experiences, personalities and relationships that enabled them to explain their current place in the world. Matt Houlbrook emphasises that self-fashioning takes place in a particular historical moment, in specific milieux.[43] The autobiographies studied here were published mostly between the 1930s and 1960s. Notably, by the interwar years, models of fathering continued to value breadwinning but had extended to include more domestic and leisure-time dimensions. A concept of family 'togetherness' was evolving in which fathers were still not as emotionally important as mothers but were, increasingly, expected to engage with offspring.[44] Authors had to explain their late Victorian and Edwardian fathers in a context that was significantly different from their childhoods. Notably, many authors took pains to explain how the Victorian paterfamilias was 'involved', caring for and attached to offspring but in ways that differed to the modern 'fun dad'.

Social conceptions of love changed, too. Claire Langhamer has identified the mid-twentieth century as a key moment in the crystallization of idealized notions of love, especially romantic love.[45] Reading emotion in working-class autobiography is hindered by most authors' avoidance of explicit expressions of sentiment or seemingly inappropriate details of private life in documents that overwhelmingly were public accounts of political selves. Citrine assiduously avoided sentiment and insights into

---

[40] Grace Foakes, *Four meals for fourpence: a heart-warming tale of family life in London's old East End* (London: Virago, 2011), 122.
[41] William Bowyer, *Brought out in evidence: an autobiographical summing up* (London: Faber and Faber, 1941).
[42] This is also revealing of attitudes towards psychology and family life. A. V. Christie, *Brass tacks and a fiddle* (Kilmarnock: Author, 1943).
[43] Matt Houlbrook, 'A pin to see the peepshow: culture, fiction and selfhood in Edith Thompson's letters, 1921–22', *Past and present*, 207 (2010), 215–49.
[44] See King, *Family men*.
[45] Claire Langhamer, *The English in love: the intimate story of an emotional revolution* (Oxford University Press, 2013).

his 'private' life. When authors did attempt to convey emotion, they tended to be fall back on cliché or tight-lipped expressions that intimated little more than stoicism. Some historians have seen authors' limited vocabularies of interiority as a difficulty of working-class narrative.[46] Certainly, language is important. Michael Roper pointed to the process by which writing is a negotiation between experience, internal states and cultural forms that permit expression of those states. In this light, we have to consider that (even) cliché can be freighted with profound significance to the person deploying it.[47] In the chapters that follow, analysis of father-child dynamics interrogates what authors chose to narrate about fathers, the language and narrative devices they used, as well as the content of stories told. The vast majority of authors focused on anecdotes about their fathers rather than recounting their feelings for them. Nevertheless, the stories indicate what mattered and, in their construction, suggest how fathers matter. Accounts of what father did were rarely just that. Rather, authors narrated their fathers' public status (the 'macro' story of paternity) to infer more intimate ('micro') evaluations of the man.

Notions of maternal love were well defined by the mid-twentieth century while increasing demands on fathers to be playmates or 'pals' also suggest an evolving conception of fatherly 'love'. It is doubtful how useful these categories of love really are, especially given that feelings defined as love often change over time and that late-nineteenth century official notions of working-class parental relationships to children were defined through obligation rather than feeling. A few of the autobiographers I discuss in this book were explicitly troubled by the gap in twentieth-century models of 'love' and the apparent lack of a verbal language of love in their childhood experience. Some authors were certain they had no love for or from their fathers; most simply never mentioned it. I have followed the lead of autobiographers and avoided the word 'love' unless autobiographers name it.

'Love' has a lot of baggage and I find it difficult, even if we acknowledge that love incorporates much that is ambiguous and messy, to talk about 'love' without the spectre of idealised love hovering in view. There is also the problem of sentimentality: Victorian popular culture seeped with sentiment and, yet, sentimental was a dirty word.[48] It seems likely

---

[46] Vincent, *Bread, knowledge and freedom*, 39–61.
[47] Michael Roper, 'Splitting in unsent letters: writing as a social practice and a psychological activity', *Social History*, 26:3 (2001), 318–39. See also, Roper, *The secret battle*, 23; and, Michael Roper, 'Slipping out of view: subjectivity and emotion in gender history', *History workshop journal*, 59 (2005), 57–72.
[48] Carolyn Burdett, 'Introduction to New Agenda: sentimentalities', *Journal of Victorian Culture*, 16:2 (2011), 187–194.

that some authors were aware of the modernist disdain for sentiment and strove to avoid mawkishness for fear it would diminish the seriousness of their stories. It is possible to identify a kind of magical enchantment with fathers for some autobiographers but this often served, especially for male authors, as a self-conscious mode of indicating the child's immaturity. Therefore, I have replaced love with 'attachment'. Although attachment has its roots in John Bowlby's emphasis on the importance of bonds formed between mothers and babies, the term has, in recent decades, expanded to incorporate the abstract and affective meanings invested in myriad social practices across the life cycle. It conveys the significance and ambivalence of bonds without necessarily carrying idealised expectations.[49] Crucially, we cannot equate an autobiographical absence of explicit languages of 'love' for fathers with an absence of individuals' profound feelings for, and about, them. W. J. Brown, for example, concluded that although he had never 'loved' his father, experience and maturity facilitated 'better' understanding of him and 'deepened my admiration for his endurance and his courage'. Brown moved from childhood resentment towards his father, towards ambivalence, to finally embrace his father as an empathetic figure of tragedy: 'Poor Father!'[50]

In charting the emergence of 'emotions' as a field of research, the sociologist Carol Smart suggests a distinction between studies of love and studies that analyse 'near to' love: care, commitment, marriage and romance.[51] For Smart, there is a danger that focussing on 'near to' love diverts attention away from affection in everyday life towards 'more readily calibrated notions of duty, obligation and even contract'.[52] Certainly, studies of the working-class father in a historical context do focus on these areas, especially men's obligations to provide, without

---

[49] This is particularly pertinent to issues of 'foster' or 'looked after' children. See Anne Collins, *Attachment* (London: Fostering Network, 2008); Susan Goldberg, *Attachment and development* (London: Arnold, 2000).

[50] William J. Brown, *So Far* (London: George Allen and Unwin Ltd., 1943), 17–19, 75–9.

[51] Of course, the history of emotions has dramatically expanded, too. 'Classic' texts include William Reddy, *The navigation of feeling: a framework for the history of emotions* (Cambridge University Press, 2001); Peter Stearns, *Be a man! Males in modern society* (New York: Holmes and Meier, 1979) and Peter Stearns and Carol Zisowitz Stearns, *Anger: the struggle for emotional control in America's history* (Chicago; London: University of Chicago Press, 1986); Barbara Rosenwein, *Emotional communities in the early Middle Ages* (Ithaca, N.Y.; London: Cornell University Press, 2006); and, Thomas Dixon, *From passions to emotions: the creation of a secular psychological category* (Cambridge University Press, 2003). See also, Linda Pollock, 'Anger and the negotiation of relationships in early modern England', *Historical Journal*, 47:3 (2004), 567–90; Martin Francis, 'Tears, tantrums, and bared teeth: the emotional economy of three Conservative Prime Ministers, 1951–1963', *Journal of British Studies*, 41:3 (2002), 354–87.

[52] Smart, *Personal life*, 54–5.

consideration of the affective dimensions of duty. But duty and obligation need not distract from feeling. Doolittle's analysis of shame in relation to men's failure to provide is a notable example of this.[53] My study explicitly focuses on the acts Smart defines as 'near to' love. Instead of calibrating duty, however, I interrogate how the performance and understanding of obligation and everyday practice can be steeped in feeling. This book suggests that authors mediated subjective identities and interpersonal relationships through reflection on everyday obligations. This does not detract from affection but examines how mundane, everyday practices are inflected with affective significance. For some authors, fathers' performance of paternal obligations was transcendental: it transformed the mundane into the beautiful, provided interpersonal validation in macro socio-economic terms, and made 'near to' acts of love into intimate acts of devotion. Conversely, men's shortcomings in performing 'near to love' practices provided an index for authors to chart their disenchantment with, and detachment from, fathers.

★

The book addresses the memories of adults who grew up in a broad range of families described in social and economic terms as 'working class': through occupation, skilled and unskilled, and income; housing, from one or two rooms in so-called slums to agricultural cottages to terraced houses with bay windows; values, beliefs and a subjective sense of being 'other' to bourgeois lifestyles and opportunities. I present urban and rural lives, including a handful of gypsy travellers. The book focuses on men who assumed the responsibility of providing for children. I incorporate the small number of authors who depicted fathers as deliberately idle or vicious. But I am keen to clarify that this book is not about the group we might variously know as the unemployable, the 'underclass' or, in more explicitly loaded and problematic parlance, the 'rough'. At the same time, I would resist saying that the book is about the group historians have referred to as 'the respectable'. Such categories are misleading at best (and there is a notable absence of such value-laden groupings for describing the bourgeois classes). Many of the authors cited here described fathers in much more complex terms than 'respectable' or 'rough'. I do, however, pay attention to the instances where authors invoked notions of 'respectability' as a public model of esteem that enabled the articulation of more personal intersubjectivities.

[53] Doolittle, 'Fatherhood and family shame'.

The book is organised thematically. As family welfare legislation and social policy reform focused overwhelmingly on motherhood, I have not felt the need to follow the chronological progression of late Victorian and Edwardian policymakers' discourse. Certainly, I did not find that Edwardian social policy reforms affected authors' stories of paternal identity and father-child relations, either through explicit commentary on those reforms or in discernible differences between authors born in the 1870s and those born in the 1900s. Some autobiographers, particularly those writing in a commemorative genre, referred to little or no chronological specificity; others situated their stories temporally in terms of birth date and made only fleeting reference to major events, notably, the First World War and, to a lesser extent, the Boer War. Most authorial chronologies had personal significance (for example, the time before and after a parent had died) or were important for locating the life in the broader (usually) political story. Labour, trade union and adult education memoirs tended to note the absence of welfare provision, particularly for unemployed men, sick pay or holidays with pay; the introduction of free education; and welfare legislation such as pensions, national insurance and, eventually, the welfare state. Most of all, the majority of autobiographers writing in the mid-twentieth century drew a line between generations: their late Victorian and Edwardian Liberal or conservative fathers were different to the notional 'new generation', that is, sons and daughters born towards the end of an era who were pivotal in making change.

Many authors began their family stories by reproducing the sexual division of labour: fathers were absent from home and childhood most of the time because they were in work. This is the cliché of working-class fathering: good men worked hard for their children. Chapter 1 interrogates this cliché and how it was used in life stories to indicate the complexities of father-child dynamics and, more particularly, the profound personal significance of men's wage labour. Work was the principal area through which authors mediated gratitude towards fathers and demonstrated, like Citrine above, their father's sacrifice and devotion to his children. Chapter 2 examines how children navigated the correlation between love and toil when they related stories of fathers' unemployment. To a point, this was easier to discuss in a twentieth-century context when National Insurance embodied models of unemployment as a structural problem rather than moral failing. Stories that focused on the pity of men's unemployment validated the introduction of welfare schemes while staking a claim for men's right to work. Nevertheless, the shame of unemployment haunted autobiographers who sought to explain how, in the absence of social welfare, fathers legitimated paternal status through alternate channels. This gives rise to a model of unemployed fathering not as failure but, rather, as fragility. This chapter also draws on the case studies of unemployed families by social investigators Seebohm Rowntree and Bruno Lasker in which fathers, and their wives, sought to validate men's household and family status in the context of unemployment.

Chapter 3 challenges the assumption that plebeian men were peripheral to home. It contests the prejudice in social histories towards narrating stories of men's presence as a negative influence on 'family' (mother and children) life. Some fathers were, of course, violent, tyrannical or disruptive; many were not. This chapter focuses on the banal everyday practices of home, such as the consumption of tea (the evening meal) and fathers' habitual occupation of household space. In paying attention to the materiality of home, it argues for a move away from scholarly analysis of working-class consumption as rooted in aspiration to examine how individuals appropriate objects to mediate social relationships. The chapter demonstrates the literal presence of men in the home, how children invested their presence with meaning and used men's time and space to engage in particular father-child intimacies, and how, even in their absence, men's things and spaces functioned to remind family of Father.

Chapter 4 turns to men's leisure to unpick how adult children gave meaning to the activities fathers selected for themselves and exceptional times when families came together, notably at Christmas and holiday. Family times provided rare moments in (some) autobiographies for outlining family intersubjectivities. Nevertheless, the chapter contests easy correlations between time and togetherness. Relatively few autobiographers recalled spending much time engaged in activities with fathers that were *for* children. Instead, they concentrated on relating men's leisure interests as indicators of his values and identity outside of work. This enabled authors to propose a father's 'authentic' self, as opposed to his generic proletarian identity, to locate him on a macro scale of esteem and, crucially, to intimate his status and significance as *my* father.

Chapter 5 examines laughter, comedy and fun in autobiography. First, it considers the genre of tragi or 'grim' comedy as a medium for narrating traumatic family experiences and managing the unhappiness of everyday life. Not only could authors wield comedy as a retrospective weapon to exact narrative revenge on fathers; the puncturing of masculine authority and vanity through the medium of comedy facilitated a kind of emotional labour, whereby children could manipulate the trauma of the past to reorder the abstract hierarchies of family life. The chapter also considers questions of who laughed in family stories, when, at what, and with whom, for insights into the affective alliances and antagonisms of family, and how these shifted over time. Finally, the chapter suggests that we take comedy and triviality in working-class autobiography seriously. Notably, an analysis of funny stories about men and babies, alongside memories of unsophisticated fun in family life, illustrate the ways in which laughter could operate as a masculine mode of attachment that enabled men to talk about children in particular ways.

The final chapter returns to authors' accounts of paternal obligation, with a focus on authority and protection. It begins by considering men's duty to discipline children and the problems of navigating chastisement as a marker of paternal obligation and affection, particularly when violence was so readily associated with the feckless father in official and welfare discourse. As with providing, however, some authors appropriated accounts of paternal authority and protection as stories of father-child intimacy. Paternal authority and protection of course could be a burden: on fathers when they failed to protect, and on children who found protection oppressive. The chapter concludes by suggesting how paternal attempts to protect or guide children could operate as powerful motifs for the ultimate rejection of fathers or, reconciliation and connectedness, in later life.

A minority of autobiographers' fathers were literally absent from very young childhood, either because they died or absconded.[54] Biological fathers and men who brought up children as their own (notably, grandfathers but, also, stepfathers, uncles or adoptive fathers) are the subject of study. I have avoided discussion of father figures, although it is notable that children without fathers, or who were detached from fathers, frequently identified a moral or intellectual father figure in making sense of their life stories.[55] Only when we situate fathers with mothers in conceptualising the working-class family can we begin to understand the importance of family, in all its formations, as a site for the constitution of self.

---

[54] See for instance, Philip Inman, *No going back* (London: Williams and Norgate, 1952); Ralph Finn, *Time remembered: the tale of an East End Jewish boy* (London: Hale, 1963); Edgar Wallace, *People*: a short autobiography (London: Hodder and Stoughton, 1926); George Reilly, *I walk with the king* ed. by Sarah Reilly (London: Epworth Press, 1931).

[55] See for instance, Percy Brown, *Round the corner* (London: Faber and Faber, 1934), 34.

1 Love and toil: fatherhood, providing and attachment

> *As he spoke he leaned over and touched the hand of the sleeping child and the little fingers closed round one of his with a clutch that sent a thrill through him... 'We've always got through somehow or other', he repeated, 'and we'll do so still.'*[1]

The quotation above, from Robert Tressell's *The Ragged Trousered Philanthropists* (1914), is from the final pages of the novel. The protagonist, Owen, is a 'good man' who works hard for his family, including the illegitimate babe he and his wife have adopted. A sick man physically, Owen is also sick with industrial capitalism. He struggles to make ends meet in a context where work is irregular, poorly paid and his ill health presents a recurring obstacle to lifting his dependents out of poverty. Through Owen, Tressell demonstrates how the good man's desire to work for his dependents was inextricable from his affection for them. Throughout the novel, Owen contemplates death as the family's real solution to their difficulties but his love for them outstrips his murderous urge. Tressell emphasises the extent to which Owen's son, Frankie, adores and idolises his father, enacted in the easy tactility between them. As the excerpt above demonstrates, Owen's acceptance of paternal responsibilities for 'this little helpless, dependent' babe adds to the financial burden of family but thrills him simultaneously. Fatherly obligation, here, is given coherence and meaning by the affective rationale and reward that underpins it. As an allegory for the ideals and frustrations of the emergent socialist movement, Owen's family story demonstrates the extent to which men's breadwinner responsibilities were charged with political and personal significance. Like many of the autobiographical fathers discussed in this book, Tressell's breadwinners struggle to survive industrial capitalism, a struggle that their families' lives reflected and reproduced. As this chapter demonstrates, for Owen and men like him, toiling for dependents was a transcendental act of devotion.

---

[1] Robert Tressell, *The Ragged Trousered Philanthropists* (London: Flamingo, 1993), 585.

The 'breadwinner model' is the lens through which most historians have analysed and evaluated working-class family life. Examination of fathers within this model, as far as it goes, tends to concentrate on their waged contributions to domestic economy and matters of respectability, power and privilege. The gap between families' economic experience and the ideology of male breadwinning is well recorded.[2] As numerous studies have shown, 'breadwinning' was a fractured process whereby men may have had the capacity to earn higher wages but household resources were supplemented by working wives and older children. Certainly, few autobiographers' fathers were 'breadwinners' in the strict sense; but this did not necessarily diminish the meanings invested in father's work. If breadwinning had objective criteria, measurable through wages earned, participation in labour markets and paid-work time, analyses of the subjective elements of breadwinning at the end of the nineteenth century coalesced around notions of 'respectability' and women's experience of financial dependency on husbands.[3] Within this model, the tasks of parenting, that is, feeding, nurturing and training, fell to women and were associated with 'mothering', a distinction embedded in poor law relief by the end of the nineteenth century.[4] In contrast, father practices were grounded in earning sufficient wages to support the family and, crucially, handing them over to the household. For sociologists and historians, this division of labour in parenting tasks also can be classified as 'caring about' (breadwinning) and 'caring for' (nurturing) children.[5]

The assumed correlation between domestic life and mothers excludes men as active affective agents although the 'provider' model is not

---

[2] For classic studies on the rise of the breadwinner ideal see, for example, W. Seccombe, 'Patriarchy stabilized: the construction of the male breadwinner wage norm in nineteenth-century Britain', *Social History*, 11 (1986), 53–76; S. Horrell and J. Humphries, 'The origins and expansion of the male breadwinner family: the case of nineteenth-century Britain', *International Review of Social History* 42 (1997), 25–64; Colin Creighton, 'The rise of the male breadwinner family: a reappraisal', *Comparative Studies in Society and History*, 38 (1996), 310–337; C. Creighton, 'The rise and decline of the "Male Breadwinner Family" in Britain', *Cambridge Journal of Economics* 23:5 (1999), pp. 519–41; J. Lewis, 'The decline of the male breadwinner model: the implications for work and care', *Social Politics* 8:2 (2001), 152–70.

[3] For good overview of objective and subjective criteria for 'breadwinning' see Tracey Warren, 'Conceptualising breadwinning work', *Work, Employment and Society*, 21 (2007), 317–36.

[4] See especially, Anna Clark, 'The new poor law and the breadwinner wage: contrasting assumptions', *Journal of Social History*, 34:2 (2000), 261–82 and M. Levine-Clark, 'The gendered economy of family liability: intergenerational relationships and poor law relief in England's Black Country, 1871–1911', *Journal of British Studies*, 45:1 (2006), 72–89.

[5] Megan Doolittle, 'Fatherhood, religious belief and the protection of children in nineteenth-century English families' in Broughton and Rogers, *Gender and fatherhood*, 31–42 and Warren, 'Conceptualising breadwinning work'.

divorced from men's family commitment. A sufficient number of social historians have drawn attention to wives' and children's claims that financial providers were 'good' men for the model to have become a cliché.[6] Scholars also acknowledge that the purchase of consumer goods or payment for services, for example, children's funerals, from wages represented one of the principal modes of men's expression of attachment to family.[7] Located within a framework of family economy, paternal providing and protection may be understood as intrinsic to a system of exchange in which wages were traded for authority and privilege. Men's status as 'good' husbands and fathers in this model depended upon the rate of exchange and most studies of the working-class family have focused on what this meant for mothers, wives and children. Acknowledging that the majority of working-class men were 'good', they worked hard and handed over wages for housekeeping, pioneering studies of working-class family life inevitably focused on the dark side of breadwinning. While trade unions harnessed the breadwinner model to champion men's claims to representation and better working conditions, the ideology worked against the occupational, political and economic interests of women. Joanna Bourke gave a lively account of women's navigation of power dynamics within the family while Ellen Ross's insightful analysis of working-class marriage noted that, statistically speaking, 'good men' were common but her discussion focused on women's difficulties and resentments towards the 'family' wage.[8] Other approaches emphasised the diffuse elements of authority associated with breadwinning, such as claims to the best food, and the deep-seated shame when men failed to earn enough.[9]

---

[6] This is the classic social history line on family and household economy. See Roberts, *A woman's place*; Bourke, *Working-class cultures in Britain*; A. Davies, *Leisure, gender and poverty: working-class culture in Salford and Manchester, 1900–39* (Milton Keynes: Open University Press, 1992); Karl Ittmann, *Work, gender and family in Victorian England* (London: Macmillan, 1994); W. Seccombe, *Weathering the storm: working-class families from the industrial revolution to the fertility decline* (London: Verso, 1993).

[7] See Ross, *Love and toil*, 192–4; Julie-Marie Strange, *Death, grief and poverty in Britain, 1870–1914* (Cambridge University Press, 2005).

[8] Bourke, *Working-class cultures*, 67–71; Ross, *Love and toil*, 72–6. See also Sonya O. Rose, 'Gender antagonism and class conflict: exclusionary strategies of male unionists in nineteenth-century Britain', *Social History*, 13 (1988), 191–208; and, Katrina Honeyman and Jordan Goodman, 'Women's work, gender conflict and labour markets in Europe 1500–1900', *Economic History Review*, 44 (1991), 608–628.

[9] See for example, S. Horrell and D. Oxley, 'Crust or crumb? Intra-household resource allocation and male breadwinning in late-Victorian Britain', *Economic History Review* 52:3 (1999), 494–521; Megan Doolittle, 'Fatherhood and family shame, 84–108; Doolittle, 'Time, space, and memories, 245–264.

Yet, there is little interrogation of the ways that fathers and children appropriated men's work as a process that mediated abstract ties or as a language for explaining fatherly attachments to the outside world, or how they changed over time. Historians' focus on mothering has perpetuated a model of household relations that privileges maternal love and toil. This chapter revisits the relationship between providing and fatherhood to assess how adult children aligned male wage labour with affective ties and what providing meant for understanding and articulating father-child attachment in a public context where autobiographers had become providers too. Particular attention is paid to the recollections of sons who were implicated in a model of parenting that valued wage earning as the principal component of father practices; for those authors committed to labour politics, stories of men's work adopted further significance. Accounts of late-Victorian and Edwardian family life produced in a mid-twentieth-century context had to navigate shifting expectations of parenting, especially parents' presumed increased emotional investment in children as birth (and infant death) rates declined and the emergence of what John Gillis called the 'fun dad' in the inter-war period, a kind of Sunday leisure fathering.[10] This is not to devalue mothers' waged or emotive labour in families or to suggest that children's relationships with mothers and fathers were the same. Rather, the chapter seeks to redress the relative neglect in histories of working-class family life of how children understood and imagined attachment to fathers.

Duty and devotion

Most working-class accounts of late-Victorian childhood focus on the role of mothers to reflect women's presence in domestic labour and time although, as Ellen Ross noted in her magisterial *Love and Toil: Motherhood in Outcast London, 1870–1918* (1993), few autobiographers writing in the mid-twentieth century associated contemporary models of idealised maternity with personal experience. Ross's mothers were neither tactile nor sentimental. Nevertheless, children's effusive regard for seemingly distant mothers demonstrated how the practices of motherhood could operate as a language of love. Maternal identities were rooted in working hard for children: 'love and toil' were inextricable.[11] Mothers' work was so integral to *being* a child that, for some autobiographers, mothers were 'not a person really' but a sensibility and service; most sick or troubled children knew they wanted their mother.[12]

---

[10] Gillis, *A world of their own making*. [11] Ross, *Love and toil*, 3–10.
[12] See for instance, Elizabeth Bryson, *Look back in wonder* (Dundee: David Winter and Son Ltd., 1966), 29; Foakes, *Four meals for fourpence*, 15–25; 37–52; Silvester Boswell, *The*

Fewer authors wrote explicitly about attachment to fathers. Nineteenth and mid-twentieth-century conceptions of fatherhood rooted paternity in financial provision, the framework for family security, self-identity and children's access to opportunities.[13] Life story conventions tended to reflect and perpetuate such assumptions, especially when authors were circumspect about including intimate detail in texts that recorded political, educational and social change. When adult children did locate fathers in the composure of their past, they turned to men's labour, and the domestic comforts purchased by that labour, as a public sign of men's family commitment. As one speaker at the 1913 'Workers of the World' conference at Browning Hall (a settlement in Camberwell that promoted labour politics and religion) noted, men did not sit at home telling their families they loved them; they went to work to prove it.[14] When miners in Durham paraded through the street in their annual gala, their dependents usually walked with them.[15] Such practices enacted publicly the dynamic between work, family and place. That such assumptions were commonplace is undoubted. They formed the bedrock of men's claims to citizenship and countless self-improvement schemes and were ingrained in working men's rhetoric about self-respect and independence. Acknowledgement of provision as a symbol of masculine commitment may be well documented but, usually, these accounts tell us more about legal and political conceptions of masculinity or of women's lives, rather than father-child attachments.

Literary critics have typically lamented the absence or limitation of subjectivity in plebeian autobiography; revelations were of class rather than the 'self'.[16] In particular, the conventions of political or self-improvement memoirs emphasised the 'respectability' of fathers. An author's reference to a father who worked hard for his family was, in the crude bifurcation between 'rough' and 'respectable', an affirmation of his public decency while the father who rejected the role of provider

---

book of Boswell: autobiography of a gypsy (London: Victor Gollancz Ltd., 1970), 88. This tendency was amplified in the Great War: Roper, *The secret battle*.

[13] Vincent, *Bread, knowledge and freedom*, 62–86.

[14] *To the workers of the world: an appeal for personal religion by eight members of parliament* (London: W. A. Hammond, 1913), 34. The conference proceedings featured papers by eight Labour MPs, including Ramsey MacDonald and Keir Hardie, and two clergymen. Browning Hall was a particularly politically active settlement house. See Robert Browning Settlement [Francis Herbert Stead], *Eighteen Years in the Central City Swarm, An account of the Robert Browning Settlement at Walworth* (London: W. A. Hammond, 1912).

[15] North of England Film Bureau, *Durham Miner's Gala*, black and white silent film, 35mm, North West Film Archive, Manchester Metropolitan University.

[16] Hackett, 'A different form of self, 208–26 and Gagnier, *Subjectivities*, 139.

was invariably feckless.[17] The 'good man' model of fathering could circumvent awkward questions about ambivalence or hostility between family members. The Labour peer Herbert Morrison's (born 1888) youthful frustration with his father's conservatism was smoothed by acknowledgement of the older man's 'good' provision (they had an enviable house).[18] Certainly, it is a mistake to equate commonplace references to 'good men' with affection. Grace Foakes (born 1901) was explicit that her father was a 'good man' in that he toiled long and hard for his family yet she did not love him; in retrospect, she thought that her father had not allowed love.[19]

While adult children's reflection on their fathers' wage labour often acknowledged breadwinning as paternal duty, it could also be imagined as an act of devotion. As the anthropologist Daniel Miller has demonstrated, conceptions of obligation can obscure the sacrificial rites of everyday life that transform duties into transcendent practices performed for subjects of devotion. In Miller's study, the obligation to shop for essential household items in the late-twentieth century is an act of devotion performed, overwhelmingly by mothers, for other family members. For Miller, duty and obligation are not exclusive to love and affection. Provisioning, a mundane chore, can become 'beautiful' when rationalised by the discourse of thrift, exercised for the family's ultimate benefit, shopping for goods to promote family members' wellbeing and, crucially, the deliberate sacrifice or limitation of individual consumer desires to invest the household shop with extra meaning. Provisioners need not enjoy shopping to transform tedious responsibility into a transcendent act of love. Likewise, subjects of devotion are not necessarily subjects of idealised love. Rather, love is a practice that incorporates a medley of pressures, including affection, obligation, resentment and ambivalence.[20]

Miller's model applies to late Victorian and Edwardian family dynamics where paternity legally meant an obligation to provide, and insecure material circumstances shaped the pattern and expression of affective lives. Set against a recurring 'slum' narrative of lower-class men as

---

[17] See for example Betty May *Tiger woman: my story* (London: Duckworth, 1929); Guy Aldred, *No traitor's gait! The autobiography of Guy A. Aldred* (London: The Strickland Press, 1955–56); Emma Smith [pseud.], *A Cornish waif's story: an autobiography* (St. Agnes: Truran, [1954] 2010); Aubrey Darby, *A view from the alley* (Cornwall: Judith Darby, 2012); John Paton, *Proletarian pilgrimage the autobiography of John Paton* (London: Routledge & Sons, 1935); Pat O'Mara, *Liverpool Irish Slummy* (Liverpool: Bluecoat Press, 2009).

[18] Herbert Morrison, *An autobiography* (London: Oldhams Press Ltd., 1960), 11–12, 16–17.

[19] Foakes, *Four Meals*, 26–36.

[20] Daniel Miller, *A theory of shopping* (London: Polity, 1998).

intrinsically profligate, men's subjugation of individual desires to work hard for their families potentially invested extra-legal and economic meaning into the performance of labour. Likewise, whilst wives might lament that men took 'pocket money' from wages earned, fathers who deliberately limited personal spends (and often used those spends to pay for boot repairs, travel to and from work and to purchase food consumed at work) invested the 'household' wage with extra significance.[21] When father shared *his* 'pocket money' with offspring, children identified an affective impulse driving the munificence, especially in otherwise 'unsentimental' or undemonstrative men.[22]

For individual narrators, attempts to articulate the devotional elements of men's work often took the form of cliché. (Lord) Bernard Taylor's (born 1895) father began working life as a farm labourer but economic necessity forced him to switch to colliery work. Taylor's pedestrian epitaph to his father was that he 'was a good man': retiring, shy and reserved. His preoccupations were work, gardening and doing the best for his family. This résumé of a man's life did not, perhaps, amount to much, especially when set against the son's achievements as politician and peer. Yet it was in the mundane qualities of the 'good man' that Taylor identified exceptional esteem for his father: 'To me he was one of nature's gentlemen.'[23] Guy Aldred's (born 1886) parents separated in his infancy and he went to live with his mother's parents. Aldred's eulogy to his grandfather's hard work, dignity, thrift and constancy testified to respectability, self-identity and the sexual division of labour. His grandmother was skilful in stretching resources; his grandfather was 'a good and considerate' provider solicitous of his family. Aldred's grandfather shone a spotlight on the biological father's shortcomings, especially when he vetoed his daughter seeking maintenance from her estranged spouse. The older man was not obliged to provide for Aldred but elected to. Providing was the process through which the grandfather became the father: 'A better parent it would be impossible to find. After a lapse of so many years I hold his memory green.' Aldred's description of boyish delight in watching his grandfather at work raised his labour from the

---

[21] Even the suffragist Anna Martin, who criticised men for taking the comforts provided by wives for granted, acknowledged that men's pocket money ('bits') paid for essential items. Anna Martin, 'The irresponsibility of the father' in Ross, *Slum travellers*, 148–60 (155).

[22] Margaret Powell, *Below stairs* (Bath: Chivers, 1968), 5; Percy A. Heard, *An octogenarian's memoirs* (Ilfracombe: Stockwell, 1974), 47; H. M. Burton, *There was a young man* (London: Geoffrey Bles, 1958), 35; Thomas Warr, *Fogs lifted. A slum child's story* (London: Simpkin, Marshall and Co., 1909), 4; Walter Southgate, *That's the way it was: a working-class autobiography, 1890–1950* (Oxford: New Clarion, 1982), 69.

[23] Lord Taylor, *Uphill all the way: a miner's struggle* (London: Sidgwick and Jackson, 1972), 4.

mundane to a political and personal sign: 'As a child, I loved to look across the street and watch him at work. To me he was a very great man.'[24]

Taylor and Aldred's commitment to championing the rights of ordinary working men invested their fathers' labour with public-political significance. Since Aldred was a freethinker committed to socialism, it is no surprise that he disdained his pretentious actor-father to trumpet the craftsmanship of the 'thoughtful, gentle, yet robust' bookbinder grandfather. Jack Lawson's (born 1881) autobiography opened with an elaborate description of a man, his physique, walk, clothes and tattoos, as he strolled along a road: 'obviously' a working man, 'one of the millions'. The commonplace was a ruse. This man was also one in a million: 'to me, he was a great man; he was my father'. For Lawson, his father's magnitude was underscored by the 'great' sacrifices he made: he performed 'killing work' in the mines 'for his children' and walked miles to and from his workplace so his offspring could live in a healthy environment. Again, this was political. A Labour MP, Lawson was deeply critical of post-war policies on unemployment and a passionate advocate of improving the health of urban children.[25]

If the 'great' man of labour biography was clichéd, this should not obscure the sincere meaning authors attempted to convey. As Michael Roper notes of correspondence from soldiers in the Great War, public conventions were adapted to individual purpose; what appeared to be 'mere' cliché could be invested with profound interpersonal significance.[26] Taylor's reflection that his colliery father was a 'gentleman' established a direct relationship between the obligatory 'for me' of men's labour and the personal 'to me' embedded in the attempt to convey to a public audience the intimate value invested in this particular man's toil. Taylor's elevation of his father to a natural elite (by the son who was a peer in an artificial hierarchy) confirmed the older man's respectability. The 'to me' invested this with extra meaning because it excluded the public and substituted social hierarchies with an imagined authentic 'natural' order. Taylor's appeal to nature also echoed his father's love for rural life.[27] Within the micro-hierarchies of everyday life, such expressions of attachment position the 'place' of an Other within a familial emotional economy that outstrips macro-level social status.[28] Taylor's

---

[24] Aldred, *No traitor's gait!*, 13, 22. [25] Lawson, *Man's life*, 9–11.
[26] Roper, *The secret battle*, 23. [27] Taylor, *Uphill all the way*, 4.
[28] See Candace Clark, 'Emotions and micro-politics in everyday life: some patterns and paradoxes of "place"' in T. Kemper (ed.), *Research agendas in the sociology of emotions* (Albany: State University of New York Press, 1990), 305–334.

epitaph to his father reflected the political valorisation of labour while suggesting that affective attachments lent a different kind of cohesion and stratification to everyday life.

Authors' insistence on taking labour that was 'for me' in conjunction with 'to me' meanings drew the public elements of men's obligation to work into a more personal realm. Reginia Gagnier's study of subjectivities in working-class autobiography notes that authors could simultaneously assert their ordinariness, epitomised by George Acorn's *One of the multitude* (1911), and claim individual agency; this did not overcome anxieties about the ego and many plebeian authors who insisted on differentiating a personal tale found it difficult to express their story.[29] A similar process is at work with reference to 'ordinary' fathers and their commonplace obligation to work. Authors who introduced 'to me' meanings into acknowledgement of their father's ordinariness conceded the unexceptional quality of working men but, simultaneously, asserted individual agency by suggesting the specificity of paternal ties. For Lawson, it did not matter that his father was illiterate and uneducated; to him, his father was one of the wisest men he ever met.[30] Likewise, the use of cliché to convey a personal relationship enabled readers to know exactly what authors meant: they might not judge Lawson's father to be 'great' but they could appreciate the dynamic that rendered one's 'ordinary' father exceptional.

Lawson associated his father's labour with caring *about* and *for* his children. An account of his strong miner father walking home from work with the infant Lawson, cradled in his arms, held explicit nurturing connotations. That he could not have remembered this, Lawson freely acknowledged: he was an infant and it seems improbable that a miner would have carried his babe from his night shift. Although fictionalised, the image highlighted Lawson's attempt to express the emotive dynamic in labour. In middle age, this memory was so real that Lawson could almost sense his father's arms holding him. The memory was a 'golden day' in the landscape of Lawson's past; a 'luxury' that brought him peace.[31] The imagined scene summarised his father's qualities and the pathway of identity that made Jack Lawson the man he was. The very sumptuousness of the story intimated the affective meanings Lawson attributed to his relationship with his father as a child and an adult.

The legal obligation of fathers to provide rendered men's wage labour an accessible, almost taken-for-granted, motif for adult children's navigation of attachment to father in the context of autobiographies

---

[29] Gagnier, *Subjectivities*, 144.   [30] Lawson, *Man's life*, 13.   [31] *Ibid*, 9–10.

ostensibly concerned with the external world and, where words such as 'love' were unfamiliar, awkward or inappropriate. David Kirkwood (born 1872) located his first conscious rush of love for his steelworker father in puberty as he and his father passed a gypsy family in the street. Comparing the gypsies to his father and himself, Kirkwood was struck by similarity and difference: a common happy companionship set against disparity in material circumstance. This was, and was not, about men's labour as Kirkwood realised that a child's attachment to a parent could develop without orthodox provision. Nevertheless, the contrast prompted Kirkwood to identify his father as an individual who made particular choices and to root his attachment to his father in pride: 'I walked beside my father. For the first time I was conscious that I loved him and that this man was my father'.[32]

Expressions of pride and admiration can act as markers that confirm the place of feeling persons within social interaction.[33] Kirkwood's link between pride in his provider father and love was partly about politics: as a Labour politician with strong trade union interests, Kirkwood conceived of men, public and private, in relation to their role as workers. The unspoken question is whether Kirkwood could have loved his father had he not provided. It is, of course, unanswerable: his father's identity was so deeply ingrained with his labour that it was impossible to imagine him without it. Moreover, in a family that was, Kirkwood suggested, embarrassed by emotion, a language of 'winning through' (survival) shaped understandings of affective bonds. Kirkwood could not think how to express sentiment towards his father without reference to 'winning through', a technique for living that depended, overwhelmingly, on paternal wages.[34] Indeed, the first sentence with which Kirkwood began his life story quoted his father's declaration that 'we'll win through yet'.[35] To dispense with work as an affective sign raised the question of how to rethink 'good' fathering and attachment outside the boundaries of conventional assumptions about masculine obligations. In this sense, Kirkwood's statement that he 'loved' his father is radical in that it deployed an explicit emotional vocabulary for the benefit of an external reader. Within the emotional community that was his family, however, such words were neither necessary nor desirable when father's breadwinning could be understood as something beautiful or, in Miller's terms, an act of devotion.[36]

---

[32] David Kirkwood, *My life of revolt* (London, G.G. Harrap & Co., 1935), 52–3.
[33] See Candace Clark, *Misery and company: sympathy in everyday life* (Chicago and London: University of Chicago Press, 1997), 229–233.
[34] Kirkwood, *Life of revolt*, 52–3.   [35] *Ibid*, 1.
[36] For discussion of the plurality of emotional communities, see Rosenwein, *Emotional communities in the early Middle Ages*.

Even children whose fathers were not employed in wage or 'respectable' labour could appropriate 'provision' to relate attachment. If David Kirkwood could not cognate love without provision, the gypsy he held as a foil to his father possibly had no such difficulty. Silvester Boswell (born 1895) may not have been the gypsy boy that Kirkwood passed in the street but there was no doubt that Boswell attached the same language of love and pride to his father's unorthodox modes of provisioning as Kirkwood attached to wage labour. Boswell clearly loved his mother; when he was taken to hospital wounded in the Great War, it was his 'Mummy' he longed for. Yet Boswell's life story was preoccupied with extolling his father's qualities. A model of gypsy manhood, he was an exceptional provider: the family had a 'plentiful' life and lived 'tip top' because his father was 'a live wire'. He invented 'contraptions', was ingenious exploiting business opportunities, expert with horses, quick witted, a champion fighter and excellent at making a tent. Like Lawson and others, Boswell located his father in a masculine taxonomy to identify his generic virtues. At the same time, his evident delight in his father's fulfilment of his obligations placed him 'above the average Gypsy man'.[37]

Boswell revelled in his ethnic identity. J. H. Crawford (born c.1890), the son of a tramp couple, had no such consolations and was more circumspect about his itinerant childhood. Crawford depicted his suffering mother with sympathy and sadness, not least because she grieved so much for the five babies who died shortly after birth. His father was a more shadowy figure. He expressed little regret for his dead offspring and, despite its hardships he was resigned to life on the road. Crawford's birth story epitomised the complex, if muted, attachments of this family. Taking refuge from a snowstorm, Crawford's mother delivered her son in a barn. On his return, Crawford's father affected dismay for the babe's arrival, reflecting that the 'poor little devil' would be better off with a family that wanted, and could provide for, children. The bitter testimony acknowledged the peculiarly harsh conditions of tramp family life and suggested deep ambivalence between father and infant. His father's actions told a more complex story: he lifted the babe in his 'big' hands to scrutinise him, made mother and child as comfortable as possible, caught and cooked a hare for his wife's supper, and then transformed the hare skin into a furry Babygro. The story, rehearsed many times through his childhood by Crawford's mother, epitomised the symbolic significance of men's deeds in the absence of verbal expressions of attachment. This was not the powerful bond of compassion and guilt

---

[37] Boswell, *The book of Boswell*, 15–6, 20, 23, 26, 88, 165.

that Crawford articulated towards his mother, for sure, but both Crawford and his mother related the birth story as a signifier of their faith in the older man and his commitment to them. Although 'gruff on the outside', Crawford's father was 'good to me': 'A handy man is father. We'll ne'er be without our bit of meat so long as he's to the fore'.[38]

It was, perhaps, easier for children to rationalise retrospectively fathers who were unorthodox or whose provision fell short, and to reimagine hard times from an affective, rather than material, standpoint. Walter Southgate's (born 1890) father kept the shoe lasts that belonged to his boot-maker dad. Serving no useful purpose to the pen-maker son, the dead man's shoe lasts appeared to have been retained for sentimental reasons. Wooden shoe lasts crudely mimicked the naked foot. That the father's hands would have smoothed and worked over the lasts for many years added further meaning to the objects. The lasts eventually were burned for fuel when Southgate's parents hit hard times. Southgate used this anecdote to highlight the precarious conditions of his childhood, sympathy for his long-suffering mother and the pity of affective economies that could not afford to keep material mementoes. The wry tone of this story emphasised the affective range of Southgate's writing: the shoe lasts were burned because his hapless father, who was full of ideas about the rights and wrongs of the working man, never earned enough. That the grandfather 'provided' fuel, despite being dead, heightened the shortcomings of the father. But Southgate's sympathetic tone underscored the extent to which frustration at his father's inadequate fulfilment of paternal obligation was tempered by acceptance and awareness of a broader context in which the middle-aged narrator could locate his political career, at least partially, in relation to his father's more abstract provision – his radical sensibilities.[39]

Risk, alienation and attachment

Many working-class autobiographies were political. As Reginia Gagnier noted, the personal elements of such texts trod a fine line with argument.[40] Nevertheless, to read such life stories in terms of political rhetoric alone risks minimising authors' personal investment in politics. For Walter Benjamin, social democracy lulled the working classes into dreaming of liberated descendants instead of focusing on the sacrifices of ancestors. In this model, the oppression and alienation of parents and

---

[38] J. H. Crawford, *The autobiography of a tramp* (London: Longmans Green and Co., 1900), 3–14.
[39] Southgate, *That's the way it was*, 12.   [40] Gagnier, *Subjectivities*, 161.

grandparents represented a source of personal outrage, potentially, the 'greatest strength' of working-class mobilisation.[41] That politically motivated autobiographies were deeply ambivalent about fathers' labour, referencing pride in skill and survival alongside pity and anger at the conditions under which they toiled suggests how fathers' labour could operate as a personalised motor towards political consciousness. Communist Party activist, T. A. Jackson (born 1879), located his political sensibilities firmly in relation to his father's occupational, intellectual and political experiences as a compositor and trade unionist. The abstract and intimate dimension of this inheritance was manifest in Jackson's 'treasured' preservation of his father's fifty-year span of London Society of Compositors' membership cards.[42]

Some autobiographers began their story with an assertion of pride in their father's working-class identity and his labouring skill.[43] Author references to plebeian ancestors of 'fine stock' and 'good proletarian stock' staked a claim for the dignity of working people.[44] Yet references to the suffering that underscored such pedigree could also indicate attachment to one's father. Fred Bower's (born 1871) father, a stonemason, went on strike just after his eldest child was born. With union funds exhausted and 'blacklegs' having supplanted the strikers, his father struck out to try his luck in America, leaving his wife and infant with his parents until he sent for them. After 'much hardship', he got work at his trade and his family joined him. This opening explained Bower's selfhood (he was active in labour politics) and the 'class-war bias' of his story; but it also identified his respect and fondness for his father. Referring to 'my old dad', Bower noted that understanding his father's experiences had taught him to hate industrial capitalism and that this was a 'noble' inheritance. This had an affective quality as Bower reiterated and elaborated his satisfaction in his father: 'Yes, I am proud of the dear old Dad'.[45]

Even autobiographies that were ostensibly apolitical could reference father's alienation from work to intimate the personal significance of his

---

[41] Walter Benjamin, 'Theses on the philosophy of history', XII. See T. Eagleton, *Walter Benjamin, or towards a revolutionary criticism* (London: NLB/ Verso, 1981), 147.
[42] T. A. Jackson, *Solo trumpet* (London: Lawrence and Wishart, 1953), 38.
[43] Vincent, *Bread, knowledge and freedom*, 62–86.
[44] See for instance, Sidney Campion, *Sunlight on the foothills* (London: Rich and Cowan, 1941), 3; Citrine, *Men and work*, 11, 17; W. M. Lax, *His book. The autobiography of Lax of Poplar* (London: The Epworth Press, 1937), 16; Thomas Bell, *Pioneering days* (London: Laurence and Wishart, 1941), 89. See also, Albert Mainsbridge, *The trodden road: experience, inspiration and belief* (London: J.M. Dent and Sons, 1940), 9.
[45] Fred Bower, *Rolling stonemason: an autobiography* (London: Jonathan Cape, 1936), 17–20.

toil. Mark Grossek (born 1888) was incredulous that his father, a tailor, worked so hard for such little pay and accepted the humiliation of his position. Even so, Grossek recalled that, as a boy, he had revelled in the warm security of evening companionship in his father's workroom when he listened 'with approval' to his father's discourses about 'whatsoever'. Grossek's critique of his father's acceptance of working conditions symbolised a generational shift in political attitudes to employment conditions and the son's social mobility. Yet, in recognising his father's backbreaking toil for meagre wages, Grossek also acknowledged the tenderness of everyday sacrifice. His recollection of the sound, as well as content, of his father's voice, his quirks and foibles, reflected and reinforced the extra-economic meanings attached to the tailor's exploitation.[46] When William Lax (born 1868) likened his father to a 'bird let loose' in his new career selling life insurance, he paid tribute to the older man's years of sacrifice in the 'drudgery' of iron moulding and his humiliation in tramping for work.[47] Harry Gosling (born 1861) thought his father was instinctively a 'daydreaming' romantic. That he worked hard and steadily to do 'everything in his power for us all' in contradiction to his 'natural' character made him a 'model father and husband'.[48] A. V. Christie's (born 1875) father wanted to be an architect but lack of funds prevented him training. Instead, his father's pen and ink study of a church interior hung on the parlour wall for years as testimony to disappointed ambition. Christie's insight into the older man's thwarted aspiration provided a compassionate, if wry, framework for rationalising his father's lacklustre career in ironmongery.[49]

Reflective accounts of men's work facilitated rumination on the multiple meanings of toil. Fred Gresswell (born c.1890) argued that although his labourer father was uneducated and untrained in a formal sense, he was energetic and an all-round expert in agriculture. Until old age, his father had never appeared tired. Gresswell then qualified this to note that, rather, he had never heard his father complain of tiredness. The qualification matters: it turned a vibrant account of a provider who worked 'tirelessly' for his family into something more complex. Labouring outdoors for long hours over seven-day weeks would exhaust most adults but to acknowledge tiredness to one's children would render the labour a burden. Instead, as a rite of devotion to his family, it

---

[46] Mark Grossek, *First movement* (London: Geoffrey Bles, 1937), 119–121.
[47] Lax, *His book*, 24–5.
[48] Harry Gosling, *Up and down stream* (London: Methuen and Co., 1927), 6–20;
[49] Christie, *Brass tacks and a fiddle*, 14.

appeared to be a joy. It was only with hindsight that Gresswell haltingly questioned the energy underpinning such devotion.[50]

Awareness of men's exhaustion or alienation from work could fuse anger at men's working conditions with bitter personal significance. The cost of father's 'for me' breadwinning gave edge to 'to me' meanings of that labour. Bernard Taylor noted acidly that, having worked hard almost to the end of his life in a job he did not enjoy, his father retired on a pittance with ruined lungs.[51] Edwin Muir (born 1887) recounted that his farmer father, so suited to the untamed Orkney idyll of Muir's childhood, could not adapt to city life and died shortly after moving to Glasgow in search of work. Years later, Muir's bitterness and grief remained raw in an autobiography that emerged from his encounter with psychoanalysis.[52]

Similarly, the injury or death of men at work facilitated particular insights into the dynamic between the responsibilities of fathering and attachment. Mining was notoriously dangerous and children's bitter reflections on the exploitation of men's lives were inseparable from the value attached to 'their' miners. Elizabeth Andrews' (born 1882) father escaped from the Maerdy (Rhondda) pit explosion of December 1885, which killed eighty-one men and boys. As children, she and her siblings 'loved to hear' their father rehearse his heroic escape from the explosion: 'To make it more vivid to us, Father would draw a plan of the pit in chalk on the kitchen floor'. Readers might expect Andrews to follow through with the detail of the miraculous escape but she does not. Presumably, her father was one of thirty men rescued just 120 yards from the site of the explosion. For Andrews, the content of the story had less significance than the symbolic value of the storytelling. In focusing on the ritualised narration of father's escape from death, Andrews's emphasis is on the importance of the miner-father, not simply as an economic factor in family survival, but also the heroic and compassionate character of fathers who went to work in the mines in the first place. As a political activist in the South Wales coalfield, Andrews recognised that mining tragedies were intrinsic to campaigns against the exploitation of cheap labour and the multiple hardships of miners' families. That Andrews recalled the ritualised retelling of her father's survival rather than the detail indicated how her family added layers of significance to the narrative over time. This was especially noteworthy because, although he survived the explosion, Andrews's father died of silicosis at fifty-seven years (two of her brothers also developed the disease). Noting the

---

[50] Fred Gresswell, *Bright boots* (London: Hale, 1956), 19–20.
[51] Taylor, *Uphill all the way*, 4.   [52] Muir, *An autobiography*, 90–3.

dreadful count of miner deaths in pit explosions or from occupational disease in her lifetime alone, Andrews's narrative had poignancy: for families, every miner's death represented the loss of someone 'precious'.[53]

In the maudlin song 'Don't go down the mine, Dad' (1910), a little boy dreams that the pit where his father works is on fire. On waking, he pleads with his father not to go to work: his chief bargaining tool is that the miner's death would break his heart. Explaining to the boy that he must perform his duty, the man departs for the pit but cannot forget his little boy's pleas and returns home. The dream comes true and it is not the boy of the song who is heartbroken but the children of his father's workmates. Sung in baritone with a *patetico* melody, the song ranked amongst the 'sentimental' repertoire of music hall. Its popularity is suggested by its representation in adult memories, the printing of lyrics on postcards with stylised images and the incorporation of the song in a magic lantern show.[54] Although 'high' culture treated the pathetic genre with disdain, the words could resonate with families who understood all too well the dangers of men's labour. Indeed, anecdotes about miner fathers who stayed at home on days of pit disasters could become apocryphal.[55] Children did not need to experience the death of a father, or even have a collier father, to find resonance in the song: such lyrics made sense to anyone who thought that the loss of Father would break a child's heart.

Jack Jones (born 1884) noted his miner father's bitterness when a mine explosion in South Wales cost 276 lives but pit owners refused to raise the men's wages. His father's disgruntlement highlighted differing scales of cost and return between provision and tragedy. Jones situated his father's views on this tension in the context of a rare moment of childhood confidence between father and son. Having overestimated his navigation skills taking an illicit excursion to the Welsh metropolis from his Valleys' home, Jones was picked up by the Cardiff police and spent the night in a boys' home. The arrival of his father to collect him the following day met with relief but, also, the expectation of punishment. His father had pawned his watch to pay the train fare to Cardiff. Travelling home, Jones sat facing his father as they passed the scene of the pit

---

[53] See especially Elizabeth Andrews, *A woman's work is never done* (Dinas Powys: Honno Classics, [1967] 2006), 8–14.
[54] See for instance, Lilian Slater, *Think on! said Mam: a childhood in Bradford, Manchester 1911–1919* (Manchester: Neil Richardson, 1984), 47; *Screening the poor, 1888–1914*, curated by Martin Loiperdinger and Ludwig Vogl-Bienek (Edition Filmmuseum, 2011); British Library sound recordings: sounds.bl.uk.
[55] Cissie Elliot in Charles Kightly (ed.), *Country voices: life and love in farm and village* (London: Thames and Hudson, 1984), 228–9.

tragedy and his father reflected on the miner's lot. That Jones was approaching an age when he would join his father at the coalface added another layer of meaning to the story, especially as his father neglected to discipline the boy and, later, admonished his wife for trying. Instead, regret for the apparent cheapness of the miner's life united father and son. That they were talking about their lives invested Jones's reflection with poignant intimacy in real time and reflection.[56] Although it was politically incendiary to suggest that employees were responsible for pit disasters, Wil Edwards (born 1888) suggested that miners (paid by the weight in South Wales) took risks they 'would not normally take' ('just once') towards Christmas in order to pay for toys for their children. Underscoring the close relationship between love and toil, Edwards's suggestion was especially affecting because, first, so many pit disasters occurred in the run up to Christmas and, second, Edwards had never known his miner father because he also died over the festive period, just prior to his son's birth.[57]

The life cycle: reflection and renegotiation

The reflective quality of life-writing enabled adult children to impose, or illustrate, affective frameworks on the mundane features of their past. Retrospection facilitated identification of life cycle milestones, but, also, enabled authors to renegotiate the dynamics of relationships past and present. For working-class autobiographers, key milestones in the shifting dynamic of relationships with fathers included the transition from childhood dependency to wage-earning independence and becoming a parent. For male autobiographers especially, adult participation in paid labour could stimulate assessments of work as an emotive mechanism in relation to being fathered. Jack Jones's mother dominated his recollection of early childhood in terms of time, contact and intimacy; his miner father was absent in the 'day's battle for bread' or asleep. Jones and his siblings knew little about their father except that he worked hard and his exhaustion was, at times, brutal. Father sometimes made unreasonable demands on resources and could appear ignorant of his children's needs. Mother, who explicitly placed her children first, sought to correct this by clever deceit and defiance. Parental priorities were, at first glance, sometimes at odds. When the miners went on strike, Jones's mother went begging for food, much to his father's humiliation; yet

---

[56] Jack Jones, *Unfinished journey* (New York: Oxford University Press, 1937), 61–9.
[57] Wil Edwards, *From the valley I came: reminiscences of the author's life up to 1926, with special reference to his mother* (London: Angus and Robertson, 1956), 4–8, 34.

strikes for better wages were premised on the need to better support wives and children.[58] Jones added nuance to this familiar model of working-class parenting, however, in his account of leaving school to join his father at the coalface.

Jones's depiction of entering the manly world of work transformed dehumanising toil into a beautiful act of sacrifice. The corporeal strength of the miner was matched by his craftsman's skill and mental agility; commonplace work practices were imbued with ritualistic significance; Jones's father was knowledgeable as he explained about coal markets, prices, wages, geology and politics; he caressed and coaxed coal into his trams but, paid by the weight, he moved it at 'a mile a minute'. For Jones, this toil had pragmatic and emotive meaning as he reinterpreted his father's exhausting labour as his love token. Jones's narrative of his first day at his father's work repeated 'My dad' almost as punctuation. Father's labour was a 'work of art' and it was, Jones says, a privilege to watch him.[59]

The inclusion of this narrative in a chapter entitled 'To meet the prince', where the royal Prince is never seen at all, confirmed the miner as heroic. Yet Jones inflected labouring pride with personal attributes. Working alongside his father facilitated new insights into the older man and his toil and, fostered an easy tactility of guardianship and intimacy whereby his father touched him and called him 'Son' and 'Johnny'; in place of habitual tiredness, Jones witnessed animation. The highpoint of Jones's first day at work was his father's appraisal of him: 'Yes, you'll do'. While the memory referenced a milestone in juvenile masculinity, Jones related this explicitly through the medium of his particular relationship with his father to demonstrate the significance of interpersonal forms of socialisation. The other miners josh the boy but his father treated him with solicitude and tenderness. As Jones notes, this 'kindly, jolly and protective' father was, and was not, the same man he had known before; shared toil made visible the hidden meanings in his father's everyday labour and exhaustion. This did not topple his mother from her position at the heart of family life but work enabled Jones to navigate his relationship with his father in real time and reflection. Through the shared experience of mining (and the revelation that providing generated corporeal pain), Jones reevaluated the enigmatic man of early childhood to

---

[58] This tension was played on by a conservative press that portrayed men as selfish and starving their children. See A. J. Croll, 'Starving strikers and the limits of the "humanitarian discovery of hunger" in late-Victorian Britain', *International Review of Social History*, 56: 1 (2011), 103–131.

[59] Jones, *Unfinished journey*, 65–9, 72.

invest the everyday sacrifice of his father's provision with interpersonal significance. Eventually, Jones rejected mining in favour of becoming a writer, adult education and community worker. He wanted his sons to access as much education as possible and have career choices, something unthinkable to his father's generation.[60] This was not to denigrate his father's occupation but, rather, to recognise the profound personal cost of such labour and want something different. Jones's paean to the miner father was, first, a tribute to the sacrifices his father made, performing (sometimes literally) crushing work in the dank subterranean world of the pit and, second, an act of conciliation for having rejected that work for himself and his sons.

The homosociality of men's jobs, politics and leisure is what, superficially at least, sustained paternal detachment, especially when 'family' was defined as mother, small children and home. Yet the homosocial culture of wage labour could work positively for boys who were invited into a hitherto mysterious world of father's work whereby fathers represented someone exciting and privileged, however workaday his toil.[61] The district nurse, M.E. Loane, noted that men drifted away from their sons for five years or so after boys turned eight. The relationship was renewed when lads began to work. For Loane, the middle-class supposition that this was because the wage-earning child had ceased to be a financial burden was 'dull' and foolish. Rather, work provided shared experiences for dads and lads to rediscover a common language: they had the 'same plane of difficulties and interests'. Fathers understood the conditions of work that were a revelation to the boy and the boy realised 'as he has never done before' his father's 'daily toil and self-sacrifice'.[62]

Lewis Jones's (born 1897) autobiographical novel, *Cwmardy*, described the protagonist Len as just a 'baby' when he entered the pit with his father, Big Jim. On first descending the pit, the boy's excitement gave way to fear and he searched for his father's hand in 'love and confidence'. Jim navigated a path between 'manly' silence, intended as reassurance, and sympathy for his son. By the end of the second day, the exhausted boy weeps with regret for his lost education and his father carries him 'like a child' to bed. Both are caught in a liminal moment where Jim is instrumental in assisting Len at work but also in navigating a man-boy identity

---

[60] *Ibid*, 64–77. Although proud of his eldest daughter, Jones did not expect his daughters to pursue careers.
[61] For example, George Baldry, *The rabbit skin cap: a tale of a Norfolk countryman's youth* (Ipswich: Boydell Press, 1974), 57; Joseph Stamper, *So long ago* (London: Hutchinson, 1960), 21, 107–8; Harry Harris, *Under oars: reminiscences of a Thames lighterman, 1894–1909* (London: Centreprise Trust, 1978), 39; Citrine, *Men and work*, 13–8.
[62] Loane, *From their point of view*, 155–6.

between the pit and home. A coming-of-age novel about the discovery of radical politics, Len's journey to political consciousness is mirrored by his relationship with his father. The pit is as an occupational, political and emotional field through which men negotiate rights, responsibilities and identities as a group and as individuals implicated in particular relations.[63] Of course, men and boys frequently worked alongside each other without necessarily being related. Yet authors made distinctions between paternalism in general and working with fathers. Barnabas Britten (born c.1880) idolised his father, a sailor: 'Yes Dad' and 'Right-O, Dad' punctuate his dialogue to affirm the older man's qualities and the boy's ambition to join his father's boat. As skipper, his father occupied a dual authority over his son but cognisance of father's work-self threw his sentimental status into relief and Britten was careful to distinguish 'the skipper' who happened to be his father, from his father, who was also skipper.[64]

Harry Harris's (born 1880) memoir, composed in 1935, paid homage to the skilled 'lighterage' men who worked on the River Thames. Harris's son, also a lighterman, contributed a preface when the text was published in 1978 telling readers that Harris was a 'man of simple tastes' who loved his family as he loved the Thames. The son's tribute to his deceased father hinted at anxiety that the manuscript focused on work at the expense of personal life. But the story of river freight was a story about family. Harris learnt his trade at the knee of his father and grandfather; his occupational pride emphasised his personal heritage. Harris eschewed explicit affective expression for the older men in favour of detailing boyhood admiration for their skills and the privilege of working with them. For Harris, the quality of a lighterman depended on the class of man tutoring him. The last sentence of Harris's manuscript referenced his promotion to foreman alongside repetition of one of his father's 'truths': 'It is better to be a "teller" than "told."' Harris's son followed his forefathers and became a lighterman. The entwined histories of fathers and sons in this homage to craftsmanship suggested that the son's prefatory reminder of family ties was superfluous; Harris's attachments were writ large into the passage of breadwinning skills and pride from father to son.[65]

Even when sons pursued different occupations to fathers, the transition of boys from school into work could facilitate peculiar

---

[63] Lewis Jones, *Cwmardy: the story of a Welsh mining valley* (Cardigan: Pathian, [1937] 2006), 137–66.

[64] Barnabas Britten, *Woodyard to palace: reminiscences* (Bradford: Broadacre Books, 1958), 191–2.

[65] Harris, *Under oars*, 2, 39. Motivation to publish his father's manuscript sprang from an attempt to defend the craftsmanship of the lighterage men against the backdrop of a trade in decline.

moments of masculine intimacy. Where boys took up apprenticeships, the transition to work adopted a more formalised and ritualistic significance. On signing his son's apprenticeship papers, William Lax's father regretted the shift of his paternal role into a new phase where all he could offer his growing son was advice (cream always rises to the top) and prayer. Despite the hackneyed character of this exchange, Lax charged the moment with sentiment, noting that his father was tearful and that the father-son communion took place before they returned home.[66] If families understood providing to be a key component of fathering, the removal of this economic relationship had emotive significance for father and child. For some fathers, other protective components of fathering provided an alternative mechanism for expressing attachment. David Kirkwood noted that his father was so affected when his daughter left home for domestic service that he made, for him, a powerful declaration of attachment: he promised to go to her if ever she needed him.[67] That he selected another pragmatic component of fathering, one that was particularly pertinent, perhaps, to girl children who were excluded from masculine rituals of shared work experience, indicated the extent to which individuals transformed duties and actions into affective testimonies.

Work could represent a source of antagonism rather than attachment. A. E. Coppard (born 1878) left school at the age of nine, despite his mother's 'deep concern' for her children's education. He helped his tailor father, who was dying of consumption, make police uniforms, but had no ambition to follow his father's trade: it was not an 'enriching profession'.[68] Sidney Campion (born 1891) left school frothing with the confidence, energy and ambition of youth. Alas, this did not (immediately) generate an exciting career trajectory but, rather, short-lived dalliances with trades while he looked about him and refined his criticisms of 'slum manufacturing'. Unimpressed with his son's 'damned foolishness' and seemingly flaky socialism, Campion Senior intervened in 'uncompromising language' to prevent his son becoming a 'waster', arranging an apprenticeship at his place of work, a wood yard. For Campion's father, the apprenticeship signified his fulfilment of paternal duty: the labourer secured his son a ticket to skilled work and a 'magnificent' salary at twenty-one-years old of £2, double his father's wage. Campion's view of this transaction was different: regardless of his 'feelings and wishes', his father had thrown him into mechanised servitude, skilled

---

[66] Lax, *His book*, 89. [67] Kirkwood, *Life of revolt*, 24.
[68] Alfred E. Coppard, *It's me O Lord! An abstract and brief chronicle of some of the life with some of the opinions of A. E. Coppard* (London: Methuen, 1957), 28–31.

or not.⁶⁹ Emanuel Shinwell's (born 1885) father ran a tailor's shop. On leaving school, Shinwell helped his father by running errands for him before striking out for independence as a message and, later, van boy. Underwhelmed by his son's occupation, Shinwell's father arranged for him to be trained as a tailor's cutter. Shinwell loathed the job, professing to possess no aptitude for the post and constantly diverted by his mania for the more thrilling world of 'blood-and-thunder' fiction. When he tried to join the army without his parents' permission, he had the 'worst row of my life' with his father. Refusing consent, his father secured him employment with a tailor. Although Shinwell 'hated the work', he conceded that the wages, at least, afforded him some independence.⁷⁰

Authors sometimes deployed clashes between relatives over a boy's future to highlight the lack of sympathy or generational and political differences with fatalistic or seemingly conservative fathers.⁷¹ Even here, reflection on such moments could throw emotional economies into relief. John Eldred's (born 1885) parents fought bitterly over his future. His mother was ambitious that her bookish son should escape manual drudgery, a potentially damning comment on her stonemason husband, let alone his desire that their boy follow his trade. As a child, Eldred was delighted that his father was building his new school; he exaggerated the importance of his father's position to his peers and sought status from helping him. The pride faltered when Eldred realised that the work was monotonous and that his after-school assistance was a prelude to an apprenticeship. Eldred's mother won the battle over his future (Eldred became a journalist) but his father succeeded in initiating his son into the world of work by requesting Eldred's company on a job the day before the boy began his working life.

Eldred reflected that, at the time, he thought this was another interlude in the parental war over his future. In hindsight, Eldred saw the gesture as his father's attempt to redeem something meaningful from defeat. The job transpired to be at a newspaper office, the locus of the boy's ambition.⁷² An awkward man, work was intrinsic to the selfhood of Eldred's father: he excelled in occupational skill where he failed in personal

---

[69] Campion, *Sunlight*, 21–38
[70] Emanuel Shinwell, *Conflict without malice* (London: Odhams Press, 1955), 21–24
[71] See for instance, Morrison, *An Autobiography*, 20–27, George Ratcliffe, *Sixty years of it: being the story of my life and public career* (London: A. Brown and Sons Ltd., 1935), 5, 35. Albert Jupp's (born c.1905) father allowed him to try his hand at several trades before losing patience and insisting his son join him in the plastering trade. Centerprise, *The Island: the life and death of an East London community, 1870–1970* (London: Centerprise Trust, 1979), 23.
[72] John Eldred, *I love the brooks: reminiscences* (London: Skeffington, 1955), 86–88.

dynamism. In this context, Eldred reflected that the stonemason's skill was his father's intended gift for his son and the rejection of that trade was personal. Viewed thus, the trip to the news offices adopted multiple interpretations: it was his father's peace offering and a form of compensation for defeat but it also represented the affective significance the older man invested in rites of passage between fathers and sons at work. Eldred identified his ham-fisted father's gift of work, in this case a preliminary insight into his ambitions, as an eloquent intimation of attachment to his son.

Overall, political and autodidactic autobiographies did not divulge the meanings of becoming a father. However, retrospective evaluations of fathers often identified an author's model of good fathering, whether a feckless father galvanised individuals into becoming 'good' providers or a steadfast dad was seen anew in light of the travails of paternal responsibilities.[73] Silvester Boswell's story ended with an intergenerational narrative of love and pride in Gypsy fathering. Boswell recounted sitting by his father's bed, 'night and day', during the two weeks the older man lay dying. Although not explicitly sentimental, the tenderness of watching the sick man was enhanced by Boswell's desire, after his father's expiration, to carry out precisely his wishes for burial. Boswell also looked to the future, turning to his sons, especially his son Lewis, so like himself and his father, to end the story with an affirmation of the gypsy man: Lewis, despite the difficulties of gypsy life, will 'turn his hand to anything' for his children. That Boswell loved to join his son on his travels and rejoiced in shouting 'Gypsy!' with his grandsons resounded with pride and pleasure in a particularly masculine conception of ethnic identity, skill and personal attachments.

Authorial confessions of failing as a provider highlighted the exemplary efforts of stalwart fathers. Jack Jones's eulogy to his miner father carried extra meaning when set against Jones's fecklessness at the outset of marriage: addicted to gambling, his mounting debts were paid by the sale of his entire household goods. Pregnant, his wife returned to her family in mid Wales. To win his family back, Jones had to prove his mettle as a provider. Although a miner, the only work in his wife's locale was 'boy labour': unskilled, low-paid bark stripping. His account of the work drew heavily on Christian symbolism: he walked in his muddy and

---

[73] For feckless dads as motors to 'good' fathering, see James Royce, *I stand nude* (London: Hutchinson, 1937) and Sam Shaw, *Guttersnipe: an autobiography* (London: Sampson Low, Marston, 1946). Other writers' contrasts between their fathers' faults and their peers' affective dads suggested a blueprint for fathering. See V. Garratt, *A man in the street* (London: J.M. Dent, 1939), 72 and Robert Roberts, *A classic slum: Salford life in the first quarter of the century* (London: Harmondsworth, 1971), 117.

torn clothes through the main street of his wife's hometown carrying a log over his shoulder listening to the jeers of onlookers who remembered his finer days. It was precisely in the humility (and humiliation) of such toil that Jones demonstrated the authenticity of his provider-father claim; the incentive to perform such labour was the privilege of holding and knowing his new-born baby.[74] Ostensibly concerned with regaining the right to father his child, Jones's account paid an implicit tribute to his father and the privilege of fathering. Indeed, the rest of his narrative noted his kisses for, and indulgence of, his ageing father alongside statements of love for his offspring and, as time passed, their children.

When the breadwinner model was subverted and mothers became principal providers, the affective qualities of providing perhaps were thrown into relief as women explained their apparent deviation from the 'norms' of mothering. Kathleen Dayus's (born 1903) experience as a working widow with children demonstrated the extent to which paid labour could generate insights into parental providing. Widowed in the 1920s and needing paid work, Dayus placed her three children in a Dr. Barnardo's orphanage. As a mother, Dayus had expectations of parenthood that were inextricable from notions of nurturing. Her story made explicit the dynamic between love and wage-toil embedded within father narratives, partly because of her compulsion to explain her 'mother' identity within an unorthodox framework. Dayus classified her waged labour as a process that enabled her to accept the removal of her children: she worked hard in her job so that, eventually, she would be able to care for them herself. After building an enamelling business through outwork, she earned sufficient money to rent a house. The provision and furnishing of this home placed Dayus in 'seventh heaven' because it materially secured her children's return. Wage labour symbolised Dayus's yearning for her children long before she succeeded in acquiring the house.

Dayus's desire to fuse providing with nurturing shaped her adult understanding of her parents and she strongly identified with her father. While cautious about interpreting 'love' from within a twentieth-century maternal context, Dayus reflected that, as a child, she believed her father loved her. This was rooted less in tactility or affectionate declarations than in her father's work. At the outset of her story, Dayus's unskilled father was unemployed. When he found work casting brass, Dayus located this within an affective framework: announcing his job, the newly employed man expected a kiss (which his wife did not grant). That her father's work involved long hours for meagre wages heightened the

---

[74] Jones, *Unfinished Journey*, 127–35.

correlation between his love and toil; work made him 'miserable, tired, dirty and wet through'. That Dayus understood the stultifying labour as devotional was symbolised through the story of his homecoming: she knelt at the tired man's feet to remove his boots and soothe his sores. Dayus's humility echoed with biblical foot-washing ritual to intimate the reciprocal affective dynamic of her father's provision and, in charting her mother's ambivalence, the lack of affective sympathy between mother and daughter.

That Dayus and her father understood the dynamic between love and toil was underscored in the account of her father's childhood: his father had abandoned his mother. The older woman never got over the shock of desertion. As Dayus's father explained, 'She loved Dad and so did us three boys'; he was 'our only breadwinner'. This could be construed as grandmother and children loved the man *because* he was their provider, rooting the dynamic firmly in economic terms. However, given that the emphasis here is on the shock of abandonment, the breadwinning appears to be marshalled as evidence that the father loved them in return. Breadwinning operated as an external sign of reciprocal affective ties although, undoubtedly, the financial loss compounded the grief of abandonment. The recollection concluded with a particular moment of togetherness as father and child cried and Dayus planted a kiss on her father's cheek to symbolise the empathy between them. That the narrative moved onto her father's pay night further highlighted the emotional economy intertwined with family wages, not least because 'father's treats' included gifts for his children.[75]

For some authors, reassessments of a father's attachment through work represented a renegotiation of their everyday childhood from a perspective of not only adult work and parenting but also of the death or dependency of their fathers. Debility and weakness could feminise older men but in autobiography at least, the vulnerabilities of older men could make explicit the affective status of men in their prime. Intrinsic to Guy Aldred's account of his grandfather was sadness that the older man did not know how much his labour signified to his adult grandson.[76] For others, the death of parents prompted a wholesale renegotiation of the dynamics of childhood. Although 'half-dead' from cancer, John Eldred's father carried on working through 'sheer willpower' until the week he

---

[75] Kathleen Dayus, *Her People* (London: Virago, 1982), 11–13. On the affective dimensions of maternal breadwinning and managing in the context of struggle see also, Anna Pertierra, 'Creating order through struggle in revolutionary Cuba' in Daniel Miller (ed.), *Anthropology and the individual* (Oxford: Berg, 2009), 145–58.
[76] Aldred, *No traitor's gait*, 13.

died, much to the astonishment of the medical practitioner Eldred paid to attend. More sorrowful was his father's anxiety that he had not 'helped you very much'. Eldred reassured the dying man that he had been a 'good' father, the only father he wished for. This acknowledged the older man's toil but it also went beyond this to intimate Eldred's adult reevaluation of his childhood.[77]

Mothers represented powerful narrators of paternal identities through either complaints about, or praise for, their husband. As the historian Carolyn Steedman noted, children choose which side they 'belong to' at an early stage. She began her 'long lesson' in hatred of her father around the age of seven, picked up initially from her mother's dislike for his coarse habits but ingrained over time by mother and children blaming him for not being good enough. Thirty years later, Steedman felt regret for the father of her early childhood who 'probably loved me, irresponsibly'.[78] As Steedman demonstrates, dynamics between husband and wife might shape children's relationships with fathers, but these were not static. Ross's *Love and toil* names the chapter on maternal nursing of sick children ('She fought for me like a tigress') with a quotation from Eldred's autobiography. As Ross notes, many mothers worked tirelessly to bring children from the brink of death and were devastated if they failed.[79] There is no doubt that Eldred's memory of being dangerously sick was dominated by his mother's struggle to save her boy and the family's subsequent understanding of this story as a monumental act of love. Yet this is the only incident from Eldred's life story that Ross uses in her study of London motherhood. Eldred's biography is not a paean to mother love; alongside the story of his career is a painful account of an unhappy family.

Eldred's father was a 'good provider' but flawed, indulging in bouts of heavy drinking and violence. Retrospectively, Eldred did not blame his father for these flaws but related them within a context whereby, as a child, he perceived his father through the spectrum of his mother's contempt for her husband. Indeed, the adult Eldred doubted that his father's drinking had been as heavy as his child self had believed. He also suspected that his mother goaded her husband to violence. Eldred did not condone his father's behaviour but infused it with sadness. His father was a large, awkward man who craved affection from a wife who had married a meal ticket. Revisiting incidents of his father's apparently

---

[77] Eldred, *I love the brooks*, 162–3.
[78] Carolyn Steedman, *Past tenses: chapters on writing, autobiography and history* (London: Rivers Oram, 1992), 21–40.
[79] Ross, *Love and toil*, 166–94.

inexplicable violence, Eldred rationalised them in light of this. In telling the story of family life, Eldred actively shifted from his mother's perspective, which had informed his childhood fear of his father, towards compassion for the older man's disappointment in marriage and recognition of his father's clumsy attempts to navigate attachment with his son. Husband and father, here, represented fluid identities, hopes and relationships in lived experience and in memory. Eldred Senior was a good man with faults but, as his son testified, the husband was different to the father.[80] When Eldred reassured his father (and reader) of the older man's goodness, then, this was not just the clichéd 'good' man model of family economies but, rather, an oblique reference to the shifting navigation of complex affective identities over time and the position of his father's waged work within a medley of pressures, duties and desires.

Conclusion

Adult children's reflections on relationships with fathers (and mothers) were not static but suggested the ongoing negotiation of interpersonal dynamics over time. Writing of affective relationships with fathers in a public context drew heavily on assumed norms of paternal duty and obligation although men who fulfilled their responsibilities were by no means always held in affection. Nevertheless, the subjective elements of breadwinning provided a key motif for adult children trying to articulate what their father meant to them. It is also possible to see some men's accounts of their fathers framed in relation to how they understood shifting father practices. Post-Great War social and economic changes, such as contracted working hours and the introduction of paid holidays, located men more firmly within family time and space, changes that were supported by shifting cultural ideals about home and domesticity.[81] Autobiographers' attempts to explain fathers' obligation to provide as evidence of men's attachment sought to bridge an assumed experiential gap. That this often had political implications did not depersonalise the accounts but, rather, demonstrated how ideologies were inextricable from personal experience. In turning to labour as a motif for affective relationships, autobiographers challenged the assumption that late Victorian and Edwardian men were peripheral to family life and that their role was predominantly financial. Rather, they used the meanings invested in work to give shape and voice to intimacy. This distinguished

---

[80] Eldred, *I love the brooks*, 161–5.
[81] Gillis, *A world of their own*, 196. See also Laura King, 'Fatherhood and Masculinity in Britain, c.1918–1960', PhD thesis, University of Sheffield (2011).

fathers from men in general and, from mothers' husbands. Male autobiographers' particular invocation of work as attachment suggests a gendered culture of expressing, accepting and reproducing affect that could also change over time.

Written overwhelmingly by adult men engaged in autodidactism or labour politics, many autobiographies expressed sympathy for the exploitation of masculine paid labour. Compassion for fathers as workers who toiled for children could generate insights into, and revisions of, father practices and identity, even where fathers fell short of fulfilling their obligations. Fathers' responsibility to work 'for me' generated nuanced perceptions of what he meant 'to me'. While recognising that men's role as legal providers and protectors of family placed them in the realm of caring about dependents, retrospective evaluations of men's work could blur the boundaries between neat distinctions of gendered cultures of parenting whilst, at the same time, underlining differences in parental styles of attachment. Authors' reliance on providing as an act of masculine devotion exploited shared languages of male identity and paternity and invested them with personal meaning. None of this suggests that the breadwinner ideal or the rights attendant on paternity did not oppress women and children, or that attachments to mothers and fathers were the same. Rather, it calls for recognition of the fluid boundaries of a sexual division of affective labour whereby, in memory at least, fathers' obligation to provide could be deeply embedded within an understanding of the socio-emotional economy of everyday life.

2 Love and want: unemployment, failure and the fragile father

> *'He stuck to this post for seven years, but the work was "killing". He had known what it was to come in dog-tired at 11.20 pm. . . It is hard on a man with so excellent a record to come down to dependence upon catch jobs.'*
>
> Dunn, aged fifty-seven, in Rowntree and Lasker, *Unemployment: a social study* (1911)[1]

On 7 June 1910, sixty investigators employed by the influential social researcher Seebohm Rowntree and his colleague Bruno Lasker, combed the residential streets of York to identify who was unemployed and why. Although England showed signs of economic recovery from a long trade depression, conditions in York lagged. The city's population was approximately 82,000. Its chief industries were the North Eastern Railway Company, cocoa and confectionary works, the building trades and flour milling.[2] Knocking on doors, surveyors identified households with one or more unemployed person(s), tracked those individuals' employment history from leaving school and sought to identify the cause of current unemployment and potential obstacles to finding new posts. The objective was to identify the economic and social factors shaping work histories, and to calculate the likelihood of unemployed individuals returning to work and at what wages. Rowntree had an established track record in researching poverty. He was a moralist and occasionally slipped into a language of eugenics but his study made an important contribution to contemporary debates about the structural causes of poverty and the socio-economic factors that trapped people in long-term poverty.[3]

---

[1] B. Seebohm Rowntree and Bruno Lasker, *Unemployment: a social study* (London: Macmillan and Co, 1911), 243–245.
[2] *Ibid*, v–x.
[3] John Welshman, *Underclass: a history of the excluded, 1880–2000* (London: Hambledon Continuum, 2006), 21–44. Studies contemporary to Rowntree and Lasker's approach include, William Beveridge, *Unemployment: a problem of industry* (London: Longman and Co., 1909); A. L. Bowley and A. R. Burnett-Hurst, *Livelihood and poverty: a study of the economic conditions of working-class households in Northampton, Warrington, Stanley and Reading* (London: Bell, 1915).

The survey returned 1,278 persons as unemployed in York on 7 June, including those who worked in casual labour but were without work on the day of the census; these individuals were underemployed.[4] Amid the statistical data, Rowntree and Lasker published eight case studies of families to represent the spectrum of what the Victorians would have called the 'deserving' unemployed. All but one of these families, a widow, had an unemployed male head of household. As the case of Dunn above illustrates, the survey highlighted the plight of the 'sturdy, honest working man' who could, and would, 'turn his hands to most things' but had 'come down' in the world through unemployment. Unlike the mid-Victorian reformer who perceived unemployment in moral terms, Rowntree and Lasker called for industrial and economic reform to address the problem of unemployment. This chapter draws on Rowntree and Lasker's case studies, not in the context of debates about shifting definitions of poverty or structural understandings of unemployment but, rather, as stories that advance particular narrative frames for imagining and talking about paternal unemployment.

The development of socio-economic understandings of unemployment in the latter half of the nineteenth century is well documented, as is the shifting relationship between married men's work, citizenship and access to relief.[5] As Marjorie Levine-Clark observed, the primary claims of unemployed married men with children on public sympathy and welfare assistance was a well-established principle by the turn of the twentieth century.[6] Scholars have been quick to highlight the problems of this breadwinner-citizen model, not least its implications for single men and women; the employment of skilled men in 'parish' labour; and the persistence of arbitrary categories of the un/deserving poor.[7] In a

---

[4] This excluded people who were out when the surveyor called and those who were employed on the day of the census but had not worked the previous or following day.

[5] Lynn Hollen Lees, *The solidarities of strangers: the English poor laws, 1700–1948* (Cambridge University Press, 1998); David Vincent, *Poor citizens: the state and the poor in the twentieth century* (London: Longman, 1991); Ernest Hennock, *The origin of the welfare state in England and Germany, 1850–1914: social polices compared* (Cambridge University Press, 2007); George Boyer, 'The evolution of unemployment relief in Great Britain', *Journal of Interdisciplinary History*, 34:3 (2003), 393–434.

[6] Marjorie Levine-Clark, 'The politics of preference: masculinity, marital status and unemployment relief in post-First World War Britain', *Cultural and social history*, 7:2 (2010), 233–252.

[7] See for example, John Burnett, *Idle hands: the experience of unemployment, 1790–1990* (London: Routledge, 1994); Susan Pederson, *Family, dependence and the origins of the British welfare state* (Cambridge University Press, 1993); Jane Lewis, 'Gender and the development of welfare regimes', *Journal of European Policy*, 2 (1992), 159–173; José Harris, *Unemployment and politics: a study in English social policy, 1886–1914* (Oxford: Clarendon, 1972); and Sonya Rose, *Limited livelihoods: gender and class in nineteenth-century England* (Berkeley: University of California Press, 1992).

family context, scholars have linked patterns of male unemployment to increases in domestic violence, shame and family breakdown.[8] Masculine authority within the family rested on fulfilment of provider obligations. When provision faltered, the power dynamics of domestic life changed.

Megan Doolittle has highlighted the relative infrequency of detailed accounts of unemployment in autobiography and the apparent difficulty with which authors attempted to navigate deeply humiliating experiences, especially regarding parochial relief.[9] Drawing on autobiography and Rowntree and Lasker's case histories, this chapter revisits the ways in which families articulated experiences of paternal unemployment in relation to men's specific status as fathers. The sociologist Esther Dermott highlights two dimensions to contemporary father-child relationships: mechanics, that is, the structural underpinning of relations, and 'intrinsic' elements, referring to the quality of everyday conduct and relationships. The mechanics of father-child relationships, such as breadwinning, are a means to an end in that they allow personal, or 'intrinsic', dimensions of relationships to thrive.[10] For late Victorian and Edwardian fathers, work legitimised paternal status and authority. As the previous chapter demonstrated, it not only validated the intrinsic dimension of father-child relationships; for many children looking back, work *was* the intrinsic element of fatherhood. For men with children, then, un- or underemployment was a failure in fathering. This problem was not exclusive to working-class men, as Valerie Sanders demonstrated beautifully with her analysis of the poet Thomas Hood's fluctuating economic fortunes.[11] It was, however, potentially far more common for working-class families to experience periods of male unemployment.

The chapter examines how working-class men and their children gave meaning to fatherhood when fathers could not (as opposed to would not) provide. Paradoxically, stories of paternal unemployment mimicked testimonies of men's devotional labour in that they drew heavily on the

---

[8] Doolittle, 'Fatherhood and family shame, 84–108. On domestic violence see James A. Hammerton, *Cruelty and companionship: conflict in nineteenth-century married life* (London and New York: Routledge, 1992); Shani D'Cruze, 'The eloquent corpse: gender, probity and bodily integrity in Victorian domestic murder' in Judith Rowbotham and Kim Stevenson (eds.), *Criminal conversations: Victorian crimes, social panic and moral outrage* (Columbus: Ohio State University Press, 2005), 181–197; and, Martin Wiener, 'Alice Arden to Bill Sikes: changing nightmares of intimate violence in England, 1558–1869', *Journal of British Studies*, 40:2 (2001), 184–212.
[9] Doolittle, 'Fatherhood and family shame'.
[10] Esther Dermott, *Intimate fatherhood: a sociological analysis* (London, Routledge 2008), 113.
[11] Sanders, *The tragic-comedy*, 35–41.

motif of sacrifice as a means of explaining father-child attachment in unorthodox circumstances. The chapter recognises the powerful social, legal and economic motors towards categorising the unemployed father as a 'failing father' and the degree to which families, and fathers, incorporated failure into paternal identities. Nevertheless, in an interpersonal and retrospective context, fatherhood as a category could possess sufficient elasticity to absorb the unemployed man. This complicated their macro status as 'failures' to posit a gentler conception of unemployed fathers as 'fragile'.[12]

Unemployment and the failing father

For adult children, accounts of fathers' unemployment usually referenced the strain of economic shortages on mothers, consequences for children, especially hunger and the premature cessation of education and the tense dynamic between spouses as the spectre of the workhouse loomed ever larger before them.[13] Some fathers refused to provide for children and were, in a sense, self-selecting 'failed' fathers. In autobiography, adult children drew direct correlations between men's failure as fathers and their refusal, or reluctance, to provide financially. The actress Betty May's father 'lived and drank in idleness', a reflection of his 'naturally cruel' and fiendish temperament.[14] Other authors located their fathers' ineffectuality within a broader context of the injustices of capitalism.[15] Some fathers worked but their 'provision' was poor because of money spent on drink or gambling. Again, adult children's reflections appropriated this 'mechanical' shortcoming in paternity as a signifier of the absence or unsatisfactory status of affective dimensions to father-child relations.[16]

Feckless men made good copy. Joseph Stamper (born 1886) railed against the bias in social commentary towards failing men.[17] Despite the

---

[12] Dermott, *Intimate fatherhood*, 113. Dermott introduces the notion of the 'fragile' father in the final chapter of her book.

[13] See Jane Humphries, *Childhood and child labour in the British Industrial Revolution* (Cambridge University Press, 2010), 172–209.

[14] Betty May, *Tiger woman: my story* (London: Duckworth, 1929), pp. 20–26. See also O'Mara, *Liverpool Irish Slummy*, discussed in Chapter 5.

[15] See for instance, Tom Barclay, *Memoirs and medleys: the autobiography of a bottle washer* (Leicester: Edgar Backus, 1934) and Joseph Keating, *My struggle for life* (London: Simpkin and Marshall, 1916).

[16] See for instance, Garratt, *A man in the street* and Jack Martin, *Ups and downs: the life story of a working man* (Bolton: Stephenson, 1973). See also Ross, *Love and Toil*, 42–3 and 56–90.

[17] Stamper, *So long ago*, 202–4.

pervasive raciness of the feckless poor, the father who deserted or begrudged financial obligations to dependents represented a minority among men. Rowntree and Lasker's survey of unemployment in York claimed that more than half their subjects had good character and physique. Only fifteen per cent of men were without work because of faults in their character. Even here, defects ranged from the classic blight of intemperance, to bad time keeping to faults that were harder to categorise as wilful, such as inefficiency. Furthermore, 'defects', physical or moral, were often the outcome of prolonged periods of unemployment.[18]

For some children, the humiliation of family poverty fostered lasting contempt for selfish fathers.[19] As Rowntree and Lasker's survey illustrated, men without regular work also manifest self-loathing and depressed spirits. The Archers lived in a small three-room dwelling in a 'pleasant' court with their three children. Apprenticed as a joiner, Archer had never thrived at his trade; by his mid-twenties, he was a mere labourer, albeit a conscientious one. In 1906, aged twenty-seven, he was dismissed from the North Eastern Railway Company as they rationalised staff. He had been without steady work for four years at the time of the survey, taking 'catch' jobs where he could find them. If he was fortunate, he earned around nine to ten shillings a week.[20] For the first year after his dismissal, his wife had earned nine shillings a week doing laundry but her health had deteriorated while a seriously ill infant required nursing day and night. The family had applied to the parish and received two grocery orders but the Board refused to give further outdoor relief. Mrs. Archer was volubly bitter: the family were 'on the rocks'; she wanted to 'make a hole in the River Ouse and [have] done with it'. Archer, who had never drunk, gambled or rowed, radiated despair ('Aye, he feels it!'). The couple 'tried and tried and better tried' to pull themselves up but felt that luck was 'dead against' Archer.

As his wife vented the couple's frustration, Archer sat hidden in 'the remotest corner of the room', 'well in the background', murmuring an 'echo' to his wife's sentiments when she proclaimed drowning preferable to the workhouse. As the surveyor noted, it was hard for Archer to watch, quite literally, his family suffer. After all, his unemployment was the source of their distress. A good-looking fellow, Archer was weary with hunger and walking almost thirty miles a day looking for work. His coat could not 'possibly hold together much longer', he had 'unspeakably'

---

[18] Rowntree and Lasker, *Unemployment*, 173–199, 301–311.
[19] Doolittle, 'Fatherhood and family shame'.
[20] At the time of the survey, the average hourly rate in York for a joiner was 8.25 pence. Rowntree and Lasker, *Unemployment*, 151.

worn shoes; his feet were blistered and swollen. His body hinted at the depression of his spirit: his shoulders had the 'very set' of a man 'who is giving up all hope'. Little wonder he had 'lost heart': he tramped daily looking for work, answered job advertisements in borrowed newspapers and had registered at the unemployment bureau. As Mrs. Archer observed, there was not much more Archer could do.[21]

Rowntree and Lasker resisted blaming families like the Archers for their loss of heart: it was inevitable that relative buoyancy buckled under rejection, privation, increasingly poor health and hunger. Casual labour pressed men into disaffection and exacerbated existing problems. Rafferty, a former brick hauler, had consumption. While his health permitted, he worked breaking stones during the summer when his breathing eased. The meanest of jobs, stone breaking enabled Rafferty to maintain some self-respect: if his illness demanded a break in work, he could always return to it. The cruel irony was that the brute effort involved in the task probably exacerbated his poor health. For two years prior to the survey, the severity of Rafferty's lung haemorrhage had prohibited this employment and his wife had taken seasonal agricultural work instead. Rafferty did 'very little but "mind the children"'. While Rafferty harboured 'vague hopes' for a new lease of life, the surveyor reflected that his life had been 'hard', he appeared to have only 'faint melancholy interest' in the world about him and, both he and his wife were sinking into a 'kind of fatalism'. The despondency of Rafferty was palpable: he 'sits silent'.[22]

At another house, in a squalid court, lived the Lovells, a couple with four children. For sixteen years, Lovell worked for the same firm of house painters until lead poisoning forced his departure. His character was irreproachable: an 'excellent workman' in his prime, 'sober, conscientious, intelligent and punctual' (though he lacked 'push'). He initially received compensation for the lead poisoning but payments discontinued after eight months and he took a post as a caretaker to keep the family afloat. The meagre wages prompted Lovell to return to house painting in pursuit of better pay. This was a cruel and 'fatal blunder': his hands were 'now so disabled', he was unlikely ever to work regularly again. He was haggard, malnourished, suffered with asthma and bronchitis and looked 'like death'. Even on his best days, the surveyors thought him unfit for heavy work. Lovell's dejected spirits gave little animation to his proto-

---

[21] This family was so indigent that the surveyor advanced them money from the fee paid for their participation in the survey although this was against the guidelines established by Rowntree and Lasker because it created a false 'budget'. Rowntree and Lasker, *Unemployment*, 254–257.

[22] *Ibid*, 245–248.

corpse appearance.²³ The men above were all fathers who wanted to work for their children. The burden of their 'failure' was written into their despondency.

Even when men remained reasonably optimistic of securing regular work, talking about unemployment, especially to men from a different social class, remained awkward. Originally trained as a plumber, case study subject Campbell had worked in York for a firm for seventeen years as an engineer and hot-water fitter before being dismissed due to rationalisation in the economic downturn. Campbell suspected that his age, forty, had much to do with his dismissal. Certainly, the York data showed that men's chances of finding and keeping work diminished significantly over the age of forty. After two months of hoping he would be taken on again, the Campbells had spent their savings and begun to pawn possessions. Campbell had once belonged to a trade union but left it during a period of 'slackness' after which he began working for his most recent employer at a wage below the union rate. Employed for years as an engineer, Campbell had long since sold his plumbers' tools. From the artisan class, he and his wife had been used to helping others and found seeking assistance for themselves 'acutely painful'.

Like the other case study men, Campbell was 'phenomenally silent'. Unemployment dealt a powerful blow to his pride and self-respect. Invited to write an account of his experience, however, Campbell became 'expansive' about the 'bitterness' and bewilderment of becoming a 'completely world-forsaken man'. Crucially, the journal highlighted the extent to which his children's dependence on his labour provided both the motor to sustaining efforts to find work and the millstone of guilt that dragged his spirits down.²⁴ In another family, Nevinson, a fifty-year-old man with two 'first-rate' character references who had never been known to refuse any work, was also a 'silent man'. When he did speak, the surveyor noted his shrewd originality but Nevinson remained mute concerning many things. Like Campbell, he was more forthcoming in a diary he composed, with his married son (a 'splendid scholar' as Nevinson proudly stated) acting as amanuensis. Even here, though, the medium of the adult son probably encouraged Nevinson to censor his narrative to avoid burdening his son or, indeed, losing face with him.²⁵

The sense that these men were 'failing' was inescapable, both in the narratives they and their families composed with Rowntree and Lasker, and in the published survey's commentary on them. Matters were even worse for the would-be provider father who became dependent on

---

²³ *Ibid*, 251–254. ²⁴ *Ibid*, 238–242. ²⁵ *Ibid*, 230–234.

offspring. The Martins were 'the best type of working people'. Martin was forty-nine-years old and had earned good wages until his firm failed in 1907. He had managed to gain a temporary post for ten months but from 1908 had only casual labour and, through the goodwill of an old friend, odd gardening jobs. Martin was industrious, honest, punctual and willing, although plagued by rheumatism. He would accept any work, and was the type of worker who picked himself up after catastrophe. He was competent and more reliable than most. His fault, or weakness, was that he lacked 'self-assertion'. However much he tramped for work, there were inferior but forceful men who would claim prospective employers' attention.

The physiological and psychological burden of Martin's unemployment on his family was profound: they were undernourished to 'an appalling degree', his children had black shadows beneath their eyes, Mrs Martin had 'frequent heart attacks' and Martin was exhausted from 'vain tramps' for work. Each family member was close to a breakdown that could be averted only by Martin obtaining regular work, even if poorly paid. The family were entirely dependent on a daughter, aged eighteen, and a son, fifteen, who brought home a total of thirteen shillings a week. Described by their parents as 'good children, none better', the surveyor thought the youngsters prematurely aged and careworn. If Martin felt responsible for his children's poor health, the unrealistically high expectation his family invested in him compounded the situation.. For thirty-two years, he had earned good money every week. After the first shock of unemployment, his family assumed this hard-working man would quickly find regular work again. Even after two years of disappointment, his family hoped 'every day' that he would put all to right. Martin was, like the other men in the case studies, quiet and subdued, exhausted and 'disconsolate'. Had he expressed bitterness, it would have been understandable: despite doing everything he should and could, his family were on the brink of 'absolute ruin'. The resilience and 'wonder' of this family, like others in the case studies, was not that the male head of household remained unemployed but, rather, that the family was still 'holding its own'.[26]

As scholars have shown, the strain of men's prolonged unemployment on women, tasked with feeding, fuelling and clothing family, was enormous. Often, their predicament was exacerbated by a desire to propitiate depressed and frustrated husbands, and to protect children from the worst excesses of domestic antagonism and want.[27] Yet some of these husbands felt the sting of children's deprivation too. Social workers and

[26] *Ibid*, 249–51
[27] Ross, *Love and toil*, 56–90; Bourke, *Working-class cultures*, 71–81.

surveyors were apt to note the depressed spirits of unemployed men with families to support. At the forefront of Edwardian innovations in social work, Florence Petty visited women at home to teach them economical, nutritional cookery. At one house, a French polisher had been unemployed for fourteen weeks. This followed hard on the heels of his wife giving birth to twins. Petty noted that the couple had 'got very low' and pawned most of their belongings. She classed the wife as intelligent and keen but noted her disquiet in seeking Petty's help. Seeking assistance tacitly acknowledged the husband's failure as a provider: it made her feel a 'sneak' and suggested her reluctance to expose his failure in a public context.[28]

Such cases hinted at the matrimonial tensions that emerged from men's lack of work but couples could be united in their anxiety about the effects of unemployment on children. In another household, Petty met a married couple with a baby. The father had steady work as a Carman (driver of horse-drawn vehicle, usually employed by railway companies to transport goods and parcels) until his firm unexpectedly closed down. Although he took 'catch' jobs whenever possible, unemployment dealt a heavy blow. If toil was the key component of men's duty and attachment to children, being without work struck at the foundation of men's place in family life. Making explicit the dynamic between love and want, Petty observed that the former Carman was 'most devoted' to his wife and baby and unemployment made him 'very depressed'.[29] Contrasting sharply with the insouciance of the feckless man, attentive fathers were assailed by self-recrimination when they failed to provide. The Economic Club in 1891 investigated working-class economies. In one case study, a thirty-year-old jobbing plumber with three (living) children had been without regular work for months, partly due to illness from lead poisoning. While the plumber received treatment in hospital, his wife turned to the parish for support. Though he was sensitive to the shame of application, what grieved the plumber most was the 'surliness' with which the overseer treated his wife and the tardiness of relief once applied for. The death of his fourth child, a two-month-old infant, at a time of hardship exacerbated the man's bitterness. His pride was wounded, but the sting of humiliation was magnified because he was 'devoted' to his wife and children.[30]

---

[28] Florence Petty, *The pudding lady. A new departure in social work* (London: Stead's Publishing House, 1912), 42.
[29] *Ibid*, 64–5.
[30] Economic Club, *Family Budgets, being the income and expenses of twenty-eight British Households, 1891–1894* (London: P.S. King and Son, 1896), 18.

Not all depressed, unemployed men generated sympathy. Sam Shaw's (born 1884) memoir gave his father short shrift: he was aimless, self-indulgent and, in Shaw's view, harboured a personal dislike for his son. An active anti-socialist, Shaw resisted blaming economic structures for his family's poverty to dwell specifically on his father's failings. Shaw pictured his unemployed father at home, seated in his chair and smoking a pipe. This was all wrong. As the following chapter indicates, public understandings of fathers' position at home operated in a dynamic relationship with their time in work. Shaw's depiction of his father in his chair, a metonym for paternal authority, and his indulgence in tobacco, placed the older man implicitly in a binary between what ought to be, that is, father enjoying leisured privileges *after* work, with what was, the failed father as burden on household. His father filled the house with manic energy, stamping his heels and muttering 'a lot about the workhouse'. The more prolonged the unemployment, the more Shaw 'saw Dad every day', a situation that, financially and interpersonally, made family life 'worse' and steadily drove his father mad.[31] That Shaw's unemployed father escalated from depression to utter loss of reason offered a powerful allegory for the creeping malaise of idleness on masculine heads of household and its ramifications for the everyday unhappiness of children.

Correlations between men's unemployment and madness had powerful rhetorical value even when used to indict men. For critics of feckless men, loss of wits, frequently associated with intemperance, was the price of self-indulgence. However, as Rowntree and Lasker showed, good men suffered too. Sympathy for workless men was increasingly common in the structural paradigm that emerged in the latter decades of the nineteenth century where unemployment was an economic rather than moral problem. Even 'moral' texts incorporated some cognisance of paternal helplessness. Frederick Hasting's *Back streets and London slums* (1888) noted the degradation and humiliation of the unemployed and men in extremely low paid jobs: they 'despised' their condition and were so 'shattered' by disappointment that they became less and less rational. Hastings cited the case of an unemployed man who could only get sporadic work as a sandwich man (standing in the street, wearing advertising boards), one of the meanest occupations. This father was afraid to be left alone with his 'little pets' because, in the absence of providing, the only thing he could think of doing *for* them was to kill them.[32] A father

---

[31] Shaw, *Guttersnipe*, 8–13.
[32] Frederick Hastings, *Back streets and London slums* (London: Religious Tract Society, 1888), 50.

who could not provide for them, and for whom death had come to represent a rational act of beneficence in the face of indigence or separation, adored these children. In such contexts, stories of irrational paternity began to look dangerously reasonable.

The sensational edge to Hastings' anecdote exposed the degree to which provision legitimated men's relationship with their children. Apocryphal stories about unemployed men's 'insanity' highlighted the intensity of paternal despair in failing children through not working for them. As the socialist Joseph Toole (born 1887) asserted in his memoir, unemployment was 'nearly as bad as cancer' and, like a tumour, should be 'cut out' from civilised bodies: 'Nothing wears a man down so speedily, nothing so makes him lose hope.'[33] However flawed the breadwinner ideal, men's internalisation of responsibility for providing for families provoked deep self-recrimination when they failed.

In *The Ragged Trousered Philanthropists*, Robert Tressell repeatedly returned to the 'impotency' and 'shameful degradation' of men who laboured for meagre wages and who could be dismissed without notice. Throughout the novel, the protagonist Owen contemplates, for the 'thousandth time', killing his family as a solution to their bleak circumstances.[34] Although Tressell identifies the problem as capitalism, Owen's suffering is rooted in his crushing sense of responsibility: he cannot procure the nourishment, medicine or environment for his wife and son to thrive. Tressell's choice of the word 'impotency', referencing the flaccid penis, powerfully aligned the family's want with Owen's specifically masculine failure. It also mirrored the ways in which public dimensions of 'manliness', through work or legal paternity, mapped onto the intimacies of family life. That Owen's child was a boy amplified the hopelessness of the future: the son is doomed to repeat the labouring masculinity of his father. For Tressell, if working people could not realise the power of collective action, the only other option available for the likes of Owen and his dependents was death. This, at least, denoted agency. Hence, Owen's death wish represents his desire to make positive choices on behalf of his son and reverse, or thwart, failure: better to die than drudge all his life.[35]

In one scene, Tressell posts a newspaper headline proclaiming 'terrible domestic tragedy: double murder and suicide' only to dismiss it as 'one of the ordinary poverty crimes'. Diffidence here is the point: it underscores the banality of working-class despair and the cheap value placed on their lives. It is some twenty pages later that the story behind the

---

[33] Joseph Toole, *Fighting through life* (London: Rich and Crown, 1935), 27.
[34] Tressell, *Ragged trousered philanthropists*, 229.   [35] Ibid., 45.

headline is revealed to be far from 'ordinary': an unemployed man has dispatched his family to death and committed suicide. Insisting on society's trivialisation of such deaths, Tressell rails against coroners' verdicts that explain such actions as 'temporary insanity', thereby depoliticising them. They are, he suggests, the rational steps of an attentive man who takes his responsibilities seriously and cannot bear his dependents to suffer. In the absence of provision, such crimes were acts of devotion. That Owen is a tender man is never in doubt: his compassion for fellow outcasts is symbolised through his rescue of a stray kitten and, later, his adoption of an illegitimate baby. Owen's kind-heartedness is embedded in his resolution to kill his wife and child gently, without pain or mess. The affective logic underpinning Owen's thought heightens Tressell's overriding claim that it is capitalism that is insane. As the suicide note in the newspaper report exclaims: 'This is not *my* crime, but society's.'[36]

Tressell had fictive licence but correlations between men's 'madness' and unemployment were not without foundation. Jade Shepherd's analysis of men committed to Broadmoor for acts of violence upon their children made explicit the legal and imaginative correlations between a father's failure to provide and acute mental illness.[37] Examining coroners' returns for suicides in Kingston-Upon-Hull in the nineteenth century, Victor Bailey identified distinct patterns of suicide associated with the life cycle. Not only were cases of male suicide statistically more likely to come before the coroner; male suicides were overwhelmingly concentrated in the middle of the life cycle (thirty-five to forty-five years old), when financial pressures on breadwinners with young families were greatest. Although the support of a spouse could ameliorate despair, more than half of male suicides were married men. Illness, drink and financial problems, including unemployment, were the major causes of suicide in this category. Indeed, Bailey opened his chapter on suicide in the prime of life with a passage from Tressell's novel musing on the 'permanent insanity' of men slaving all their life for wife and children with nothing to show for it.[38] Some magistrates, at least, sympathised with the despair that drove men to seek oblivion. In 1870, a police magistrate reprimanded but discharged John Johnson, an unemployed sailmaker, aged forty-seven, accused of attempting suicide. Johnson had

---

[36] *Ibid.*, 87–92.
[37] Jade Shepherd, 'One of the best fathers until he went out of his mind: paternal child-murder, 1864–1900', *Journal of Victorian culture*, 18:1 (2013), 17–35.
[38] Victor Bailey, *This rash act: suicide across the life cycle* (Stanford University Press, 1998), 186–210.

been out of work for months and his family were starving.[39] Although he counselled Johnson that suicide was a sin, the magistrate's dismissal of the case hinted at resigned compassion for the man's hopeless predicament.

If medical, legal and religious paradigms rooted suicide in individual weakness, families who experienced the suicide of a male head of household could reclaim victims from ignominy by harnessing the logic of *felo de se*. At the age of seventy-two, Allan Taylor's (born c.1890) grandfather-provider was sacked, probably because of age, although Taylor does not give a reason. The older man had worked since the age of eight, averaging sixty-four hours a week at his loom for the princely sum of sixteen shillings. Taylor's grandfather embodied his work: a 'wee snippet' of a man, his spine curved like a 'bridge' from years bent over a loom. The grandfather's masculinity was in no doubt: he had sired twenty-two children, supported the nineteen that lived, and continued 'fathering' into old age by providing for his fatherless grandchildren, including Taylor. The loss of his job struck at the kernel of his selfhood, a blow that was mirrored in the older man's symbolic loss of himself when, on being sacked, he got plastered with drink. Paradoxically, this intemperate hiatus underscored the steadfastness of the older man. The shock of grandfather's intoxication, when grandfather *never* drank, paralleled the astonishment of his unemployment. As Taylor notes, idleness and dependency presented an impossible situation to a man whose identity was grounded in working for his family. Two days later, his grandfather left the house to 'look for work'. He was not seen again until his body washed up on the shore a week later.[40]

From the brink of failure: reclaiming the unemployed father

In macro terms, unemployment and suicide were monumental failures on the part of fathers: unemployment indicted men for failing to provide; suicide smacked of abandonment and stigmatised survivors. As Tressell demonstrated so powerfully, though, individuals need not be hidebound by political or economic logic, especially when they perceive that logic to be deeply flawed. On a micro level, family commentary on men's 'failures' as fathers could reproduce dominant understandings of male unemployment and simultaneously subvert them. Allan Taylor's story

---

[39] *Lloyds Weekly News*, 1 May 1870, 12.
[40] Allan Taylor, *From Glasgow Slum to Fleet Street* (London: Alvin Redman Ltd., 1949), 29–30.

of his grandfather's suicide suffused compassion for the older man with contempt for a society that treated him so shoddily. He also invested his grandfather's demise with agency: the death might have been accidental but the family positively claimed it as suicide. Taylor acknowledged that, as a journalist, he was often accused of exaggeration. The story of his grandfather's suicide certainly had a fantastic element, not least because his widow claimed to have foreseen the death in her tealeaves. His grandmother's clairvoyance added a quaint note to a biography charting a material world where the Glasgow tenement baby could achieve adult professional success. For all that, the older woman's divination rang with authenticity: self-effacement was the logical conclusion for men who 'work like slaves for starvation wages with the constant dread of unemployment and actual want hanging over us like a pall'. The mutilated face of his grandfather's corpse (the family had to rely on a distinctive tattoo to identify the body) held a mirror on unemployed men's metaphorical loss of face and replicated the violence of capitalism. The grandmother's confidence that her spouse committed suicide subverted the shame of his unemployment and felo de se, still a crime when Taylor published his autobiography (1949). Suicide gave the grandfather authority, both in terms of concluding his biography and in enacting a final devotional rite, that he would not be a burden on his family.[41]

Even where men resisted the pull of suicide, the desire for death enabled fathers to fantasise about doing something for offspring. Although paternal deaths effectively deserted dependents, there was pragmatism in the hopeless man's longing for expiration: widows with children were more likely to access outdoor parochial relief than were women burdened with an unproductive man.[42] Two families in Rowntree and Lasker's case studies named a desire to die. For one father, Lovell, this was a realistic 'contingency' as he suffered terrible ill health. With Lovell alive, the family 'dreaded' applying to the parish because they anticipated being told to 'come inside'. If Lovell died, his widow probably would be granted outdoor relief.[43] Another family, the Archers, had been told they must enter the workhouse to access parochial relief. The couple agreed that they would rather drown than suffer such defeat.[44] Such statements gave rhetorical emphasis to despair while articulating the couple's desire to take hold of fate. Some men with families tried to enter the workhouse alone. In December 1880, *Lloyds Weekly Newspaper* reported on the case of thirty-eight-year-old labourer, John Ives, father of five children, without work for almost a year due to

---

[41] *Ibid.* [42] Doolittle, 'Fatherhood and family shame'.
[43] Rowntree and Lasker, *Unemployment*, 252. [44] *Ibid*, 255.

illness and partial paralysis. He tried to enter the workhouse alone to spare his wife and children the indignity but the relieving officer refused to manipulate the system. Two weeks later, the man had a seizure and refused a doctor, telling his wife that he wished to die. In all probability, dying would enable his wife to claim outdoor relief. Their children were starving.[45]

Autobiographies that proclaimed labouring men's attachment to family and their right to work could inflect paternal degradation with personal significance, investing the unemployed man's humiliation with noble potential. A principal motif in authors' claims for workless fathers' dignity and devotion was their willingness to go 'on the tramp'. William Lax reflected that unemployment 'meant the dislocation of family life'. Just before Lax's birth, his unemployed iron moulder father left his pregnant wife in Wigan while he tramped to Manchester in search of work. Lax, an accomplished speaker in his roles as nonconformist minister and Mayor of Poplar, used short, stilted sentences ('Trade was bad'; 'My father was out of work'; 'He went on tramp') to convey the 'anxiety' and suspense of unemployment while simultaneously depicting his unemployed father as a blameless man of action.[46] The inclusion of the anecdote as a preamble to Lax's birth story signified the material and ideological importance of men's obligation to provide. That Lax could not have remembered this suggests how, in family contexts, stories of men seeking work were retold, long after the event, as celebrations of men's constancy and dedication. As Valerie Sanders noted, men's primary duty in providing for family gave fathers a 'central but precarious' role in family fortunes: so much depended on how seriously he took this responsibility and how far he was subject to forces beyond his control.[47]

Tramping was, simultaneously, a signifier of men's eagerness to work, as evidenced by the practice of trade unions organising tramping circuits through much of the nineteenth century, and a 'low' practice, associated with 'regular roadsters', reliant on casual labour, vagrancy wards and hand-outs to live free from responsibilities.[48] Emanuel Shinwell's unemployed father tramped from 'place after place': from London, he

---

[45] *Lloyds Weekly News*, 5 December 1880, 2. [46] Lax, *His book*, 19.
[47] Sanders, *The tragi-comedy*, 15.
[48] The most comprehensive account of the tramping system remains Eric Hobsbawm, 'The tramping artisan', *Economic History Review*, New Series, 3:3 (1951), 299–320. As Hobsbawm points out, by the end of the century, this system of seeking employment was utilised mostly by single young men. For press commentary on the tramp problem at the turn of the twentieth century see, Julie-Marie Strange, 'Tramp: sentiment and the homeless man in the late Victorian and Edwardian city' *Journal of Victorian Culture*, 16:2 (2010), 242–258.

sought work in Nottingham, Leicester, and Newcastle before eventually settling in Glasgow. Alive to the fine line between the tramping workman and the tramp who cut loose family ties, Shinwell stressed that his father was 'forced' to leave home because of the trade depression at the end of the 1880s. Tramping was what family men did when their circumstances left no alternative. Once he reached South Shields in the north of England, where he had relations, his father sent for his seven-year-old son to join him. This relieved the financial burden on Shinwell's mother, working as a cook in London, and signalled to Shinwell's reader that, although separated from his dependents, his father remembered his obligations to them.[49]

Even when fathers' tramps were unsuccessful, for the child narrating the story, the effort men expended, walking 'miles and miles', mattered.[50] Joseph Stamper's father tramped from St. Helens in Lancashire to Belfast, seeking work as an iron moulder. As Stamper wryly notes, so did all the other unemployed iron moulders in England. Unsuccessful, his father had to work his passage back tending cattle bound for a slaughterhouse on the Wirral. The implicit parallel between man and beast here amplified the brute economics of capitalism. Although tramping gave the illusion of freedom, men were just as bound to their obligations as cattle were for slaughter.[51]

That earnest, respectable men took to the road in search of work augmented just how meaningful this potentially humiliating experience was to adult children reconstructing childhood experience. When one author's father did succumb to the call of freedom, his subsequent capitulation signified the complex nexus of attachments and responsibilities in family. Alfred Coppard's father, a journeyman tailor based at Folkestone, deserted his wife and children, leaving them in 'sore straits'. He absconded a hundred miles or so to Brighton. The abandonment was temporary, and Coppard offset the callous departure with the outcome: his father obtained new work, invited his family to join him and 'all was to be well again'. Coppard's tone has a tempered cynicism, not all of which centred on his father. The move to Brighton was sensible in that both parents had kin there, but, little would 'be well' when journeyman tailoring was far from 'enriching' and unemployment 'endemic'. Although doubtful how far they anticipated it at the time, his father was also dying. In this light, his desertion and return suggested mutual

---

[49] Shinwell, *Conflict without malice*, 16–19.
[50] Rose Gibbs, *In service: Rose Gibbs remembers* (Royston: Archives for Bassingbourn and Comberton Village Colleges, 1981), 4.
[51] Stamper, *So long ago*, 200.

dependency between husband and family: he worked like 'a slave' to support the dependents he might have given up; his wife and children reciprocated, nursing him through sickness. Coppard acknowledged the appeal of freedom to a sick man in his twenties with three children to support. Paradoxically, the abandonment underscored the significance of recall: this man wanted to cut loose but, seemingly, changed his mind. Coppard adored his 'beautiful' mother who fought for her children as wife and widow, but he also was attached to his father, mourned his death and, in later life, liked to imagine his father's face before him.[52]

Autobiographical accounts of fathers tramping for work indicated men's family commitment and exposed the inherent problems of an economic system that generated so much casual labour, a theme echoed in Rowntree and Lasker's survey. Sciatica plagued one man, Nevinson, who was nearly fifty years old. Although he confined his tramps to York, Nevinson 'worked' hard at it. Some days, he left home as early as three or four in the morning. He spent most days walking 'round and round' until evening, trying to pick up any available work. If he returned without having secured paid work, he undertook household tasks such as mending his 'little boy's boots' or chopping wood he had found. Rejected repeatedly, Nevinson conceded that he was 'fairly sick of walking about'.[53] Archer was in physical pain from relentless tramping: his worn boots revealed blistered and swollen feet. A tramp of twenty-eight miles in one day 'nearly did for him'.[54] The former engineer, Campbell, was also physically weak and sore from tramping.[55]

Although men's tramps gave the semblance of routine and testified to commitment, the labour of tramping accentuated hunger and, with constant rejection, sharpened the teeth of despair. These men must have looked less and less like able workers. For the families they returned to, their blisters, hunger and fatigue from tramping were badges of endurance, fortitude and devotion. Men's boots carried a host of negative connotations associated with domestic violence.[56] The decrepitude of unemployed men's boots and the tenderness of their feet, however, implicitly held Rowntree and Lasker's tramps as foils to the brutes in stout boots to amplify these men's integrity. If adult children invested men's waged labour with affective meaning, paternal suffering from the quest for work similarly resonated with emotive significance to facilitate the agency and dignity of jobless fathers, at a public and personal level.

---

[52] Coppard, *It's me, O Lord!* 9–31.   [53] Rowntree and Lasker, *Unemployment*, 230–5.
[54] *Ibid*, 254–8.   [55] *Ibid*, 238–243.
[56] See Slater, *Think on! said Mam;* and Joanne Bailey, *Unquiet lives: marriage and marriage breakdown in England, 1660–1800* (Cambridge University Press, 2003).

Akin to tramping narratives was the story of fathers who deskilled in order to do 'anything' to provide something, although trade unions advised that skilled men hold out for skilled work.[57] The Economic Club's study of the plumber demonstrated how impractical it was for the family man to wait for skilled work. The plumber described his approach to finding work as 'three-branch', a strategic navigation between holding out for skilled wages and the necessity of taking unskilled labour to keep his family ticking over. First, he tried local connections for plumbing jobs. When these failed, he applied directly to firms and householders. His third branch, working as a porter at auction rooms or taking 'whatever' paid, demonstrated his versatility. The plumber's dilemma highlighted the problems of this strategy, not least because he sometimes had to turn down skilled work because he had pawned his tools and had nothing else on which to raise a loan.[58] Nevertheless, his resourcefulness underscored his identity as a 'devoted' father and husband.

Similarly, adult children narrated paternal flexibility in taking 'anything', so long as it paid something, as testimony to men's faithful dedication to family. The Labour politician Ben Turner (born 1863) paid tribute to his 'sweet tempered' father, a radical weaver and trade unionist, a model of manhood. His father experienced several periods of strike activity and unemployment during Turner's childhood. During one prolonged period, his father was 'driven' to quarrying to keep family resources ticking over. At other times, his father broke stones for road building or cut peat on the moors. The impact of such labour on his father's body was heartbreaking: 'It made us children weep to see my father's bleeding hands.' Turner's anecdote had political resonance, especially written during the inter-war depression when trade unions were battling over schemes to put unemployed men to work in exchange for relief. The potential indignity of such labour was also deeply personal. Turner's stigmatic imagery highlighted the degree of paternal sacrifice, especially as the work bore little correlation to the weaver's skill or physique. Unless the reader missed the affective significance of the tale, he stated that 'no children had more loving parents than we'. Turner's tears for his father's hands transformed the indignity of unskilled labour into something beautiful, valorising even the meanest of work, stone

---

[57] Even temporary deskilling precipitated a decline in men's overall earning capacity and could encourage men to accept skilled work at lower wage rates. Rowntree and Lasker highlighted many examples of men who took 'anything', including 'rough' work for which their physiques were entirely unsuited to keep families ticking over. See Rowntree and Lasker, *Unemployment*, 32–3; 44–5; 96–7; 243–5.

[58] Economic Club, *Family Budgets*, 19–20.

Love and want: unemployment, failure and the fragile father   67

breaking. This carried extra significance for Turner who, as a father with two children, also experienced unemployment: it was the 'hardest' period of his life; 'the most heart breaking experience in the world'.[59]

The decline of artisan trades pitched Michael Llewelyn's (born 1888) father, a skilled blacksmith, into alternative work as a quarryman at the age of forty. This could, and perhaps should, have been humiliating. A slur by a local dignitary on his father's 'fall' to the 'filthy' labour of quarrying moved Llewelyn to rage: 'I could have brained him'. There was no need. As his father stated, there was no shame in 'honest' toil. For Llewelyn, the beauty of quarrying, so different from the blacksmith's craft, was underscored by the memory of his father's work as shared space and time: he spent 'many happy hours' at the quarry, watching his father, catching fish in the nearby stream and pondering what grand buildings would emerge from his father's stone.[60] There was filial pride in paternal humility. Anthony Grundy's (born 1880) parents made a disastrous attempt at running a hotel, losing considerable money in the process. Despite trying 'very hard' to gain employment, his father could only find unskilled, seasonal labour on farms in his native village. Grundy's story of his father's diminished status marked the son's pride in the older man's willingness to 'do anything' to keep the family afloat.[61]

Rose Gibbs's (born 1892) father was a soldier in the Boer War. Home on leave, he and his young son, just recovered from the amputation of his foot following a railway accident, had their photograph taken. A reward for the 'brave' boy's courage in hospital, the photograph aligned soldier father and plucky son to suggest the ways in which paternal approval validated children's (particularly boys') experiences. The photograph had added poignancy when set against subsequent events in these 'brave boy' narratives. The gallant soldier's final return from Africa was as a wounded man. Physically impaired, no one would give him a job. He 'walked for miles and miles' in search of work but desperation drove him to the parish guardians where he exchanged labour for a three-pound loaf. Aside from entry into the workhouse, this labour was one of the most humiliating forms of 'work' men could undertake. Gibbs's adjectives conveyed the cruel irony of the wounded soldier, whose infirmities precluded paid work, performing backbreaking work for parish bread: he wielded a 'heavy' pick to break 'huge' blocks of stone. 'At last', Gibbs noted, 'someone took pity on him' and gave him a job in a brass

---

[59] Ben Turner, *About myself, 1863–1930* (London: Humphrey Toulmin, 1930), 42–43; 75.
[60] Michael Llewelyn, *Sand in the glass: an autobiography* (London: John Murray, 1943), 83.
[61] Anthony George Grundy, *My fifty years in transport* (Buckingham: Adam Gordon, [1944] 1997), 5.

foundry.[62] The 'at last' intimated the prolonged anxiety of her father and those depending on him. It also created narrative tension for worse was to come: shortly after gaining employment, her father was wounded again in an industrial accident. The dry resignation of Gibbs's authorial voice alongside her identification of someone else's pity worked to maintain a normative father-child dynamic by removing Gibbs from the potential condescension of sympathy. Rather, Gibbs highlighted the chasm between social and cultural assumptions about men's roles and responsibilities: the contrast between father in his soldier's glory and the weak man tramping for work or wielding his parochial pick to feed his family evoked the silent heroism of the unemployed dad. That this man's son also was physically wounded further reinforced the sense of inevitable tragedy afflicting men who deviated from the 'able-bodied' norm of labouring masculinity.

The meanness of filthy work could be transfigured into profound acts of devotion when children emphasised the versatility and humility of fathers. Some authors even reconfigured begging as a positive identifier of 'breadwinning' status. Begging was an offence under the 1824 Vagrancy Act, which assumed that vagrants and beggars were deliberately idle. Statistical returns for the prosecution of beggars, however, show a correlation between trade depression and begging.[63] Begging declined in line with recruitment for the First World War but for men like Fred Davies's (born 1908) father, a blind man, war made little difference to his ability to support his family. As a boy, Davies led his father to his 'pitches' every night of the week. Indeed, he called his life story *My father's eyes*. His father carried a tin can and wore a sign that identified him as disabled and distinguished him from the loafer.

Even though the household economy relied on charitable organisations and Davies described his family as 'poor', he portrayed his father as a moderately successful breadwinner. The begging was for 'money for food and clothes', it took place at routine times and places, and involved long hours (twelve on a Saturday) in all weathers. Davies remembered his father as a difficult man and begging together had been full of 'ups and downs'. Nevertheless, Davies's assertion that he missed his father 'very much' after he died (when Davies was fourteen), mirrored the extent to which, for all his ambivalence, he could configure his beggar father in mechanical and intrinsic terms as a 'good' father. When his father's begging went well, he paid for family treats such as cow heel and

---

[62] Gibbs, *In service*, 4.
[63] Lionel Rose, *Rogues and vagabonds: vagrant underworld in Britain, 1815–1985* (London: Routledge, 1988).

stew; whenever he visited the Blind Aid Society, two to three times a year, the family had a slap up meal the following day. This was unconventional but provision nonetheless.

Davies affirmed his father's positive status by referencing external agents' esteem for the older man. When begging all day in an affluent town, a 'lady' allowed his father to use her toilet. Arrested on one occasion for begging with a child and causing an obstruction to pedestrians, Davies invested the experience with dignity: the Chief Constable of Manchester, a 'real gentleman', provided father and son with tea and biscuits before making out a card granting them permission to beg. Such were the markers of civility that Davies manoeuvred to legitimate his father's status in a context where the beggar typically was viewed as a rogue. Indeed, Davies wished that he had kept the Chief Constable's card as a souvenir. Davies described a stone pillar where his father stood every Saturday: 'The pillar is still there today, sixty-odd years on, and the dark mark on the pillar, where he leaned his back every Saturday for four years, is still showing.' There is tenderness in this recollection: the smudge evoked the constancy and weariness of the older man and the obligations that tied father and son (his eyes) together while the shadowy imprint on the pillar provided a metaphor for the twilight world of fathering through begging.

Davies hinted at shame in his family circumstances only twice. First, when he had to go to the Blind Aid Society in his father's place to receive items of (unsuitable) boy's clothing, an act that marked Davies personally as a recipient of charity on account of his father's shortcomings. Second, Davies recalled an encounter with an uncle, the manager of a railway depot, whom he approached for a job only to be firmly rejected. Davies recalled how his mortification brought tears to his eyes. His disappointment was acute: working on the railway, wearing a smart uniform, was the pinnacle of boyish ambition. The thing that really rankled, however, was the uncle's contempt for the boy and, more to the point, his poor parents.[64] The gift of memoir was that Davies could reverse the indignity. If his poor relations affronted the uncle, Davies's recollection cast him as a miserable figure whose social status counted for little against his lack of humanity. In the micro-hierarchies of everyday life, Davies outlined a moral universe where his father, though a beggar, fulfilled his paternal obligations as best he could; a man of whom Davies was proud.

Where men found little or no work at all, their contribution to domestic labour, especially when wives became principal breadwinners,

[64] Fred Davies, *My father's eyes: episodes in the life of a Hulme man* (Manchester: Neil Richardson, 1985), 7–15.

enhanced their status as working for their family. Campbell 'always found some little item wanted attention' and took 'satisfaction' in performing tasks at home, such as repairing his children's boots or fixing a smoking chimney, and making a 'good job'.[65] As his position as provider slipped, Lovell's assumption of childcare tasks made him 'feel that he is of some use, even when he is not "working"'.[66] Rafferty, too ill for waged work, undertook to 'mind the children'. The surveyor described them as healthy, happy and fearless offspring, despite the family's privation.[67] For sick men, there was probably little to do but stay at home. That some men found the assumption of 'maternal' and feminine tasks demeaning is undoubted. During a long stoppage at the coalmine, Jack Jones's father continued to provide by 'scratting' for coal, which he could exchange for groceries. As the family of eleven grew desperate, Jones recalled the quarrels between his parents about how to make ends meet. When his mother asserted that she would beg and sell strike ballads around the steelworks, Jones's father went 'wild' with fury: in begging from the earnings of other breadwinners, his wife and children fundamentally changed their relationship to the paterfamilias (and other men). His father, meanwhile, feared his authority would collapse altogether if he ended up keeping house. Such complaints exposed male contempt for women's work. Although grateful to his mother for feeding them during this period, Jones's celebration of the return to order seemingly confirmed his father's disparagement of topsy-turvy gender roles: as soon as the strike ended, his father 'slogged away' in the pit to provide the 'scores of things' the family needed.[68]

Although the loss of masculine wages struck a blow to paternal status, men's performance of typically 'maternal' acts could boost their legitimacy at home and confirm their attachment to family members. Historians have typically identified self-sacrifice in food distribution as a key component of maternal identity. Ellen Ross noted that while the provision of basic foodstuffs was man's most fundamental duty to his wife and children, the transformation of provision into nourishment formed the lynchpin of women's labour and identity. Food was emotional: mothers' shortcomings in feeding children provoked tears, hungry children's cries clawed at mothers' hearts and the preparation of food was inextricable from children's esteem for their mothers. The sound and sight of hungry

---

[65] Maud Pember Reeves noted that boots were the biggest clothing expense in families; most fathers in Lambeth, London, repaired their children's boots. Maud Pember Reeves, *Family life on a pound a week* (London: Fabian Society, 1912), 63.
[66] Rowntree and Lasker, *Unemployment*, 253.   [67] *Ibid*, 246.
[68] Jones, *Unfinished journey*, 78–83, 84.

children was heartbreaking.⁶⁹ In the York survey, the Archers' nine-month-old baby was 'half starved', never still and its perpetual crying tore the 'very heart' from its mother.⁷⁰ But it seems unlikely that fathers were insensitive to children's hunger or careless of their responsibility for it. Children's hunger was one of the principal signifiers of men's failure to provide. Rose Gibbs constructed her father's unemployment in direct relation to her hunger.⁷¹ Frederick Hastings declared that he knew men who had been driven mad by their children's clamour for food and the lack of a wage wherewith to supply it.⁷² For Sam Shaw, hungry children's demand for father's 'bread' was a powerful literary device to demonstrate the physiological and psychological nexus of fathering and want. After a long stint of unemployment, Shaw's father began pawning possessions to obtain money for food. His excursions from the pawnbrokers met with 'invariable' calls of 'Got a loaf, Dad?' In getting 'straight to the point', this question signalled his children's expectation that father should provide 'bread'. Shaw's use of 'Got a loaf, dad?' as the chapter title, and his repetition of the question throughout, magnified the degree to which men's literal and metaphorical 'bread' legitimised their relationship with children. As an adult, Shaw 'shuddered' that 'so much' bread was wasted, for it reminded him of his father's 'haunted' look whenever he returned home without a loaf.

That the spectre of his father's failure haunted the elderly Shaw (who had provided for eight offspring) suggested the imaginative and emotive burden of men's breadwinner obligations. Shortly after this sequence in Shaw's story, his unemployed father was committed to a lunatic asylum, whereupon local guardians replaced his father's loaf with 'parish' bread, the inadequacy of which highlighted the poor substitution of the state for a father. Although Shaw was indifferent to his father *per se*, the 'loaf' story underpinned the abstract comfort of family obligations fulfilled. For all his father's failings, Shaw blasted the state for ripping the ties of family asunder. When Shaw was committed to an Industrial School at the age of ten for selling matches without a license, on his father's instructions, he captured his loneliness by contrasting the soulless borstal with his siblings at home, asking 'Got a loaf, Dad?'⁷³ At once, this device portrayed the origin of Shaw's committal to the borstal (had his father been an adequate breadwinner, Shaw would not have been selling matches) and what he lost in the process.

---

⁶⁹ Ross, *Love and toil*, 27–9. ⁷⁰ Rowntree and Lasker, *Unemployment*, 255.
⁷¹ Rose Gibbs, *In service*, 4. See also James Vernon, *Hunger: a modern history* (Cambridge (MA) and London: Belknap Press of Harvard University Press, 2007).
⁷² Hastings, *Back streets*, 61. ⁷³ Shaw, *Guttersnipe*, 8–13, 51.

The distribution of food among family members signified obligations and attachments. Mothers typically skimped on calories to prioritise the nourishment of husbands and children. The best and largest share of food, especially meat, usually was allocated to male breadwinners, a system of distribution known as the 'breadwinner effect' because of men's labour supposedly demanding more calories. Welfare schemes also replicated this allocation pattern, especially during industrial action.[74] Undoubtedly, some men were selfish and expected hearty meals from scant resources but, as Ellen Ross observed, men's habitual consumption of extra calories did not mean they were greedy 'monsters'. Rather, they 'unthinkingly' assumed privileges due because of breadwinning. The paterfamilias who carved the Sunday roast 'dramatized' the fact that his wages paid for it; when he enforced strict 'manners' at table, he enacted breadwinner authority. Ross points to the flawed logic of the breadwinner effect, noting that women's domestic labour, including pregnancy and lactation, demanded comparable caloric intake. Men's assumed right to better food depended on women's low status and wives' desire to propitiate spouses. But the 'breadwinner effect' was not always about masculinity: young adult wage earners in families were also allocated greater food resources. Similarly, men's food share diminished as their wage status crumpled.[75]

Most contemporary commentators assumed that labouring men needed more calories and protein not only to sustain work, but to secure it, too. Rowntree and Lasker repeatedly noted men who looked 'underfed' and were unlikely to find work when competing with more robust specimens of manhood.[76] Eleanor Rathbone's study of casual labourers in Liverpool noted that intelligence and character, values prized by the bourgeois social worker, held little value in jobs that required brute strength.[77] To compete effectively for wages, men needed to look nourished. Maud Pember Reeves repeatedly emphasised that men's diets kept families afloat: to starve father was 'bad economy' with repercussions for all family members.[78] The Economic Club's account of the plumber's

---

[74] Ross, *Love and toil*, 34. Andy Croll persuasively suggests that this went beyond sexed worlds of food to reflect the politics of supporting strikes or the 'victims' of men's industrial action. Croll, 'Starving strikers', 103–131. Some welfare schemes offered meals for men on the tramp or in low paid occupations; other schemes prioritised food parcels for unemployed married men with children. See for example, *Lloyds Weekly News*, 25 January 1880, 5.
[75] Ross, *Love and Toil*, 27–55.
[76] Rowntree and Lasker, *Unemployment*, see 44–5 and 48–9, for example.
[77] Eleanor Rathbone, *Report on the results of a special inquiry into the conditions of labour at the Liverpool Docks* (Liverpool Economic and statistical Society, 1903–4), xiii.
[78] Reeves, *Family life*, 68 133, 124, 143.

family noted the extent to which couples subscribed to gendered food distribution. Following two weeks of 'enforced idleness', the plumber began work on an empty stomach. He and his wife believed this weakness led to his development of lead poisoning, necessitating admission to hospital and plunging the family into dire straits.[79] We know this was flawed logic, but when wives gave men the greater share of food, they did so at least partly from a sense that the family's hopes sailed with him: calories invested in men's strength generated a better return for everyone.

Awareness of the emotive significance of food was not the preserve of mothers. The navigation of food distribution in families with an unemployed (or underemployed) male breadwinner suggests that calorie consumption represented a moral, material and emotional dilemma for mothers *and* fathers when children were hungry. Rowntree and Lasker's study of unemployed families in York highlighted accounts of men's willingness to forego food for their children. In the Rafferty family, father ate 'next to nothing' while Lovell had dry bread so his children could have dripping.[80] Nevinson had been without regular employment for three years at the time of the study. Most of the family's meals consisted of bread and margarine or dripping. He could be persuaded to eat the 'last crust' only if his wife convinced him there was another loaf for her and their children. When a neighbour brought a bowl of oats one evening, the Nevinsons allocated it to their children. That Mrs. Nevinson encouraged her husband to eat in the belief that there was more bread for her and the children suggests that both spouses were alive to their food dilemma. Reluctance to consume calories his children needed articulated this man's discomfiture in claiming 'breadwinner' rights when he failed to provide. His wife's insistence that he eat something reflected her hope that he would find work and her bid to reassure him of his position within the family. Indeed, the only work Nevinson was likely to get was labouring, for which he would need strength.

Mothers were, perhaps, especially sensitive to, and articulate about, the emotive significance of hunger and keen to challenge surveyor suspicions about their husband's character. When asked if her husband supped beer to supplement his food (assuming working people classed beer as a foodstuff), Mrs Nevinson's anger was palpable. In regular work, Nevinson 'liked his glass of beer as well as any one'. With prolonged unemployment, his priority was bread. As his wife fumed: 'You don't find a man who goes out many a morning at five o'clock fasting,

---

[79] Economic Club, *Family budgets*, 19.
[80] Rowntree and Lasker, *Unemployment*, 245–8, 251–4.

because he wants to leave what crust there is for the children and me, dropping into the public with the first shilling he earns'.[81] For Mrs. Nevinson, her husband's choices about the provision, consumption and sacrifice of food were replete with devotional connotations.

In the Archer household, the unemployed father tried to compensate for the lack of material provision by foregoing his share of food: 'Father ate nothing through the day, leaving what there was for us'. Archer's wife used stories of his nutritional sacrifice to illustrate the level of the family's want and her spouse's status as a good man. One particular story epitomised the Archers' complex navigation of priorities, ties and obligations. On the day of King Edward VII's funeral (20 May 1910), there was half a loaf in the house, but Archer set off tramping for work without breakfast: 'He wouldn't touch it'. He left the house optimistic that such a 'grand day' must bring work somewhere. His wife laid a table for lunch with the remaining bread and weak tea but Archer refused to cross the threshold: 'He looked through the window, and I called him in, but he just shook his head and went away again.' As Chapter 3 demonstrates, food rituals in working-class homes enabled families to acknowledge fathers' rights and authority but, also, provided a space for tactile and affective engagement. Mrs. Archer's preparation of the table suggested an attempt to maintain practices of togetherness that reassured Archer of his status and embedded him within an everyday family dynamic. That he felt unable to enter the house was, as Mrs. Archer assumed, a powerful indicator of this father's self-loathing: bringing no wages home, he felt he had no place at his family table.

When Archer finally returned home that evening, his wife described him 'looking more like a ghost than a man'; a revealing phrase that exposed the difference between the working man and his unemployed shadow. He had earned two pence carrying a portmanteau. In celebration, Mrs. Archer recklessly sent a child for fish and chips. As many social workers would have clamoured to tell her, two pence might have gone further. But well-intentioned social workers so often missed the point. For Mrs. Archer, the shared supper held symbolic value. Archer was exhausted, depressed and hungry but had stayed out all day until two pence legitimised his return home. The family togetherness of the meal celebrated his resilience and commitment, offsetting his failure with family gratitude for his determination to succeed. Mrs. Archer's note that the meal brought real pleasure to each family member highlighted parental pleasure in children's consumption of food and the affirmative

---

[81] *Ibid*, 231–5.

practices of teatime. It is unlikely that Archer, inhibited by shame and silence, would have told this story. As a mother, sensitive to the significance of food sacrifice, Mrs. Archer was alive to the emotional work of her husband's food provision, rejection and consumption.[82]

Some men were explicit about the abstract significance of food. In the diary composed for Rowntree and Lasker, the plumber Campbell noted that he tramped for work on 'not very much' food. As the weeks went by, Campbell was more anxious to find work 'being out from early morning until late at night with a stomach as empty as a soap bubble'. When faced with losing their home through non-payment of rent, Campbell resented the landlord taking scant resources that he would have preferred to 'spin out' in a 'good way' in food for his children. His emphasis on nutritional inadequacy intimated the family's want and marked the affective framework in which Campbell positioned his unemployment. Despite his physical weakness, knowledge of 'those depending upon me at home' drove his tramping. A proud man, Campbell instinctively recoiled from seeking welfare but being 'without food for the children' was a 'matter of great importance'.[83]

For some adults, food consumption offered a template for explaining how parents negotiated nurture. Joseph Stamper reflected that his parents stood as 'buffers' between their offspring and the world. Stamper could recall his mother 'cracking' with financial anxiety only once. Hidden in the scullery, Stamper heard his mother weeping while his unemployed father murmured reassurances. Minutes later, his father appeared with his Sunday suit, wrapped in newspaper, destined for the pawnbrokers. Asserting authority and responsibility, his father 'wagged his whisker' at his wife's protests and proceeded to hock the clothing. When the family ate that evening, Stamper reflected that he was the only child to know they were eating his father's suit. This profane transubstantiation, of father's clothes into victuals, realised the family dynamic around food. As a moment of togetherness, teatime signified unity, identity and parents' respective roles in the provision and preparation of food. That Stamper portrayed this meal as having a secret significance for his parents emphasised the spousal partnership that sought to protect and provide for children and the intimacy of 'family' food more generally.[84]

(Sir) Reader Bullard (born 1885) opened his autobiography with his birth, narrated from his unemployed father's perspective. Aged thirty-five, his father walked eight miles to Walthamstow docks in hope of

---

[82] *Ibid*, 254–8. [83] *Ibid*, 238–43. [84] Stamper, *So long ago*, 200–1.

securing labouring work. Failing to catch the foreman's eye, he returned home to find that his wife had given birth to a son (Bullard), a sibling for the couple's five-year-old daughter.[85] It was the father's birthday and he named his boy after its grandfather. It could hardly have been a day for happy returns, Bullard concluded. His birth account set the tone for his childhood: the family lived on a 'narrow margin' but he grew up in 'decent' surroundings and never went hungry. Here, hunger acted as a marker between the struggling and abject classes but also of parental priorities. In reflection, he suspected that his nourishment was at the expense of his parents who, in all probability, did go hungry. His parents' desire to shield their children from hunger threw the ambivalence of Bullard's birth story into relief: children were a financial burden but parents' sacrifices on their behalf testified to attachment. That Bullard's father named the babe after his father lent this scenario extra poignancy: it affirmed a lineage of paternal obligation and gratitude while signalling the dock labourer's ambition for his son. Given Bullard's commitment to self-education, the name 'Reader' was truly portentous.[86]

Unemployment and fragile fathers

Bullard's account of his father's unemployment, like Taylor's story of his grandfather's suicide, fused compassion with a desire to give unemployed fathers agency and dignity. In doing so, they identified how, when provision faltered, families could appropriate alternative elements of fathering, such as food sacrifice, tramping or deskilling, to underpin and illuminate the intrinsic elements of father-child dynamics. Yet it was not always possible to depict unemployed fathers as figures of dignity. Paternal unemployment could be shattering. Elizabeth Bryson lamented that 'my father's heart had broken when he thought he had failed his children'. Her parents responded differently to the family's subsequent hardship. Mother, whose identity was rooted in stretching household resources, rose to the challenge of poverty. For Bryson's father, the sense of responsibility for pitching his family into crisis was crushing.[87] If men's labour 'for me' had 'to me' significance, the lack of work threatened to destabilise father's affective status. Although this might throw other dimensions of father-child attachment into relief, it

---

[85] Bullard notes that his father's return home was on the principle that the willingness of casual labourers to hang around all day encouraged employers to rely on casual labour instead of giving men jobs.
[86] Reader Bullard, *The camels must go* (London: Faber and Faber, 1961), 17–18.
[87] Bryson, *Look back in wonder*, 89.

could also fundamentally alter, at least in retrospect, the intrinsic dynamic between father and child. Bryson did not value her father less because he stopped being a successful provider. In hindsight, her father's financial failure signalled a turning point in their relationship: father slipped from his heroic pedestal to become a much more fragile figure; his daughter matured from an unquestioning child enchanted by her father to a young woman solicitous of his care.

For Kathleen Woodward (born 1896), recollection of her father's unemployment enabled her to highlight affective sympathy between father and daughter in the face of her powerful mother. In his prime, Woodward's father had been a skilled lithographic printer but ill health precipitated his slide into casual labour and, eventually, financial dependence on his wife. That Woodward described this as 'endurance' suggested his humiliation. Her father possessed a 'virile and manly' conception of his obligations; his inability to fulfil them 'slowly crushed the life out of him'. His weakness was physical and emotional as Woodward recalled his tearful supplications; what had he done to deserve such suffering. Nevertheless, unemployment unlocked different components of fathering. If her father was stung by the impotency of dependency, Woodward pointed to the augmentation of his finer domestic qualities: he was 'exquisitely gentle and sensitive', refined and fastidious. He was a salve, in childhood and biography, against the coarse grit Woodward identified in her mother.[88]

Authors who sympathised with fathers conveyed the emotional complexity of men's failure to provide both in real time and upon reflection. Joseph Stamper's recollections located a detailed family story within a broader framework of observations on social, economic and political life. Anecdotes about his father's unemployment provided a vehicle for Stamper's commentary on the condition of workless men. Stamper's father took his young son on walks about the municipal park, pausing to engage groups of elderly men minding grandchildren. Stamper's description of 'decayed old working men' highlighted the emasculation of the older workless male: they were 'castrated and desexed', transformed by age and dependency from robust workers into creaking nursemaids. Stamper barely mentions that his father, too, was unemployed and performing nursemaid duties. If work made men, the unemployed father minding his boy was, potentially, even less of a man for he was, supposedly, in his prime. In another anecdote, Stamper's father took him to see a family sold up. As bailiffs emptied the house, the mother stood

---

[88] Kathleen Woodward, *Jipping Street* (London: Virago, 1983), 11.

'with her children around her' while father, excluded from their tight unit, 'stood with them'. Stamper pointed to the man's dual catastrophe: his lack of work was responsible for the disaster; in turn, cognisance of personal responsibility prevented the father sharing his dependents' suffering. Stamper's clear memory of the weeping mother's face contrasted to the blank features of the father to amplify the extent to which work validated men's status; without it, they were faceless ciphers.[89]

Stamper's objective in these anecdotes is to demonstrate how far men's inability to provide threatened to emasculate and exclude fathers from family. Yet, the primary agent of sympathy in these stories is Stamper's unemployed father who simultaneously exposes the failure and pity of workless men. Imagined as the truth teller here, Stamper Senior was also teaching his son (and his son's readers) about labouring masculinity. In doing so, Stamper staked a claim for the myriad dimensions of fathering and the specific value of his unemployed father. Stamper made this explicit towards the end of his memoir when he recalled his father's abortive tramp to Belfast in search of work. The older man said little of the trip, simply shaking his head as he stepped over the threshold of home. His despondency was mirrored in his appearance: he looked 'right buggered'. The pathos of weary defeat was offset by Stamper's recollection of the family's bewilderment that the exhausted man had walked eleven miles from Liverpool to St. Helens because he spent his last coppers on a cheap gift for his wife. The implied reprimand did not detach Stamper from sympathy for his unemployed father. If anything, it highlighted the importance of an affective dynamic in a context of male unemployment whereby the non-provider made a sacrifice in order to bring home *something*, even if this amounted to a tawdry souvenir.[90] This had added significance in Stamper's personal history because he, too, experienced tramping unemployment.[91]

Sympathetic recollections of paternal unemployment aligned adult children with men's distress rather than pitching them as victims of masculine fecklessness. Paternal unemployment made for harsh material lives but the lasting emotive impact of these periods in life could be profound. It is debateable whether Edwin Muir's father died because of his unemployment, but Muir's narrative of his father's death certainly established a correlation between his father's fruitless search for work, his demise and the adult Muir's unresolved grief. Muir's parents left the coastal village of his early childhood in search of better work

---

[89] Stamper, *So long* ago, 52–3. [90] *Ibid*, 200.
[91] See Joseph Stamper, *Less than dust: the memoirs of a tramp* (London: Hutchinson & Co., 1938).

opportunities for his father and older brothers in Glasgow. Muir's father rapidly tired from 'trudging' the streets, his workless despair exacerbated by his longing for the sea. Lost in the tidal waves of urban life, the older man sickened and died. The adult Muir's rage against this futile death is palpable as he recalls his childish cry of 'It's a lie!' on being told that his father had expired. Yet, removed from his natural habitat and dislocated from his provider purpose, his father's death was almost inevitable. Indeed, Muir's tears on disputing his father's demise suggest the boy's concession that the news was true. Muir's repetition of the word 'wretched' throughout this narrative, the emphasis on his rural parents' inability to adapt to urban conditions, the confusion of his youth and the 'meaningless waste' of his family's virtues testified to Muir's assertion that he could not write about this, 'even now', without 'grief and anger'. Although he 'climbed out' of the black depression of those years, psychoanalysis had 'violently' thrown it back into his consciousness.[92] There was little dignity or consolation to be redeemed or reclaimed. The father's increasing physiological fragility in the city mirrored the psychological violence that unemployment and want visited upon him and, in his grief, his son.

Emma Smith (born 1894) was an illegitimate baby. Her childhood was divided between her maternal grandparents, the workhouse, abusive foster parents and sojourns in institutional homes. A blistering account of poor children's vulnerability, Smith's autobiography suggested much unresolved wretchedness in her adult life and she expressed profound regret that she had been unable to provide much in the way of relief for her grandfather, afflicted by blindness, as he aged and became more vulnerable.[93] Smith's sadness at her 'failure' to support her grandfather mirrored her unspoken disappointment that he had not provided for her. There was no blame attached to failure here, just searing regret: Smith was a neglected and abused youth; her grandfather, a blind beggar, had done all he reasonably could for his grandchild. He and his wife cared for Smith whenever possible but their resources were thin, and Smith's mother repeatedly thwarted them.

Smith imagined the elderly man stood beneath a railway arch, wearing a sign about his neck that proclaimed his blindness, holding a tin can in one hand and boot laces in the other (the sale of laces circumnavigated the suggestion of begging). The railway arch froze her grandfather's

---

[92] Muir, *An autobiography*, 81–2, 101–2.
[93] For a while after she married, Smith was able to send her grandfather some money each week but this ceased when she and her husband migrated (unsuccessfully) to Australia.

image in time while, simultaneously, focusing on the nadir of Smith's life. Her sustained affection for the older man brought his memory close. But as she always pictured him at these times from stages in her life when she was living (miserably) apart from him, the memory also sharpened her recall of the obstacles to their togetherness, in real time, through his lack of provision, and in retrospect, through his death. Like Muir's inconsolable 'even now', the recollection of that 'dear pathetic figure' made Smith want to weep, 'even at this age'.[94] The endurance of bitter sorrow magnified the degree to which Smith's tragedy was inextricable from that of her grandfather. In weeping for the old man's humiliation and powerlessness as a beggar, so Smith wept for herself. Again, physical vulnerability was both the origin and symbol of men's fragility as fathers in macro terms. At the same time, Smith's sympathy with her grandfather made explicit the non-provider components of fathering: her grandfather represented affective refuge in a hostile world, in spite of his financial failure. The pity of failing to provide was that it had such devastating consequences, which underscored the importance of provision as a mechanism for supporting attachment and magnified the powerful emotive components of father-child relationships that existed within and alongside financial responsibilities.

Conclusion

Throughout the nineteenth and twentieth centuries, financial provision was the legal, political, social and affective keystone of fatherhood. When fathers were unable to provide, it threatened to destabilise their status, in a public context of citizenship and in the private realm of family dynamics. Fathers, in this context, easily were understood as failing. Some children undoubtedly were contemptuous in adulthood of fathers who had not done enough to support families. For the commentators examined here, however, fragility rather than failure defined unemployed fatherhood. Paternal unemployment need not characterize a father indefinitely nor were families in thrall to a macro narrative that assumed the unemployed father was, de facto a failure. In a retrospective context, adult children viewed periods of paternal unemployment within a long trajectory of the life cycle, often from the perspective of having also experienced periods of unemployment or financial strain. Others sought to invoke an elastic conception of fatherhood where the removal or inadequacy of provision struck a blow at paternal identity but, by no

---

[94] Smith, *A Cornish waif's story*, 53 (and 84).

means, eclipsed other acts of sacrifice or care, even seemingly 'insane' deeds or desires, that could be appropriated as 'fathering'. Narrators' desires to identify alternative modes of paternal provision illuminate the significance of mechanical aspects of fatherhood for making sense, in a public context at least, of men's commitment to, and affection for, family. Simultaneously, the sheer plasticity of 'providing' demonstrates that the mechanics of fathering extended beyond handing over one's wage.

When providing faltered, father-child dynamics might come under strain but, in a long view, could survive and become manifest in alternative ways. Even when children were unable to reclaim the dignity or agency of workless fathers, emphasis on pity and compassion redeemed such men from being failures to position them within a conception of fragile fatherhood. The faltering mechanics of fathering did not diminish paternal attachment but, rather, changed its dynamic. The historian Wally Seccombe outlined the financial and material strategies of working-class families to 'weather' the economic storms of life.[95] The imaginative strategies of families to challenge unemployed men's status as failing fathers suggests that the affective attachments of working-class families could also 'weather the storm'.

---

[95] Seccombe, *Weathering the storm*.

3 Man and home: the inter-personal dynamics of fathers at home

A day in the life of a coal miner, a short film sponsored by the London and North Western Railway Company (1910), began and concluded with footage of a miner leaving and returning home.[1] The interdependency of domestic and waged labour was writ large in these scenes, as the miner's family waving from the garden marked his departure while his little girl running to greet him, as his wife and son waited by the garden gate, heralded his return. The homecoming scene ended with the consolidation of the family group at the front door and their movement into the cottage interior. That the film moved on to depict a middle-class family in the domestic interior, engaged in family togetherness before a roaring fire (mother embroidering, father and daughter engaged in tomfoolery) indicated the limits of cinematography at this time, especially as the lighting inside miners' cottages was typically inadequate.[2] It also showcased the fruits of the miner's labour, demonstrating the codependence not just between domestic and waged labour but, also, between middle-class comfort and plebeian work. Yet the film's depiction of the miner's homecoming, with the effusive greeting from his family, drew implicit parallels between the middle-class togetherness that could be filmed and the imagined working-class domesticity that could not.[3] In this sense, the film staked a claim for the positive but invisible family lives of working men. This chapter penetrates where the film crew could not and steps inside the working-class interior to examine how father-child practices, identities and attachments were

---

[1] *A day in the life of a coal miner* (1910), Kineto Films. 35mm, black and white, silent film. North West Film Archive, Manchester Metropolitan University.

[2] There was another practical dimension here: until the introduction of pithead baths, most miners' first action on returning home was to bathe.

[3] For notions of family togetherness, see Kerry Daly, 'Deconstructing Family Time: From Ideology to Lived Experience', *Journal of Marriage and Family* 63:2 (2001), 283–94 and Tamar Kremer-Sadlik, Marilena Fatigante and Alessandra Fasulo, 'Discourses on family time: the cultural interpretation of family togetherness in Los Angeles and Rome', *Ethos*, 36:3 (2008), 283–309.

navigated and negotiated, in real time and in reflection, in rituals and spaces associated with men's time at home.

The provision and standard of working-class housing in the nineteenth and early twentieth century has long attracted the interest of social, economic and urban historians. More recently, scholarly attention has turned to material culture and to home as a geographical and imagined space distinct from categories of household and dwelling.[4] Assumptions about the sexual division of labour have tended to identify home as women's realm, especially in working-class culture where space was limited and men spent long hours in work and, supposedly, commercial forms of leisure. The surge of interest in masculinity in the last two decades has done something to correct this. John Tosh identified a bourgeois culture where 'a man's place' could be located in domestic and more public, homosocial contexts.[5] Scholars Eleanor Gordon and Gwyneth Nair have expanded this to demonstrate how thrusting men of business utilised a provider role to navigate the dynamics of home while Valerie Sanders has suggested how cultural icons like Charles Dickens, Matthew Arnold, Charles Darwin and Charles Kingsley could morph into playful comrades in a domestic sphere.[6] As Karen Harvey observes, examining how men made homes and how homes made men can expand categories of 'home' and 'domesticity'.[7]

The location of working-class fatherhood within a domestic context suggests that although men were physically absent from home most of the time, their presence pervaded retrospective accounts of domestic life. The most obvious signifier of man and home was the relationship between breadwinning and, with women's skill at managing domestic budgets, accommodation standards.[8] Home represented the

---

[4] See for example, Claire Langhamer, 'The Meanings of Home in Post-war Britain', *Journal of Contemporary History* 40:2 (2005), 341–62, Inga Bryden and Janet Floyd (eds.), *Domestic space: reading the nineteenth-century interior* (Manchester: Manchester University Press, 1999), Michael McKeon, *The secret history of domesticity: public, private and the division of knowledge* (Baltimore: John Hopkins University Press, 2006), Alison Blunt and Robyn Dowling, *Home* (London: Routledge, 2006).
[5] Tosh, *A man's place*.
[6] Gordon and Nair, 'Domestic fathers and the Victorian parental role', 551–6; Sanders, *The tragi-comedy*.
[7] Karen Harvey, 'Men making home: masculinity and domesticity in eighteenth-century England', *Gender and History*, 21:3 (2009), 520–40. See also Karen Harvey and Alexandra Shepard, 'What have Historians done with Masculinity? Reflections on Five Centuries of British History, 1500–1950', *Journal of British Studies* 44 (2005), 274–80
[8] See for instance. T.J. Hunt, *The life story of T. J. Hunt: an autobiography* (London: T. J. Hunt, 1936), 6–7, Thomas Bell, *Pioneering days* (London: Laurence and Wishart, 1941), 92–3, James Royce, *I stand nude* (London: Hutchinson and Co., 1937), 219; Arthur Gair, *Copt Hill to Ryhope: a colliery engineer's life* (Chester-le-Street: Crichton, 1982), 31.

mechanical-intrinsic dynamic of men's relations with children: fathers' absence from home in work indicated their fulfilment of financial obligations; their time at home facilitated the enactment of qualitative aspects to father-child bonds. The literal ties between breadwinning and housing also carried abstract meaning: the wretched home could be invoked as evidence of men's fecklessness or structural inequalities while domestic comfort symbolised a 'good' man's respectability.[9] Indeed, scholarly analysis of working-class homes and possessions has overwhelmingly been situated within a framework of conspicuous consumption and 'respectability'. 'Things' were freighted with social ambition and jealousies.

Historians' and contemporaries' preoccupation with 'luxury' goods (all things being relative) has presented puzzling conundrums over the saving and spending patterns of those with restricted incomes.[10] As archaeologists on the 'Living in Victorian London' project observe, this is a materialistic understanding of Victorian working-class lives that overlooks the banal, shabby stuff of everyday life. It privileges a bourgeois perspective on working-class ownership of items and overlooks the nuances of plebeian aesthetics, the role of objects in the formation of identities and everyday practices and the ways in which individuals use objects to mediate relationships between people.[11] This is not to dispense with 'respectability'. Clearly, some working people acquired an aspidistra as a token of their labour and thrift; families valued pianos as symbols of self-improvement as well as entertainment; others looked at the china on their mantelpiece as the material equivalent to modulating their vowels. Yet for all that, scholarly focus on 'respectability' and respectability as social jealousy, at the expense of other potential meanings, is skewed.

More recently, Megan Doolittle examined 'Father's chair' and the grandfather clock to assess how everyday objects shaped gender and age identities and how such things were remembered across generations. For Doolittle, family practices around everyday items reveal relationships of power and contestation while demonstrating the fluidity and diversity of family life.[12] Doolittle's analysis exemplifies how paternal responsibility for provision mapped onto the dynamics of home, overwhelmingly

---

[9] For feckless men's homes, see Betty May, *Tiger woman: my story* (London: Duckworth, 1929), 20; Shaw, *Guttersnipe*, 1–7; Aldred, *No traitor's gait!*, 10; Barclay, *Memoirs and medleys*, 7–12.

[10] Paul Johnson, *Saving and spending: the working-class economy in Britain, 1870–1939* (Oxford: Clarendon, 1985).

[11] Alistair Owens, Nigel Jeffries, Karen Wehner and Rupert Featherby, 'Fragments of the Modern City: Material Culture and the Rhythms of Everyday life in Victorian London', *Journal of Victorian Culture*, 15:2 (2010), 212–25.

[12] Doolittle, 'Time, space and memories, 245–264.

in men's favour: providing (however paltry) earned men the right to claim privileged seating, leisure and ownership of luxury goods such as grandfather clocks. In men's absence from home, their things embodied their authority and privilege. In *The Comfort of Things* (2008), the anthropologist Daniel Miller presented a series of portraits, stories of individuals and the things in their home that mattered to them, to challenge a narrative of consumption as corruption. Miller's vignettes illuminate how objects embody individual aspirations for sure, but he also explores how the stories people tell about their things are intrinsic to their struggle to make their lives meaningful. For Miller, we appropriate objects to explain social processes and relationships.[13]

This chapter fuses Doolittle's and Miller's approaches to consider how memories and practices around tables and chairs, consumer goods and domestic spaces, could mediate the quality and character of father-child relationships. The idea of home in the nineteenth century was increasingly dislocated from public life, encouraging the notion that houses gave shelter, but also that homes offered protection from the exterior world and reflected the moral character of its inhabitants. Indeed, much contemporary criticism of 'slum' life was the supposed permeability of boundaries in the dwellings of the poor.[14] For many of the autobiographers here, 'home' was at once a material space that they could invoke to talk about family economy, the politics of everyday life and character, but also an imagined place where the unique qualities of family life were drawn. Homes and the mass-produced things within them provided authors with a private context in which to unpick individual relationships. As Helen Bosanquet acknowledged in 1906, it was a mistake to assume that the 'monotonous, dreary' streets of working-class districts necessarily represented monotonous, dreary lives.[15]

Teatime: ritual and family togetherness

As the *Day in the Life of a Coal Miner* film illustrated, the location of men's work away from home during the industrial revolution and after meant that fathers' time at home and 'homecoming' became highly ritualised.[16] Men who worked daytime shifts generally returned home at a routine hour

---

[13] Daniel Miller, *The comfort of things* (Cambridge: Polity Press, 2008); Daniel Miller, *Stuff* (Polity Press, 2009).
[14] Martin Hewitt, 'District visiting and the constitution of domestic space in the mid-nineteenth century' in Bryden and Floyd, *Domestic space*, 121–41.
[15] Helen Dendy Bosanquet, *The family* (London: Macmillan and Co., 1906), 324–34.
[16] Gillis, *A world of their own making*, 179–200. I consider men's time outside waged labour in Chapter 4.

to consume their evening meal. In families where members returned home at differing times, men might take their food alone and the family meal substituted for breakfast or Sunday lunch.[17] For many, however, men's return from work was marked by women's preparation of tea (the evening meal) and father's occupation of his chair. These spaces and goods denoted the importance of men's labour: their wage earning was reflected in their additional calorie consumption and the reservation of privileged seating.[18] As Chapter 2 illustrated, these benefits could also prove sites of recrimination when men's provision faltered, not least because food, rites and objects were freighted with interpersonal significance.

Teatime located men at the core of household space. Even affluent working-class families lived overwhelmingly in one room, making the literally named 'living room' the locus of family space. Until the development of houses with separate kitchens equipped with heating ranges or cookers, cooking and eating food took place alongside the spaces for children's play, assorted household tasks and family members' relaxation. The crowded and potentially chaotic nature of such spaces received much critical attention, from contemporaries and historians alike. Yet the demands on living space also suggested that, in some families at least, a series of rites that ordered time, space and family interaction regulated households. In this light, teatime was an organised ritual that located fathers at the heart of family dynamics in a particular way.

Tables in working-class homes, whether circular or square, were modest in size, frequently multi-purpose and facilitated physical proximity between seated family members, chairs permitting, facing each other in convivial arrangement. A photograph taken by Manchester City Mission, c.1910, depicted a family at tea in their furnished room in a rented house. The material goods on display were sparse and of poor quality but probably typified the homes of many unskilled workers with young families. The photograph showed a young man in shirtsleeves and waistcoat seated at a small, square table laid for tea. His infant sat in a high chair at his side facing the camera and his wife stood behind their child. Place settings suggest that the man and his wife faced each other with their infant seated at table height between them. Another City Mission photograph depicted a tenement room with a small square table drawn to one side of the cooking range with a pair of chairs (one with arms) arranged either side of the range; an infant played on the floor between

---

[17] See the fond father, Welldon, in the Economic Club, *Family Budgets*, 56–8.
[18] See Ross, *Love and Toil*, 27–55. See also Chapter 2, 'Love and Want', pp. 70–6.

the chairs. At teatime, the room was probably rearranged with the table drawn out and the chairs placed at the table.[19]

Some tables collapsed when not in use, with retractable leaves that folded or slid, in order to save space. Photographs from Edward Cadbury's study of women's homework in Edwardian Birmingham depicted living rooms with small square tables with folding leaves accompanied by one or two simple straight-backed chairs; a slightly more elaborate chair was usually in the corner of the room next to the cooking range. When not in use, the table stood against the wall of the dwelling to make space for work in the centre of the room.[20] Arranging moveable or expanding tables for tea adopted the guise of a ritual centred on creating time and space for food consumption and family togetherness. Even when men were unemployed, families who maintained routines of eating together, however paltry the food, affirmed their 'family life'.[21] Likewise, families who preferred to eat without the attendance of friends or visitors, regardless of food quality or quantity, cemented perceptions that teatime was family time.[22] Indeed, exclusion from such rites was recognised as a cruel form of exercising power over vulnerable family members.[23]

Tea tables offered an interface for the working father's return to the domestic. Elizabeth Bryson recalled her excitement when her father returned from work:

I ran to meet him when he came home, clung round his knees and swung on his hands and climbed up until he hoisted me on to his shoulder to enter the house in triumph. I was a great giant who had to stoop to get through the doors.

Bryson's invocation of the fantastic (the giant, heaven, triumph) and her emphasis on her father's manly attributes (height and strength) portrayed breadwinning masculinity as heroic; she was 'enchanted' by it. This underlined the sexual division of homes whereby fathers could be exotic creatures in domestic settings. In his later life, following a decline in fortunes, Bryson's father worked from home (in a room that doubled as Bryson's bedroom). The setting, a 'house' on the third floor of a building (a shop was on the ground level and offices on the first two floors) in the city centre, offered a gloomy contrast to Bryson's earlier language of

---

[19] John Rylands Deansgate Library. Manchester City Mission, 'Look on the Fields', 1910. Wood Street Mission Archive, WSM 14/1.
[20] Edward Cadbury, Cecile Matheson and George Shann, *Women's work and wages: a phase in an industrial city* (London: T. Fisher Unwin, 1908).
[21] See Rowntree and Lasker, *Unemployment*, 249–51. I discuss these at length in Chapter 2.
[22] Roberts, *The Classic Slum*, 116.
[23] Foakes, *Four meals for fourpence*, 169. This example was of the 'cruel' treatment of a grandfather who had to sit apart from family at meals.

paternal gallantry. Yet, as the threshold between domesticity and work, breadwinner and dependent blurred, Bryson sought to maintain the ritual of father's homecoming: she strove to 'catch his eye and to get back a little of the old twinkle' as he emerged from the small room for his favourite tea; 'no matter how cluttered' the table, she 'soon cleared it'.[24] The accumulation of clutter in the daytime might underscore the extent to which the faltering provider had no rightful place at table. Nevertheless, Bryson's emphasis on father's entitlement to his favourite foods, and her insistence on making space for him, enabled her to reconstruct his 'homecoming' as a sign, to father and reader, that father-child dynamics were not solely dependent on men's fulfilment of provider obligations.

Authors who wrote sympathetically of working-class culture were alive to the importance of teatime as a component of family togetherness. Robert Tressell underscored the benevolent character of his protagonist, Owen, in *The Ragged Trousered Philanthropists* (1914), in a homecoming scene where wife and child listen intently for his tread on the stairs to their flat. His son Frankie runs to meet Owen, Tressell emphasising the joy of the child through his exclamation 'Dad!' accompanied by 'rush' and 'fling'; the boy is rewarded with a kiss before the family sit to tea. For Tressell, homecoming rites authenticated relationships and facilitated togetherness whereby household members discussed their affairs and fathers engaged with children. Characters' inattention to family rites forewarns readers of trouble ahead. At the outset of the novel, Easton is an attentive husband and father who cradles and worries over his babe at teatime while discussing financial affairs with his wife, Ruth. As the family's finances falter, they sacrifice domestic intimacy for material survival and take in a lodger. For Tressell, the commoditisation of 'family' rites and space has tragic consequences. Not long after the lodger moves in, Easton begins to be late for tea. As his wife and infant await his return in vain, Easton loses legitimacy as husband and father to the lodger who takes his place at the tea table. That the lodger subsequently impregnates Easton's wife highlights just how far the tea table functions here as a symbol for multiple masculine privileges.[25]

External observers noted when families sat down together and usually identified such habits with kin who appeared fond of each other.[26] Conversely, Robert Roberts (born 1905) knew that his father had 'Olympian contempt' for his children because he never indulged them over the tea table as other 'kindly' fathers did. The noted omission of Roberts

---

[24] Bryson, *Look back in wonder*, 7, 89.
[25] Tressell, *The ragged trousered philanthropists*, 48–62; 84–5; 180–1.
[26] Economic Club, *Family budgets*, 6–8, 59–61 and 62–7.

Senior underscores his son's disdain for an ambivalent father; simultaneously, it suggested that fondness and 'jollity' between fathers and offspring at tea was the norm in the Salford 'slum' of Roberts's youth.[27] Although some men ate in silence or read the newspaper, men's teatime offered a temporal and spatial interlude for family time. As Lillian Slater's (born 1906) father sat for tea in his Manchester terrace, his children stood around him as he talked over their day and fired general knowledge and arithmetic questions at them.[28] Slater used this ritual to signify her father's interest and delight in his children: it cemented her claim to a happy family life and confirmed that she mattered to her handsome, smiling father. Harry Watkin's (born 1909) dad allowed his children to dip bread into his gravy or smear his brown sauce onto bread. Seated at the centre of home with privileged foodstuffs, this Manchester manual worker became heroic as he dispensed edible gifts: 'We thought dad was great'.[29]

For one Bolton woman (born 1898), father's homecoming marked the children's teatime. As a family of nine, it was impossible to eat together at a small table. While the children's meal was served, father sat, in work clothes, in his chair drinking tea and reading aloud from the newspaper until the children were fed and it was his turn to eat.[30] This was a father whose presence at teatime confirmed his authority but who also deferred his needs to those of his offspring while seeking to entertain them. As he was the agent from a different world, one of paid work and industry, it was entirely appropriate that father dispensed news from beyond the domestic sphere. George Hardy's (born 1884) father could not read but as his wife read the newspaper to him, the older man interjected with 'biting' opinions from a 'worker's point of view'. Remembering the routine, Hardy used the contrast between his mother's 'gentle' voice and his father's ripostes to emphasise their different characters: she was stoical in survival while his father was 'strong and stocky' in body and opinion.[31] Practices of reading aloud might suggest men's lack of engagement but, given the sheer amount of information in newspapers, it seems probable that fathers edited and ad-libbed in line with their perception of children's interest, a process that also enabled offspring to gain insight into men's values and ideas. This was not always welcome. Harry Burton's (born 1895) father was an avid reader (although an adult

---

[27] Roberts, *The classic slum*, 117.   [28] Slater, '*Think On!*', 65–6.
[29] Harry Watkin, *From Hulme all blessings flow* (Manchester: Neil Richardson, 1985), 55.
[30] Bolton Archives and Local Studies (BALS), Oral History Collection, Ref: AL/JJ, Tape 23a.
[31] George Hardy, *Those stormy years: memories of the fight for freedom on five continents* (London: Lawrence and Wishart, 1956), 12.

Burton was sniffy about the quality of his reading materials). Evenings at home were typified by father constantly interrupting family members' attempts to read (better literature) with 'Listen to this' as he read aloud from his paper.[32]

Some men saw the tea table as a transitional space where they could offload the working day. Addressing an audience of working men in 1913, the (Labour) M.P. Frank Goldstone asked listeners to reflect how often they returned home to let the day's cares and woes spill over the tea table. Occupational worries often had implications for family members and men tended to prioritise their burdens making wives reluctant to share seemingly trivial domestic problems. Likening families to pulleys, Goldstone suggested that families who shared their troubles were closer and stronger.[33] That Goldstone chose a mechanical metaphor underscored the relationship between men's workplace, interpersonal dynamics and the domestic interior. Talking over troubles implied a degree of companionship between husbands and wives while the prioritisation of work worries signified the extent to which the family unit depended on men's labour. Walter Citrine's father, a master rigger, was a 'big, burly and courageous man'. Nevertheless, he 'brought all his troubles home'. The seaman's family undoubtedly feared for him, but his revelations about life at sea were, at least partly, a form of melodramatic entertainment that made his children hang onto their father's every word.[34] For Jack Lawson, fathers talked so much of 'the day's work' that children of both sexes knew technical terms of the coal pit 'as well as if we worked there'.[35]

Children could anticipate father's return to impart domestic news or ask questions. This could carry a disciplinary element ('wait 'til your father gets home') but, equally, was likely to represent a desire to share good news or to seek father's advice or authority.[36] Margaret Penn (born 1896) was ten-years-old when she discovered that she was adopted. Informed by a 'malicious' woman that she was a 'love child', Penn could not persuade her mother to discuss the matter until father returned from work. In Penn's recollection, her father immediately sensed that something had unsettled wife and daughter and demanded to know 'What's to do, Mother?' Seated in his rocking chair, having made a start on his 'tasty tea', he determined that the trouble must out. The deferred revelation of Penn's birth until father's teatime reflected his authority as head of household. On a pragmatic level, teatime offered a suspended moment,

---

[32] Burton, *There was a young man*, 35, 40.   [33] *To the workers of the world*, 46–56.
[34] Citrine, *Men and work*, 17.   [35] Lawson, *A man's life*, 31.
[36] For disciplinary elements of fathering, see Chapter 6.

apart from busy chores, that fixed father in one place and brought family members together. Penn's reconstruction of the disclosure at teatime also enabled her to intimate the affective dynamics at work in this family drama. She retrospectively imagined the older man consuming his 'favourite' dish for this tea, an edible reflection of her gratitude, both for his honesty with her and the adoption. Indeed, the memory contrasted the innate goodness and affection of the farm labourer who adopted Penn as a three-week-old baby with her 'bad lot' biological father who had hotfooted to Canada. As Penn noted, her big-boned, illiterate adoptive father loved all his children, including Penn, impartially and had never shown her 'anything but affection'.[37]

Of course, not all children anticipated fathers' return with pleasure. Sam Shaw dreaded his father's return from work if the older man called at the public house en route: his father was violent and abusive when in his cups.[38] Jack Martin's (born c.1900) father brought a blanket of oppression on the household with his return.[39] Even if men were 'good' husbands, running households on father time could be oppressive for wives (though doing 'killing work' to keep family was hardly a breeze either).[40] As fathers were the authoritative figureheads of family, their homecoming could be charged with anxiety. Nina Gorst's novel, *The Thief on the Cross* (1908), about a young unmarried mother, Ede Ridgefoote, portrayed the return of Ede and her baby to the 'slum' family home as a moment of hard-faced refusal to be ashamed before neighbours or her mother. Ede's only pulse of discomfort is in the anticipated confrontation with her father, Joe, on his return from work. Gorst played on negative conceptions of working men to create an expectation that the moment would be charged with violence and regret: Ede, the eldest, is Joe's favourite child, and Joe is an unskilled, inarticulate but powerful man. Ede's brassy confidence culminated in this suspended moment, waiting at the kitchen hearth for the older man's return. Instead of anger, however, the confrontation is tender as Joe pulls up his chair and reads the scene before him. Reconciliation and resignation are equally subdued. Joe rises from his chair to stroke the cheek of the baby in Ede's lap before taking it from her to cradle. The expected antagonism dissolves as Joe laments 'Poor little devil' and asks Ede to get his tea.[41] For Gorst, praised in one review for her 'unflinching realism', it is in the everyday practice and space of domesticity that battles between father and

---

[37] Margaret Penn, *Manchester fourteen miles* (Firle: Caliban, 1979), 5–9.
[38] Shaw, *Guttersnipe*, 5.
[39] Martin, *Ups and downs*, 43.   [40] Lawson, *A man's life*, 10.
[41] Nina Gorst, *The thief on the cross* (London: Eveleigh Nash, 1908), 44–7.

daughter are fought and resolved.[42] The exchange of the baby from Ede to his grandfather and Ede's complicity in making tea for Joe signify acceptance of the daughter and her illegitimate child into the family, Ede's acknowledgement of paternal authority and the capacity for domestic practices to intimate interpersonal exchange.

Father's chair: space, time and intimacy

That Gorst situated the encounter at the hearth with Joe seated in his chair is significant. For middle and working-class commentators, the hearth was the metaphorical heart of home while armchairs were overwhelmingly associated with the privileges and authority of masculine breadwinners. To a point, it is difficult to imagine where else commentators would situate working-class men at home unless they wished to portray irregular family arrangements. Armchairs indicated men's rightful domestic place and, simultaneously, the need for fathers to make families 'right'. Thomas Faed's painting *Home and Homeless* (1856) highlighted the legitimacy fathers conferred on home and family life.[43] On one side of the painting, a single mother huddles in the corner of a garret, cradling her babe, whilst an older child hesitantly approaches the other side of the painting where a loving family group congregate around a table, at the centre of which is father, in his chair, cradling his infant.

Domestic chair design was gendered, with women's armless chairs enabling tasks such as sewing and men's armchairs facilitating sleep, reading or relaxation.[44] Lillian Slater's parents probably represented many couples, most nights of the week: father sat reading the newspaper to mother who sat darning socks.[45] The position of father's armchair next to the cooking range denoted the priority accorded men's rest when they returned home from work (although it is doubtful how much of a privilege this was in homes that were stiflingly hot in summer). A photograph of a man at home in his living room in Hellidon, Northamptonshire (c.1900) showed a typical spatial arrangement for male leisure: the man sits in his armchair drinking tea, in the corner of the room by the fire, next to the table pushed against the wall. A book rests open on the table and his newspapers hang from the wall behind him.

---

[42] 'Slum heroism', *The Bookman* 34: 203(1908), 191–2.
[43] Held by National Galleries Scotland. For image, see www.nationalgalleries.org/collection/artists-a-z/F/4759/artistName/Thomas%20Faed/recordId/20407.
[44] Doolittle, 'Time, space and memories'.
[45] Slater, '*Think on!*', 62. See also Watkin, *From Hulme*, 14–15, BALS, Tape 100, AL/JJ/1a/027 and BALS, Tape 60a, AL/JW/1a/002.

The mat at the man's feet denotes the relationship between work and relaxation, suggesting a desire to keep dirty boots off the rug, while a covered orange box appears to be an improvised footrest, enhancing the comfort of the chair.[46]

That the best chair was reserved for the breadwinner indicates the status and privilege accorded male providers; as a costly item of furniture, the armchair was a tangible embodiment of the wages men earned.[47] Many families made an outlay for just one armchair although a thriving trade in second-hand furniture (and used-goods emporiums such as 'Furniture Town' on the Holloway Road, London) ensured that some kind of armchair was a realistic purchase for most working people. Upper-working-class families might reserve additional upholstered chairs for parlour use. Expanding credit facilities also enabled families to furnish homes beyond the absolute necessities.[48] Criticised in one review for 'terrible condescension', Henrietta Barnett's book on working-class homemaking (1885) nevertheless reflected and reinforced long-established notions of 'essential' furnishings for a modest home: a bed, chest of drawers, table and chairs, fender and fire tongs, a mat, modesty screen and an armchair. Given Barnett's plea that wives make homes more appealing than the pub, it seems likely that she perceived the lone armchair as critical in securing special male space and comfort within the family domain.[49]

As Doolittle notes, transgression of the chair's privileged use tested and reinforced the male authority embedded within it: 'If you were in me dad's chair when he came home he would tell us to get out'.[50] The spatial arrangement around father's armchair reinforced the authority associated with it. In Alice Foley's (born 1891) house, a copy of *Racing Handicap* hung above father's armchair denoted his pleasure and expenditure on betting; a leather strap on the same hook signified his disciplinary role.[51] As a symbol of authority and privilege, the chair could also function as a symbol of men's right to work. A visual depiction

---

[46] Gary Boyd-Hope and Andrew Sargent, *Railways and rural life: SWA Newton and the Great Central Railway* (Swindon: English Heritage, 2007), 86.
[47] Doolittle, 'Time, space and memories'.
[48] Newspapers like the *Daily Mirror* carried a broad range of furniture adverts and credit arrangements. An upholstered easy chair advertised in 1905 retailed at thirty shillings. See for example, *Daily Mirror*, 3 February 1905, 15; 15 June 1905, 12; 25 January 1905, 10; 2 May 1910, 8.
[49] H. Barnett, *The making of the home: a reading book of domestic economy for school and home use* (London: Cassell and Co., Ltd, 1885/6), 4–7, 19–22. See also 'Review: Mrs. S. A. Barnett, *The making of the home*', *Academy*, 716 (Jan 1886), 57.
[50] Quotation from BALS, Tape 32b, AL/JJ/1a/ 028.
[51] Alice Foley, *A Bolton childhood* (Manchester University Press and WEA, 1973), 5.

(c.1905) of a homeless family by a Liverpool charity (that operated, amongst other things, a homeless shelter) pictured the father standing tall behind his wife and children, holding a bundle of household goods and carrying a tub-shaped armchair over his shoulder. As a literal and figurative weight, the chair reminded viewers that men's provision had a yoke as well as a prize.[52] Rowntree and Lasker's study of unemployed families in York (1911) noted the case of a man, Archer, who walked miles daily in search of work. As he 'sank' into it, his armchair offered imaginative refuge. This was checked, however, by the hard materiality of the wooden seat and, positioned in the 'remotest corner of the room', the view: Archer looked on his three listless children crying with hunger.[53]

A metonym for paternal authority, father's chair could also provide insight into father's character. Dolly Scannell's (born 1904) father fashioned his chair from an old barrel, odd bits of velvet and donated paint. For him, his chair symbolised his thriftiness. To his children, the chair was an aesthetic 'monstrosity' but uncommonly comfortable and they vied to claim it in his absence. Any child sitting in father's chair would leap from it as soon as they heard his footstep at the door. This was not because of father's potential rage but, rather, having roundly mocked the homemade chair, his offspring refused to give the older man the satisfaction of their approval.[54] In Scannell's portrayal of family life, the hideous chair seemed to reflect her ambivalence towards her father: its ugliness mirrored the coarseness of his character even while her memories of him were mostly related through friendly teasing that poked fun at Scannell just as much as her father. Slightly shambolic and careless of the aspirations of Scannell and her mother, neither father nor his chair looked up to much. They were, nevertheless, reassuringly constant and familiar. For others, father's habitual occupation of his chair rendered it the most meaningful space in which to anchor his character. Neville Cardus's (born c.1890) 'first aesthetic emotion' recalled his infant self, seated beneath a table, absorbing the sensory experience of home: the womenfolk ironed clothes while his grandfather (the father of the house) sat in his armchair reading and proffering political views. This memory of the older man, with the lamplight catching the bumpy outline of his head, was a potent narrative prompt to relating his history and gentle, if 'wholly Victorian', personality.[55]

---

[52] Liverpool City Archives, League of Welldoers, M364 LWD 7/1 LWD Publications, 1893–1936.
[53] Rowntree and Lasker, *Unemployment*, 254–7.
[54] Dolly Scannell, *Mother knew best: an East End childhood* (London: Macmillan, 1974), 70–1.
[55] Neville Cardus, *Autobiography* (London: Collins, 1947), 13–4.

The broken chair proffered a symbol of feckless fatherhood. This was a well-trodden motif in temperance and Evangelical fiction that typically depicted the slovenly abodes of men who drank but rewarded sober fathers with a 'nobler and better life' symbolised through scenes of smartly attired fathers seated at the family hearth, reading or surrounded by adoring offspring.[56] Silas Hocking's popular novel, *Her Benny* (1879), told the story of two Liverpool 'street arabs', a brother and sister. Hocking makes explicit the dissolute character of the children's father, even before he introduces him to readers, through an inventory of the furniture in the home: a table, stool and a chair with a broken leg. That there is a chair at all intimated that the children's father was not always feckless and perhaps retained a flicker of human feeling towards his little girl, Nell. The broken leg signals a broken father: since the death of his first wife, this man had sunk into profligacy. When Benny resolves to run away with Nell, Hocking emphasises his adoption of a paternal mantle by depicting the boy standing on his father's chair, reaching into a cupboard to take food.[57]

In households with multiple chairs, a hierarchy of seating operated: father had first claim on chairs, followed by older children in work while children still in school stood.[58] When the *Illustrated Police News* ran a story in January 1885 about a violent quarrel between a father and his adult son, the identity of the protagonists in the drawing was made clear by their respective chairs: the son stood before a chair of simple construction with no arms while the father leapt from a tub-shaped Windsor chair.[59] Families appear to have been complicit in reserving seating specifically for men's use when men were at home, sometimes because children and spouses feared recrimination over transgression of father's privilege as Doolittle suggests, but for others, because rituals associated with father's chair enabled men to engage with family life in ways that underlined and extended beyond financial provision. Walter Southgate recalled that his father's mass-produced Windsor chair, acquired on credit, was 'sacred to my father's use'; he liked to sit and pontificate

---

[56] See for instance, Thomas Hamer, *Nellie Barton or her father's ransom* (London & New York: Frederick Warne, 1885), p. 63 and Nelsie Brooks, *Nothing like example and George Ranford's Happy Christmas Eve, or, facts for young working men* (London: S. W. Partridge, 1874), 71–8.

[57] Silas Hocking, *Her Benny* (Liverpool: Gallery Press, [1879] 1968), 19–22. *Her Benny* sold over a million copies and was translated into different languages. Hocking, a Methodist minister and Liberal Party activist, published more than fifty books during his career.

[58] BALS, Tape 32b, AL/JJ/1a/ 028. See also Thomas Jones (Ed.), *Old memories: autobiography of Sir Henry Jones* (London: Hodder and Stoughton, 1922), 22–4.

[59] *Illustrated Police News*, 10 January 1885, 1.

from it. When a debt collection firm sent threatening letters for payments due, Southgate's mother turned the demands into firelighter papers. His father, 'blissfully' unaware of the looming financial crisis, lit the fire with them before taking up residence in his chair to put the world to rights.[60] There is a wonderful irony at work in this story. That his mother found the money to keep the bailiffs at bay testified to her resourcefulness and the extent to which this breadwinner was oblivious to the finer financial detail of domestic life. But the story intimates other things about family dynamics: Southgate's mother wanted to avert an economic crisis over the chair without her husband's knowledge because she did not want to worry him or quarrel but, equally Southgate suggests, to ensure that enjoyment of his chair did not pall. In this sense, retention of the chair for father's comfort in a crowded East London house with four children (another three died young) was an unknown burden on a man whose breadwinning as a quill-pen maker fell short of requirements but whose perceived right to enjoy his chair outweighed competing demands.

Although husbands without children probably had special seating, too, references to 'husband's chair' are noticeably absent from historical and contemporary commentary on working-class homes. George Gissing's description of Sidney Kirkwood's bachelor lodgings in *The Nether World* (1889) detailed bed, table, cupboard, washing facilities, crockery, sundries, books and prints but made no mention of a chair.[61] The absence of named chairs for childless men illuminates the importance of labelling a chair that belonged to 'Father' as a signifier of paternal status, privilege and authority. In a two-person household with spousal relations conducted on different footings of power and intimacy, it perhaps was unnecessary for individuals to name their chair.

For children, the privilege associated with father's chair could invest it with physical intimacy, too. A jobbing plumber with three children, surveyed in a study of working-class budgets (1891–4), was dogged by ill health, irregular employment and debt. The family lived in a two-room, second-floor dwelling in a densely populated area of Southeast London, their furniture was 'trifling' and each member was malnourished. The surveyor described the father as 'devoted' to his family: his children were this man's 'chief pleasure'. Eschewing the view from the living room window over a bustling street or, indeed, participation in street life, the family turned inwards for their entertainments. Although hungry, anxious and exhausted by the search for work, the man spent early evenings seated, coatless, by the fire with his younger children, aged

---

[60] Southgate, *That's the way it was*, 65, 102.
[61] George Gissing, *The nether world* (London: J.M. Dent and Sons, [1889] 1976), 59–60.

three and five, on his knee. He would sing, whistle, play a flute and have 'a game with 'em in my way'. The man was proud of his family life, stating that he had no need for commercial entertainments because he had 'pantomime enough' at home. The chair, then, was the stage for the performance of pleasure and security in family life against a backdrop of adult apprehension. To the external observer, the tactile and touching dynamic between father in his chair and the children on his knee was the embodiment of the man's attachment. The observation that the man sat coatless related to other comments on the poor quality of the family's clothing and bedding but also highlighted the informality and physical, sensory intimacy of the seating arrangement.[62]

Even hard chairs could provide a psychological retreat if they underscored paternal identity. When the surveyor for Rowntree and Lasker's study of unemployment called at the Lovell household, a 'disconsolate and squalid' court dwelling, they found the unemployed and undernourished father at home minding his four children while his wife had gone to work. Invited inside, the surveyor noted that the concentration of four children in a small kitchen gave the appearance of many more offspring but these children appeared to have been encouraged to remain indoors and had some old, broken toys to occupy them. Lovell picked a rosy-faced child, aged two, in his arms and sat in his 'hard' looking chair with her on his lap. The survey reported that he looked too ill to work, was depressed and half-hoped for death. The detail about the child and the chair bore no relation to the financial circumstance or respectability of the family. The surveyor observed that Lovell probably sat down because the child was heavy. Even seated, the task of holding the child looked burdensome to the weak man. That he continued to hold her suggested a desire to secure her quiet but also possibly, because in relating a story of bitter poverty, occupation of his chair confirmed a masculine identity while the tactile act of holding his small child embodied the pity of the father who wished for better things.[63]

The routine occupation of father's chair underpinned the family calendar, responsibilities and tangible relationships. Elizabeth Bryson's mother sat in a low chair to perform everyday tasks. Her father was 'installed' in his chair mostly on Sundays when his young daughters climbed on him, 'one of us on each knee', and family members would 'sing our favourite Hymns'. The elevation of father's knee as special space and time did not diminish the girls' affection for their mother but demonstrated that Sundays were exceptional in that father was at home

[62] Economic Club, *Family budgets*, 17–22.
[63] Rowntree and Lasker, *Unemployment*, 251–4.

at all.[64] That his chair rocked and had arms facilitated a nurturing embrace for the working man to enfold children within his position as head of the household. It is possible to argue that men's occupation of their chair symbolised the 'performance' of breadwinning paternity. But in contexts like this, such approaches seem counterintuitive. Bryson certainly invested her father's chair with masculine authority but her memory privileged the chair as a shared space for affection and attachment.

Men could inhabit their chairs daily but be different fathers at different moments in time. Mrs. B., born in Barrow (1904), recalled that her parents' chairs were made of straight wood, a sign of their cheapness; quality chairs were constructed of curved timber. A boilermaker with poor health and irregular employment, her father was a 'moody man' who would sulk about the house for no apparent reason. Her happiest recollections of her father were after his weekly trip to the pub. When tipsy ('half canned' on two glasses of beer), he became as 'soft as butter'. Mrs. B. recollected these moments as playful and associated not with the pub so much, but, rather, her father's return to his chair. The mellowed man permitted his children to climb on the arms of his chair and play at hospitals, bandaging the limbs of their captive patient.[65]

For Elsie Pettigrew (born 1909), growing up in Liverpool, her father's chair was associated with shared moments of history and intimacy that set her father's role as provider against his boyhood experiences of hardship. With Elsie sat on his knee, he would 'tell me about the hard life he had had'. This maudlin ritual involved her father sharing stories of his mother's death, his escape from a cruel uncle, privation and the death of his first wife. The routine nature of the encounter, a 'sad fairy story' that made them both weep, suggests that Pettigrew and her father had expectations about the role and function of his chair for their particular father-daughter intimacy.[66] In repeatedly relating a story of loss, poverty and heartbreak, Pettigrew's father was possibly expressing how much his little girl meant to him. Certainly, despite the melancholic content of the story, Pettigrew used it to emphasise her affection and sympathy for her long-suffering father. There was also, potentially, a moral lesson implanted within a story that, while undoubtedly sad, ended with survival.

Recollections of Father could fix him in his chair to indicate the ways in which seating facilitated father-child togetherness. The illegitimate

[64] Bryson, *Look back in wonder*, 7, 10.
[65] Elizabeth Roberts Oral History Transcript, Barrow collection, Mrs. A.2.B. Held at University of Lancaster.
[66] Elsie Pettigrew, *Time to remember: growing up in Liverpool* (Liverpool: Toulouse, 1989), 15.

Emma Smith spent her childhood between the workhouse, charitable institutions, her abusive, itinerant foster parents and contented interludes at the home of her grandparents. Smith's happiest memories (there were not many) of childhood featured her 'beloved' grandfather, who 'always sat in a polished armchair' placed by the fire. In recollection, she and her brother either sat on his knee as he sang folk songs, or she stood with her hands on his knees, watching him. She recalled that when her grandfather left his chair, it was to wind the clock that ticked solemnly in the corner of the living room.[67] That memories of 'home' were anchored by grandfather's chair suggest Smith's longing for stability and affection: the chair was a constant in a world that involved perpetual upheaval and disruption. The clock, representing the passage of time, contrasted with Smith's stasis as she stood watching her grandfather and his fondness for folk tradition, emphasising Smith's sense of the old man's faithfulness. Even at the end of her life story, Smith remained deeply unhappy and unsettled.

One of the key questions pertaining to chair memories is whether such intimacy could occur around any other furniture or domestic space. Bedrooms also might be spaces of intimacy (although, like sofas, they were often shared with others) but working-class writers rarely discussed them from a sense of propriety. In contrast, father's chair was an advocate for father's qualities, in terms of his absence from home but also because of the specialness of the time he spent in it. It is notable that women's autobiographies pay particular attention to the intimacy of father's chair. This might bolster arguments that fathers invested more affection in daughters, in the expectation that they would dutifully care for them in their dotage.[68] Even if this was the case, the detailed attention to father's chair in autobiographies suggests that women attached less cynical meanings to the dynamic, emphasising instead that working men could be nurturing and demonstrative. The dominance of feminine memories does not suggest that boys did not climb on father's knee or enjoy friendly contact with fathers in their chairs. Rather, as district nurse M.E. Loane suggested, men became more self-conscious about open displays of affection as boys left childhood.[69] Male autobiographers tended to locate intimacy with fathers in accompanying him in 'man' tasks or, eventually, joining him at work.[70] References to father's chair

---

[67] Smith, *A Cornish waif's story*, 17.
[68] See also Rogers, 'First in the house, 126–137.
[69] M. Loane, *The Queen's poor: life as they find it in town and country* (London: Edward Arnold, 1906), 22.
[70] See Stamper, *So long ago*, 21, 107–8; Jones, *Unfinished Journey*, 34, 44, 67, 72, Gresswell, *Bright boots*, 18, Gosling, *Up and down stream*, 16–19 and Lax, *His book*, 89.

recur in autobiographies far more than in oral history interviews. Even in unstructured interviews, interviewer assumptions about gender roles within the family and home shaped discussion. In contrast, autobiographers who reflected at length on how to convey the dynamics of family personalities and relations were more likely to look beyond the tasks people performed to shape their family stories.

Men's chairs supported the spine and arms to suggest comfort, even without cushions or rockers. Made of wood, chairs were smooth with a warm materiality. Designs that included arms were sturdy to maximise the inherent strength of wood. Chairs that rocked enabled men to engage in a motion more commonly associated with the nursing mother. The structure of father's chair might have been intended to encourage relaxation and reading but it also lent itself to tactility: with a high back, fathers sat upright, resting their elbows on the arms of the chair. In doing so, fathers mimicked a chair to be sat or climbed upon. If they were tall men, they became physically accessible when seated at a height where children could engage their attention. Paternal authority probably looked less imposing when men sat down. Loane related visiting a family where the father was a 'morose, surly-looking man' whom she sought to avoid, partly from consideration that his home should offer a restful contrast to the relentless outside world. Seated unobtrusively in a dark corner one evening, however, Loane observed the man return from work and sit on the 'only easy-chair with a heavy sigh'. His youngest child, a boy of ten, 'went up to him, and, resting a hand on each knee, swung himself to and fro silently, but with evident satisfaction'. The father and son shared a short, straight-faced joke, whereupon the 'boy shouted with laughter, jumping himself up and down faster than ever, and a smile twitched one corner of the man's mouth'. For Loane, this was evidence that despite the man's surliness he was, 'after all', a father. The 'easy chair' was pivotal to the intimacy of this exchange for it was not the joke that brought a smile but, rather, 'the pressure of those grimy little hands, and the boy's weight on his tired knees'.[71]

As a space that facilitated physical proximity and multisensory intimacy, chairs were instrumental in the non-verbal navigation of feeling. That surly, powerful men could engage in such intimacies with children might suggest that the domestic interior feminised men.[72] Studies that depict the working-class home and family as mother and children infer that men at home were, somehow, men out of place. It is a short step to assuming that men at home, engaged in activities more readily associated

---

[71] Loane, *The Queen's poor*, 107–8.
[72] See Joseph Kestner, *Masculinities in Victorian painting* (Aldershot: Scolar Press, 1995).

with mothering, were not really men; plebeian manhood was somehow at odds with affective parenting and domestic interest. Focusing specifically on Luke Fildes's *The Widower* (1874) and Thomas Faed's *Worn Out* (1868), Terri Sabatos contends that middle-class artists' portrayal of humble widowers nursing their children in domestic settings emphasised masculinity by drawing attention to the fathers' large bodies, hands and beards. Rather than feminising men, Sabatos suggests, these images drew labourers into a middle-class conception of masculinity whereby fathers' interest in, and engagement with, children was taken for granted.[73]

Although Sabatos is not interested in chairs *per se*, it is worth examining how the chair in the paintings she analyses is instrumental in identifying fathers as affective agents. Fildes's *The Widower* depicts a man seated before a fireplace with his dead child on his lap; younger children play on the floor while an older daughter prepares tea.[74] The mean furnishings and the cramped room indicate the family's relative poverty. The chair enables Fildes's powerfully built father to hold the dead child gently, one arm wrapped about the upper body. With his other arm, the father holds the child's hand to his mouth to kiss. The contrast between the bulk of labouring fatherhood and the fragile corpse of the child emphasises the father's tenderness and strength. The worn out teddy bear that lies on the child's lap mirrors the arrangement, reinforcing associations between nursing and comfort while reminding viewers that affection for, and from, shabby creatures need not diminish the emotive value of the embrace. The older daughter's preparation of tea in the background references the meanings inscribed onto paternity in public and private contexts. That tea is suspended in the moment of death does not diminish the father's masculinity. Rather, it heightens the emotional crisis when the structures of the external world are temporarily irrelevant and father and daughter meet as equals in grief.

As Sabatos notes, the colourful hues of Faed's painting suggest a less distressing scenario than Fildes's dark, foreboding interior. In *Worn Out*, the father again sits in a chair, but the chair is alongside the bed in which a child sleeps.[75] Again, the chair is pivotal to facilitating intimacy between father and child. The labouring man sits, head thrown back in deep sleep, with a bowl at his feet. The table still folded at the end of the bed implies that, instead of the usual teatime routine, the father ate at the

---

[73] Terri Sabatos, 'Father as mother: the image of the widower with children in Victorian art' in Broughton and Rogers, *Gender and fatherhood*, 71–84.
[74] The image can be accessed at www.victorianweb.org/painting/fildes/paintings/2.html.
[75] The image can be accessed at www.christies.com/LotFinder/lot_details.aspx?intObjectID=4051698.

child's bedside. The bag of tools thrust behind his chair, his exhaustion and the coat that doubles as a blanket on the child's bed suggests that this solicitous father assumed nursing on his immediate return from work. A candle lit but burned down indicates that the man has sat there all night. One of his arms rests on the chair while the other nestles against the sleeping child. The child's head is turned toward its father; its small hand clutches his shirtsleeve. Given middle-class anxieties about working-class sexuality, it would have been inappropriate for Faed to depict the father lying on the bed with the child – although there is no other sleeping arrangement in what appears to be a one-room dwelling. Rather, by positioning the chair central to the encounter and including signifiers of the father's labour, Faed highlights the interplay between the mechanics of masculine paid labour and the intrinsically sentimental, nurturing work of fathering.

It is worth noting that Sabatos also considers Arthur Stocks's *Motherless* (1883) in her analysis of labouring men as lone parents.[76] This image is located outdoors. Nevertheless, in squatting by his wife's grave, the father kneels with one leg and rests his plump infant on the other, thereby mimicking a chair for the child. Seated thus, the father holds the child steady with one hand and tenderly kisses its head, again drawing attention to the way in which even improvised seating arrangements supported tactile relations. Sabatos is cautious about accepting the legitimacy of middle-class artists' depictions of working men's affective agency but the memoirs and commentary cited above suggest that, here at least, they were not misplaced. To assume that paternal indulgence of intimate tactility and domestic togetherness feminised men and made them more like mothers is to perceive plebeian masculinity in particularly narrow terms.

Stuff, space and sentiment

Historical studies of middle-class housing indicate how rooms designated for specific purposes were gendered in decor and furnishing.[77] Father's chair is an example of how this gendering operated in working-class homes where space was at a premium. Of course, the emotional dynamics of father's chair were not universal. Some men were

---

[76] The image can be accessed at www.lookandlearn.com/history-images/P000108/Motherless?img=2&search=yew%20trees&cat=all&bool=phrase.

[77] See for example, Jane Hamlett, *Material relations: domestic interiors and middle-class families in England, 1850–1910* (Manchester University Press, 2010) and Deborah Cohen, *Household Gods: the British and their possessions* (New Haven and London: Yale University Press, 2006).

simply unapproachable.[78] Others returned home from work exhausted, craved only sleep and had little time or patience for domestic travails.[79] Grace Foakes recalled her father as a stern man, but with hindsight, reflected that he must have been extremely tired given the hours he worked (sometimes two days and one night with no break).[80] Here, father's time at home was remembered not for the conviviality of his presence but rather because his absence exacted a heavy price.

Likewise, while father's chair and tea table routines were common features of working-class homes, it would be wrong to assume that these were the only objects through which autobiographers chose to mediate affective attachments. Paternal identities could be rooted in father's things (reading materials, musical instruments or family mementos). Consumer items within working-class houses have long been associated with the aspirations of families striving to demonstrate their values through material goods. There is a danger, however, that the 'bourgeois rhetorics of improvement' condition this view, overlooking 'subtle distinctions' in how different social groups used material goods.[81] Objects arbitrate social relationships, facilitate the reconstitution of identities and carry complex meanings. Some authors appropriated the 'equivocal objects' in working-class homes as vessels for articulating parental identities and roles: literally, things were the 'stuff' of relationships.[82] These were not always positive reflections. Robert Roberts's social survey cum autobiography utilised 'respectability' as a pejorative term to highlight not so much thrift and gentility, but, rather, the shallow vanity that acquisition of material goods symbolised. Roberts was self-consciously writing against what he called the 'cosy' picture of working-class life portrayed by the likes of Richard Hoggart.[83] Yet the account of his father's pride in the material clutter of home also generated insight into

---

[78] See for example, O'Mara, *The autobiography of a Liverpool slummy*; Martin, *Ups and downs*, 43 and Garratt, *A man in the street*, 4.

[79] See example BALS, Tape 136a, AB/LSS/A/028, BALS, Tape 100, AL/JJ/1a/027, J. R. Clynes, *Memoirs 1869–1924* (London: Hutchinson and Co., 1937), 27 and BALS, Tape 71b, AL JW/1a/006.

[80] Foakes, *Four Meals for Fourpence*, 30.

[81] Alastair Owens, Nigel Jeffries, Karen Wehner and Rupert Featherby, 'Fragments of the modern city: material culture and the rhythm of everyday life in Victorian London', *Journal of Victorian Culture* (2010), 15:2, 212–225 (222) and Diana di Zerega Wall, 'Sacred dinners and secular teas: constructing domesticity in mid nineteenth century New York', *Historical Archaeology* (1991), 25:4, 69–81.

[82] Deborah Wynne, *Women and personal property in the Victorian novel* (Aldershot: Ashgate, 2010) and Elaine Freedgood, *The ideas in things: fugitive meaning in the Victorian novel* (Chicago and London: University of Chicago Press, 2006).

[83] Richard Hoggart, *The uses of literacy: aspects of working-class life* (London: Penguin, 2009).

Roberts's particular disaffection for his father and the degree to which the older man was detached from family dynamics.

Roberts's 'old man' took satisfaction in displaying the bric-a-brac of home to baffled guests, treating them to a tour of his possessions, declaring that a living room print of the Battle of Quatre Bras was an heirloom that had been in the family for two hundred years. As Roberts observed, this meant the family possessed the print over a century before the battle took place (1815). Roberts's aside pierced his father's pretensions and drew the reader into a sniggering alliance with Roberts against his father's stupidity. There is perhaps another reference here: Quatre Bras was of strategic importance to the Duke of Wellington's eventual triumph at Waterloo. The failure of Roberts's father to understand the history of Quatre Bras mirrored his strategic failure in family life where indolence and fondness for drink routed his belligerent pretensions. Similarly, father's 'cheap' bits of pottery exposed his misplaced vanity: 'the gondoliers, the two massive dogs (with pup) hugging a hollow bust of William Gladstone, the bowl of China cherries!' The 'outsize' of the dogs with their puppy suggested skewed sentiment based on appearance and largesse rather than sincere affect. That even Gladstone was hollow underscored the sham values on display. The absurdity of china cherries and gondoliers in a Salford slum highlighted all that was corrupt about conspicuous consumption but, more specifically, the distorted values of Roberts's father.

Roberts's stories about his father's pride in material goods relayed the position of the older man within domestic life. Roberts related how his father, in a drunken rage, smashed all his prized china with a beer bottle. This act of violence should have inspired fear. Instead, Roberts gave the anecdote a slapstick quality, rendering his father's belligerence ineffectual and absurd. The comic value of the action accelerated when the explosion of his prized pots stunned 'the old man' sober. Roberts takes this further with witty tit-for-tat: his mother notes drily, 'Well, you've improved the look of it at last!', seconded by Roberts's brother who observed that the scene was like an explosion in a public convenience. The dialogue reduced the raging father to impotency and indicated the detachment between father and family. His mother's note demonstrated that her husband's sensibilities were skewed, in domestic and aesthetic terms. His brother's comparison between father's pottery and public washrooms derided father's aesthetics but was deliberately vulgar, too. It is reasonable to suppose that in drawing the comparison, Roberts meant to liken his father's rage to more corporeal explosions that confirmed the older man's status as a shit.[84]

---

[84] Roberts, *The Classic Slum*, 34.

Some things were staggeringly commonplace but enabled individuals to relate affective ties. The social worker Florence Petty visited one couple with five children living in two rooms; they had few items of crockery although the room was not badly furnished. The father, a labourer, was often unemployed and they seemed to survive from the mother's occasional nursing and charring. Still, the home was clean, tidy and the woman had decorated her shelves with scalloped paper edging. Teaching the woman to make puddings, Petty's notes recorded that the enamel cup they used to measure flour had belonged to the woman's father. This recycling of home wares was not unusual, especially in households with small and irregular incomes. Nevertheless, that Petty noted the cup's provenance suggested the housewife's desire to draw her father, through reference to 'Father's Cup', into everyday life and, here, an encounter with a relative stranger. As a daughter, she likely at some point would have made the drinks that filled the cup. The vessel had pragmatic value, to be sure, but the story attached to it suggested that, as a thing, it held flour and a mutual history of caring.[85]

Studies of memory and material culture demonstrate how individuals amplify the sentimental significance of particular objects in mourning.[86] When his father died, Michael Llewelyn was in Russia. Llewelyn gave a rich description of his father's books, their bindings, covers and contents, in place of the usual funeral narrative. The smell (tobacco), silence and ambience of his father's study evoked the man so powerfully that Llewelyn could feel his father there still. The books were a marker of Llewelyn's pride in his blacksmith/quarryman father's learning while memories of his father reading or sharing stories from his books to entertain his children further invested the objects with sentimental value. Llewelyn's elaborate description of the books exemplified his father's qualities as a respectable, self-educated man while intimating to readers the exceptional and affective value of the man as a father.[87] Just before his death, Joseph Barlow Brooks's (born 1874) father asked his two sons to choose whether they would like his violin or his Crimean sword. Both items related an extraordinary story about their father's life experience and identity. Brooks chose the violin, to his father's 'great pleasure', even though the boy could not play. The instrument was a material emblem of his father's personality and, specifically, recalled moments of togetherness when father played for his children. The possibility that Brooks

---

[85] Petty, *The Pudding Lady*, 55.
[86] Elizabeth Hallam and Jenny Hockey, *Death, memory and material culture* (Oxford: Berg, 2001).
[87] Llewelyn, *Sand in the glass*, 105–6.

would learn to play gave father and son satisfaction. A gift to be used confirmed the object's practical value and suggested the maintenance of sentimental associations with each handling. When Brooks's mother, estranged from her husband, sold the violin to pay towards his funeral, the loss compounded Brooks's bereavement and underscored his mother's affective disengagement from her spouse. When Brooks played on the violin in his memoir, it was to relate pity for, and attachment to, the father who, in spite of his flaws, cared for his sons and wanted them to remember him.[88]

If male autobiographers were hesitant in relating childish habits of sitting upon father's knee to a public audience, stories of father-son attachment mediated through memories of men's possessions were less compromising. Fred Bower described his stonemason father as an able, sober, conscientious man fond of music. Much of Bower's early life story turned on the determination, opportunism and unionism of his father. The inexorable grey of household grind offset a 'red letter day' when a delivery van left a mysterious parcel addressed to father. The contents, a 'gorgeous melodeon', testified to mother's thrift for she had saved for weeks to purchase the gift. The melodeon provided a vehicle for Bower to relate the reciprocal dynamic between his parents: the gift denoted appreciation of the husband's labour and the desire for his provision to continue. Bower amplified his father's worthiness as recipient by observing that, on returning home that day, he was 'toil-worn and weary as usual'.[89] The contrast drawn between the beautiful box and Bower's 'grimy' father in their 'humble' house pitched the mundane against the extraordinary to reflect the difference between the man as worker-provider and the man at home, as husband and father. When his father played the melodeon, he 'soared with the gods'. That he played for his children while Bower's mother prepared tea underscored the extent to which memories of the instrument constituted the identity of the working man in a fathering context. As with his memories of teatime and father's chair, Bower appropriated the melodeon to convey his parents' characters and explain how a musical instrument facilitated and reinforced his family's interpersonal, spatial and temporal arrangements. Bower's claim that the melodeon 'brought more beauty into our cramped and frugal lives that any gorgeous piped organ' was typical of his pride in working-class culture. It also gestured toward the multi-layered understandings of objects. The 'sacrilege' of burning the much-loved instrument once it

---

[88] Joseph Barlow Brooks, *Lancashire bred: an autobiography* (Oxford: Author, 1950), 13.
[89] According to Robert Roberts, the melodeon was the most popular instrument after the mouth organ. They cost between 2s 11d and 14s 6d. Roberts, *The Classic Slum*, 32.

stopped working indicated, first, how closely objects could be associated with individuals, for Bower is explicit about loving his father deeply and, secondly, how things are vehicles for relating the affective, otherwise historically invisible, dynamics within family stories.[90]

Simple objects could exemplify defining features of a father's life to intimate ongoing relationships between fathers and children, past and present, to lend coherence to life story trajectories. T. A. Jackson, Communist Party activist, 'treasured' his father's fifty-year set of compositors trade union membership cards.[91] Jackson had served an apprenticeship in printing but subsequently was unable to find work and changed occupations. Despite the rupture between father and son in trade terms, the older man's trade union cards represented his political and intellectual legacy of commitment to radical politics. The cherished cards mediated a father's identity, the abstract 'capital' bequeathed to the son and the tenacious bond between the two men. Silvester Boswell prized his father's pledge card, signed when Boswell was still a boy. To the adult Boswell, this small card represented his father's positive expression of attachment to his offspring: taking the pledge was a 'life changing' decision to improve the moral and financial quality of family life.[92] Walter Southgate was dismayed that his father's trade as a quill pen maker brought so little remuneration, not least because the decline of quill pens prohibited Southgate from following his father's occupation. Nevertheless, after his father's death, Southgate was sufficiently skilled to take over supplying Lloyds of London with quill pens. Southgate had spent enough time in boyhood watching and emulating his father's skill to be able to reproduce his craftsmanship, albeit as a hobby rather than livelihood. That Southgate worked with his father's penknife, more than a century old, enhanced the connections between father and son, craft and identity, object and memory.[93]

In the same way that some children drew on diverse objects to relate father dynamics, others looked to spaces beyond Father's chair to intimate men's fathering practices. Some men sought space that appeared to remove them from the kernel of family life. The shed was a male site contained within the larger boundaries of domestic-family space. This had practical and moral dimensions: sheds provided storage for items, such as gardening tools, not entirely suited to the domestic interior; the provision of legitimate 'man' space within the domestic boundary but removed from the bustle of domestic activity provided an alternative to

---

[90] Bower, *Rolling stonemason*, 32.
[91] T. A. Jackson, *Solo trumpet* (London: Lawrence and Wishart, 1953), 38.
[92] Boswell, *The book of Boswell*, 27. [93] Southgate, *That's the way it was*, 146.

the public house. Octavia Hill's ideal home for the working-class family included a shed specifically for men.[94] Although gardens and sheds often separated men from the domestic interior, time spent in such spaces denoted men's investment of time in tasks that made direct contributions to family life and household economy. As Joanna Bourke observed, this rendered the boundaries between masculine and family space permeable, especially when children were included in men's pastimes.[95] One father went so far as to build a covered passageway between the living room and his shed to enlarge domestic space and facilitate easy traffic between the two.[96]

Men's space also could link with family life in ways that were more abstract. Jack Jones identified the coalface and the pub as the locus of his father Dai's selfhood. Prior to joining his dad in the mine, Jones depicted his father almost entirely through his pervasive presence at home: through the artefacts of his labour (pit clothes hung to dry, a tin bath on the wall), the consumer goods furnishing the home (Dai's chair) and description of the house that used the miner for scale (the stairs were low because Dai stooped to ascend them; upstairs rooms were cramped because Dai did not straighten up; windows were the size of Dai's handkerchief).[97] Mother managed everyday home life but father occupied particular space within it: notably his chair and the smoking shanty outside the house. The spatial organisation of home mirrored the sexual and emotive division of labour: Jones's mother was the nucleus of emotional strength and support. The chair and smoking shanty provided spatial refuge for Dai from the hubbub of family life where, he later complained, his wife had first claim on his offspring's affection. Yet, in securing 'father' space within the home, Dai's children knew exactly where to find him. His chair and shanty provided liminal space between maternal domesticity and masculine workplace (or public house) where family or personal matters could be broached on father's terms. Likewise, Dai's movement beyond 'his' spaces could be invested with significance. For Jones, a highpoint in his childhood was his father's visit to the sick boy's bedroom to read to him. Not only did the act of his father reading aloud, with some difficulty, signify paternal solicitude and a child's delight in special attention, Dai's unusual inhabitation of child-space lent the event a particular intimacy. Later, when Dai was dangerously ill and his sons sat by his bed during the night, Jones again invested the

---

[94] Octavia Hill, 'Blocks of model dwellings: influence on character', in Charles Booth (ed.), *Life and labour of the people in London* Volume 2 (1891), 262–69.
[95] Bourke, *Working-class culture*, 86–8.   [96] BALS, Tape 32b, AL/JJ/1a/ 028.
[97] Jones, *Unfinished journey*, 21.

unorthodox occupation of domestic space, in this case, the parental bedroom, with intimate significance: inhabiting such space with the older man prompted his sons to reflect on the sick man as father and as their mother's husband.[98]

As with chairs, the negotiation of spaces within the home could be invested with affective consequence. For many, Sunday use of front rooms was not only about sequestered space, but, also, segregated time.[99] Edwin Muir recalled that Sunday nights in his family's rural home were among his 'happiest' of times. His father read the Bible aloud and led prayers from his chair, which gave Muir a feeling of 'complete security and union'.[100] Set against the upheaval of his father's subsequent unemployment and the family's removal to a Glasgow slum, the memory testified to all that was lost when, alienated by inner-city life, his father died and Muir's security collapsed. One Bolton woman (born 1898) recalled that the front room of her childhood home was her father's domain: a silent space in which he could rest after work. As she and her siblings grew older and began courting, this privileged space became contested: they wanted to sit in the front room with paramours. Her father complained that as with 'everything', the house used to be his but 'wasn't anymore'. The front room became the site over which this father's anxiety about the burgeoning femininity of his daughters played out; the parlour was a symbol of his waning authority over, and potentially diminishing significance to, these young women. For all this father's complaints about access to the front room, he was complicit in his daughters' use of it. Described as very strict, he preferred his daughters to sit there with male friends rather than go out where he had no means of surveillance. This was a gesture towards authority and a sign of his sustained protectiveness of his daughters, regardless of their age. His principal irritation was that the young people made a 'hullabaloo' by playing and singing in the room. But he did not proscribe their singing or use of the room. Indeed, his daughter linked her use of the front room to memories of family gatherings there: as a family of singers, they used the front parlour as a special space for family entertainment. The key difference here was that father had been excluded from these gatherings in spatial and emotional terms: he was no longer the hero of the scene or the man his daughters were singing for. That his daughters took him supper in his bedroom at ten o'clock in return for use of the front room suggests

---

[98] *Ibid*, 33–4; 93–4; 288.
[99] See for example, Andrews, *A woman's work is never done*, 9; Bryson, *Look back in wonder*, 15 and BALS, Tape 58, AB/LSS/A/045.
[100] Muir, *An autobiography*, 26.

a degree of negotiation over the parlour, but also the possibility of some acknowledgement that the room was charged with memories of relationships and identities that were in flux.[101]

Conclusion

Locating the working-class man in his home instead of the workplace or organised leisure complicates the gendered dynamics of working-class domesticity. Home was not simply woman's place because it was the locus of female labour. Rather, it might be more useful to view working-class homes as domains that could be appropriated and invested with fluid gender identities and affective significance. In memory certainly, domestic space and things provided ways to understand and explain the family unit, the differing roles of parents and the family's interpersonal dynamics. Following the working-class father through the front door of his home illustrates the extent to which working-class children, however much they valued their fathers' provision, identified fathers in extra-economic dimensions. Breadwinning was the pivotal component of fathering in a public context and it was, as the previous two chapters demonstrated, inextricable from how children gave meaning to their relationships with fathers. Examining men at home illuminates the intrinsic elements of father-child dynamics that breadwinning nurtured. In autobiography at least, authors' reconstruction of domestic space, ritual and furniture facilitated the public narration of attachment to a tired and soiled man who spent most of his time away from home. To return to Karen Harvey's call to consider how men made homes and homes made men, the presence of fathers within the home could make home 'right' in legal and moral terms. For many children, their fathers' presence made home a space for family togetherness that included men, through rites and practices that underscored paternal status but, also, through activities more commonly associated with mothers. This expands categories of 'home' and 'domesticity' as intergendered spaces. In addition, it stakes a claim for expanding categories of plebeian masculinity to include the nurturing, tactile father at home.

[101] BALS, AL/JJ, Tape 23a.

4 Front stage values, back stage lives: family togetherness, respectability and 'real' fathers

> *'I speak advisedly of the mother alone as the trainer of her children, because the father, in work has no time, out of work no heart.'*
> Father Robert Dolling, *Ten Years in a Portsmouth Slum (1896)*[1]

Robert Dolling's *Ten Years in a Portsmouth Slum* (1896) gave account of the work of the Winchester College Mission in his parish, St. Agatha's, Landport, Portsmouth. The book outlined the innovations and successes of the mission (for instance, the opening of a gymnasium), a character sketch of the 'slum' district and its inhabitants, the role of the Church of England in combating social problems and a plea for religious tolerance. Dolling's use of the word slum was contentious. He conceded that, when he wrote the book, the district was characterised neither by acute deprivation nor by moral degradation. The district nurse, M. E. Loane, who had worked in Landport, disputed that the area had ever been the squalid pit Dolling claimed.[2] Another source of discrepancy between the priest and district nurse was the significance of fathers in the family. Dolling thought the future of 'slum' dwellers depended, first, on creating a positive moral environment and, second, on mothers who were pivotal to providing proper moral training for children. Dolling excluded fathers from consideration because he assumed men were absent from children's lives: they had neither time nor heart for such tasks. Dolling did not pass judgement on these men. He assumed men's peripheral role in family life was normative. Loane was perplexed by the blithe assumptions made by Dolling and other philanthropic workers that working-class fathers were detached from, and disinterested in, children. Was the plebeian father less affectionate or solicitous than the bourgeois father? Loane did not think so.[3]

---

[1] Robert Dolling, *Ten years in a Portsmouth slum* (London: Swan Sonnenschein & Co., 1896), 50. The book was published after Dolling resigned his post following a dispute with the Bishop of Winchester over Dolling's unorthodox Anglican practices (such as offering masses for the dead). The book was a justification of Dolling's ministry and a plea for religious toleration.
[2] Loane, *From their point of view*, 92–3.   [3] *Ibid*, 144.

That working and middle-class fathers were largely absent from children's lives, especially in contrast to mothers, is undoubted. As John Tosh observed, similarities between biological fathers and Santa Claus at the end of the nineteenth century were striking: both were absent for most of the time while heightened expectations accompanied their fleeting visits. The most common reference to child contact with fathers outside wage labour time was at teatime, and when fathers took up residence in their chairs (Chapter 3). Yet, despite an overall contraction in men's working hours at the end of the nineteenth century, few autobiographers referred to time spent with fathers playing or in activities that were *for* children. Families also were competing for men's leisure time with commercial providers, self-improvement projects or homosocial activities.[4] Many men worked overtime, did odd jobs for payment in kind or worked at household tasks, such as cottage and allotment gardening, boot repairs and home maintenance.[5] In contrast, contact with mothers suffused most children's everyday experience. Indeed, women's labour was so constant that notions of maternal 'leisure' time were shaky.[6] Many authors cited here were male and took for granted the sexual division of leisure, as well as labour, between their parents. No doubt, many unthinkingly replicated those divisions in their marriages.

Writing from a mid-twentieth-century perspective, when working hours had contracted further and legislation introduced the right to paid holiday, autobiographers were cognisant of changing expectations of fathers and, particularly, the emergence of 'fun dad' who made time, on Sundays at least, for his children. Laura King's study of fathering in the mid-twentieth century shows the increased importance of 'father time' in popular culture and the expansion of play as a component of

---

[4] Many male leisure pursuits were homosocial. See for example, Mike Huggins and J. A. Mangan, (eds.), *Disreputable pleasures: less virtuous Victorians at play* (London: Cass, 2004); Mike Huggins, *The Victorians and sport* (London: Hambledon, 2007); and, Martin Johnes, 'Pigeon Racing and Working-class Culture in Britain, c. 1870–1950', *Cultural and Social History*, 4:3 (2007), 361–83.

[5] See for example, Slater, *'Think on!' said Mam*, 6; Watkin, *From Hulme all blessings flow*, 57; Hardy, *Those stormy years*, 11; T. A. Westwater, *The early life of T. A. Westwater: railway signalman, trade unionist and town councillor in County Durham* (Oxford: Ruskin College, 1979), 19. Men's leisure labour is a common theme in oral history interviews too. See, BALS, Tape 58, AB/LSS/A/045; BALS, Tape 32b, AL/JJ/1a/ 028; BALS, Tape 71b, AL JW/1a/006; and, BALS, Tape 136a, AB/LSS/A/028. See also Bourke, *Working-class culture*, 86–8.

[6] Claire Langhamer, *Women's leisure in England, 1920–60* (Manchester University Press, 2000), Davies, *Leisure, gender and poverty;* and, Chinn, *They worked all their lives*. Melanie Tebbutt identified women's leisure in their street life. See Melanie Tebbutt, *Women's talk? A social history of 'gossip' in working-class neighbourhoods, 1880–1960* (Aldershot: Scolar Press, 1995).

fathering and child development.[7] Given the emotive importance of family togetherness in the twentieth century, the lack of what we might call 'quality' time with late Victorian and Edwardian working-class fathers might confirm the peripheral significance of fathers within family. For some adult children, in bourgeois and plebeian households, such was the case. As Valerie Sanders demonstrated in her study of George Henry Lewes, paternal pleasure in children was by no means taken for granted.[8] Some fathers were irritated by the noise and chaos of children or deemed warmth, frivolity and tenderness as inappropriately feminine. John Tosh suggests that the 'distant' father exemplifies the ambivalence with which most middle-class Victorian fathers approached their offspring. Yet, as he takes pains to show, it is a mistake to confuse aloofness with affective detachment. Some fathers' interest and attachment to children simply manifested in indirect ways, through the fulfilment of obligations, in correspondence or conversations with spouses.[9]

This chapter extends the critique of the seemingly 'distant' father to challenge further the easy correlation implicit in Dolling's model between the lack, or limited character, of father-child togetherness and men's detachment. It begins by examining how fathers' presence or absence from family time shaped a sense of 'family togetherness' and, simultaneously, how exceptional times, such as holidays or Christmas, shaped and exposed the inter-subjectivities of family. The chapter also examines how autobiography appropriated men's activities outside waged labour to narrate men's values and, more to the point, the significance of those values within interpersonal dynamics. Authors who wrote about fathers at leisure were rarely just telling a story of what men did in their spare time. Many of the authors cited here, labour leaders, civic dignitaries, adult education pioneers, writers and trade union activists, inevitably indexed their fathers' 'respectable' leisure pursuits. Conversely, some exposed men's 'rough' pleasures to identify paternal fecklessness. This chapter does not revisit scholarly debates on the definition, boundaries or class ownership of 'rational' recreation and 'respectability', nor does it rehearse familiar debates about consumption and respectability as opiates of working-class radicalism.[10] Instead, it examines how

---

[7] King, 'Hidden Fathers?' and, King, 'Fatherhood and masculinity', 75–118.
[8] Sanders, *The tragic-comedy*, 50–6. [9] Tosh, *A man's place*, 97–8.
[10] See for instance, Brad Beaven, *Leisure, citizenship and working-class men in Britain, 1850–1945* (Manchester University Press, 2005); Peter Bailey, *Leisure and class in Victorian England: rational recreation and the contest for control, 1830–85* (London: Methuen, 1978); Gareth Stedman Jones, 'Working-class culture and working-class politics in London 1870–1900', *Journal of Social History*, 7: 4 (1974), 460–508; Neville Kirk, *Change, continuity and class: labour in British society, 1850–1920* (Manchester

authors appropriated activities that carried macro weight as indicators of 'respectability' to invest fathers with unique and intimate qualities, and to explain the significance of fathers in children's development, even when, temporally, father-child togetherness was limited. Finally, one of the ways in which children distinguished *my* father from plebeian men in general was by delineating the personal significance of his self-selected activities. The chapter interrogates how stories of paternal pastimes, even when they mimicked waged labour, offered a prism through which authors could constitute an 'authentic' man behind the breadwinner.

Family togetherness

By the mid-twentieth century, definitions of family had extended beyond a group of people sharing living space, or linked by blood, to a concept grounded in intimacy, qualitative relationships, imagined pasts and idealised futures. Within this context, 'family time' carried extra significance. Family members, aided and abetted by shifting legal, economic, consumer and social practices that increasingly separated work time from leisure, invested 'family time' with symbolic significance: 'togetherness' promoted a semblance of family stability and stimulated intersubjectivities. 'Family time' provided moments, in real time and reflection, when familial roles and identities were most clearly defined. In this context, John Gillis argues, memories of family time were as, if not more, meaningful than the actual experience of togetherness. Cognition of the significance of 'together' memories intensified the pressure in families to create memorable times.[11] For authors reflecting on late Victorian and Edwardian childhoods in the twentieth century, such models of togetherness were problematic: many children simply did not spend much leisure time with their fathers.

While men's providing could constitute abstracted 'family time', depictions of concrete working-class togetherness hinged on ritual practices associated with the passage of time: daily through teatime, weekly via church attendance or shopping and annually through birthdays, Christmas and summer holidays.[12] Gillis suggests that ritual time is

---

University Press, 1998); Martin Hewitt, *The emergence of stability in the industrial city: Manchester 1832–67* (Aldershot: Scolar Press, 1996); Andrew August, 'A culture of consolation? Rethinking politics in working-class London, 1870–1914', *Historical Research*, 74:184 (2001), 193–219; Andy Croll, *Civilizing the urban: popular culture and public space in Merthyr, 1870–1914* (Cardiff: University of Wales Press, 2000).

[11] John Gillis, 'Making time for family: the invention of family time(s) and the reinvention of family history', *Journal of Family History*, 21 (1996), 4–21.

[12] Chapter three engaged with the daily ritual processes of men's homecoming; for reflection on the 'family shop', see George Bourne, *Change in the village* (London: Gerald Duckworth & Co., 1955), 31–2.). Few autobiographers wrote of birthdays,

when families most imagine themselves as 'family': it simultaneously strengthens group identity and heightens individuals' family role and responsibility. In autobiography, narratives of ritual time enabled authors to separate the special character of family time as a foil to everyday experience, highlight the character of 'family' in contrast to the norm of mother-child togetherness and indicate intersubjectivities.

In life stories that sought to give account of social, economic and educational conditions in general, the specificity and intimacy of family time could obscure claims to representative narrative. For other authors, stories of family time (extra to teatime) offered a litmus paper of family life to be cast under the spotlight and scrutinised. Alice Foley's recollections of family time were characterised by the pleasure, excitement and conviviality of ritual togetherness, checked by constant anxiety over father's temper and his penchant for drink. Foley's introduction to her family Christmas lured readers into a fug of seasonal goodwill: special food, games and father, who performed character parts with feeling, reading Dickens's *A Christmas Carol* (1843) aloud. The cosy scene was qualified with a note that father had been bribed with whisky to participate. This was a gamble. Father's consumption of spirits, festive and otherwise, may have secured his presence but hardly guaranteed his mood. The anxious uncertainty of father's temper reoccurred on New Year's Day when he took his children to the fair. Again, father's volatility and the fickleness of his 'togetherness' qualified the promise of pleasure. If he won at the coconut shy, he and the children rejoiced in triumph; if he lost, he would accuse the stallholder of fraud and begin a slanging match. Her father could be protective, elbowing people out of the way to make space for his children, but he was also careless, leaving them to watch circus performers while he nipped for a drink.[13]

The Christmas in Foley's story was not, in the end, ruined by father. The significance of the recollection was that family was fraught with tension. Christmas, as a specific ritual moment freighted with emotive and cultural connotations, epitomised the everyday stress of her father's personality on his spouse and offspring. In referring to *A Christmas Carol*, Foley drew an implicit contrast between her troubled family and the happy but stretched Cratchits, where the father, Bob, epitomises fond fathering and whose presence makes family togetherness. Indeed, the Cratchit family dinner was one of Foley's favourite scenes from the book.

although a number referenced Christmas, particularly in terms of charity received. Loane claimed that few families were so poor by the end of the nineteenth century that they did not acknowledge children's birthdays. Loane, *The Queen's poor*, 49.
[13] Foley, *Bolton childhood*, 27–8.

In contrast, her apprehension of father's capriciousness at Christmas drew a boundary, in real time and reflection, between father and 'family' to mirror the conflict of Foley's childhood: she wanted to love her father but her instinctive sympathy for him, like her desire for togetherness, was checked by his selfishness and Foley's loyalty to her steadfast mother.

Harry Watkin also turned to Christmas to contrast his father's ambivalence with his mother's devotion. Here, family did not come together in spatial or emotive terms. Instead, Christmas exposed the differential values his parents attached to children, sacrifice and the seasonal significance of family. One Christmas, Watkin and his siblings received a 'hopeless wreck' of a tricycle that someone had given their father. Perhaps his father intended to repair it, but, as it turned out, 'he never looked at it'. More pathetically, Watkin recalled his despair one other Christmas when he realised that his mother, newly delivered of another baby, had not procured him a present, having prioritised her younger children. His mother was distraught at the idea of a giftless child but his father was indifferent, asserting he had no money for presents. Watkin 'supposed' that his father then sought refuge in the beer house: it was the only place Watkin could imagine him going. The supposition added to the misanthropy of paternal indifference for, if he did go to the pub, he must have had *some* money. The pathos of this story escalated when Watkin tied the anecdote to his revelation that Santa Claus was a sham. The crumbling myth of a jolly paternal figure prefigured the blow to the boy's belief in his biological father, although, as with Watkin's sustained participation in the idea of Santa Claus, he continued to find solace in other elements of his father's parenting.[14]

Elizabeth Bryson invoked Christmas to illuminate the way her parents worked together, in different capacities, at family togetherness. Selecting the 'poorest' Christmas of childhood might indicate a low tide of family life; in a story that charted one girl's rise from poverty to profession, such scenes had distinct narrative value. This 'poor' Christmas held sentimental value. Without even having to mention Dickens's *A Christmas Carol*, Bryson's festive family togetherness 'on sixpence' was immediately reminiscent of the Cratchits who make merry despite Bob's meagre earnings.[15] In Bryson's Christmas carol, the family's fulfilment of festive togetherness, despite their relative poverty, epitomised her claims for a

---

[14] Watkin, *From Hulme*, 48–9. For the connection between fathering and Father Christmas, see Neil Armstrong, 'Father(ing) Christmas: fatherhood, gender and modernity in Victorian and Edwardian England' in Broughton and Rogers (eds.), *Gender and fatherhood*, 96–110.

[15] Like the Cratchits, the MacDonalds were poor partly because there were too many bairns.

happy childhood where mother stretched resources and father indulged his children in play. These roles echoed throughout the autobiography, but, as a specific moment in the ritual calendar, Christmas resonated with love and sacrifice in a religious sense and as a supreme moment of family 'togetherness' in a secular, commercial sense. This memory was freighted with 'all the emotion of childhood'. It encapsulated the family life that 'bubbled up inside of us', amidst material hardship, like 'sweet-tasting water, clean and sharp and fresh'. That family attachments 'bubbled' suggested the vitality of togetherness, then and in memory, while the pure liquid motif, with all its suggestion of invigoration and necessity, enabled Bryson to stake a claim for the importance of her family's dynamic to her adult success.[16]

For other authors, accounts of family time provided a foil to everyday drudgery. Herbert Morrison's family took an annual holiday in 'humble' lodgings in lacklustre Ramsgate, along with thousands of other working-class families. As a child, Morrison 'eagerly anticipated and long remembered' the holiday as 'glamour' in an otherwise bleak landscape.[17] Morrison's gentle mockery of the annual shindig spoke volumes about his authorial urbanity. More importantly, the allure of unspectacular Ramsgate threw the sheer banality of family roles and responsibilities all year round into relief. Mark Grossek's father, a tailor, earned pitiful wages. Still, he annually 'squandered' two week's pay on one week's 'reckless' holiday. Recounting these excursions, Grossek affected bewilderment at the 'spendthrift' and 'madcap' extravagance of 'idleness' that 'frittered' his father's savings. Grossek's mimicry of late-Victorian exasperation at working-class patterns of saving and spending amplified just how far irresponsibility was the point: holidays heightened the contrast between the 'dead level' of father's everyday drudgery and the importance attached to family time that father's pay secured.

Grossek's memory of the holiday was vivid although, like Morrison, he smirked that his younger self had thrilled at the mudflats, sewage and 'bilge' of the Edwardian Southeast coast. As an adult, Grossek took the trip by steamer again but the 'heady vim' that characterised his boyish holiday had evaporated. His lament, 'ichabod' (glory is gone), referenced the decline in boats at the wharf, but resonated with his inability to recapture the 'feverish whirl' of those childhood excursions. Diffidence

---

[16] This autobiographical fragment served as a self-contained story that Bryson, an emigrant, broadcast at Christmas (1938) on New Zealand radio where her family story acquired an extra layer of meaning as an evocation of Bryson's Britishness. Bryson, *Look back in wonder*, 48–52.

[17] Morrison, *An autobiography*, 20.

demonstrated Grossek's maturity and sophistication. It also prompts his affluent reader to marvel just how dismal everyday life was if a week of mudflats generated such delight. Simultaneously, incomprehension at Grossek's thrill magnified just how exceptional those times, and memories, were. Grossek's sham disapproval of holiday 'extravagance' in a context of his father's everyday exploitation augmented the cruelty that, for many families, togetherness exacerbated the financial responsibilities of fathers. That Grossek's autobiography was published in the context of mounting agitation for holidays with pay can hardly be coincidental.[18]

Scholars have drawn attention to the holiday as emblematic of mothers' constant domestic labour: caring for children did not cease because families were on holiday. Nevertheless, holiday memories could also highlight the importance, and burden, of men's family responsibilities. Joseph Stamper noted that many husbands desperately sought casual work to keep family economies ticking over during the seasonal closure of works.[19] This 'holiday' time was hardly pleasurable but a constant reminder of men's obligations. Even relatively mundane family time could reinforce men's levels of anxiety about provider obligations. Teatimes characterised by food shortage rapidly slipped from a rite of affirmative togetherness into fraught opportunities for recrimination. Ritual events or treats that demanded payment could similarly generate breadwinner tension. In the diary he kept, James Turner (born 1857), a Halifax labourer, fused accounts of time with his children with reports on financial stress. An entry in early December 1881 began by noting that his children 'seemed to enjoy' their walk with him but immediately ran on to list various household debts and his worries about having enough work over Christmas. In another entry, Turner reported the 'good fun' of fireworks for his children on Guy Fawkes' night but followed this by asking what was to become of them: he could not make ends meet, owed his mother five pounds and, had further debts (four pounds) for groceries and coal. In Turner's writing, family pleasures confirmed and confounded his paternal responsibilities.[20]

Harry Harris's family took an annual holiday to Yarmouth, which required a 'lot of saving and careful spending'. Given father's modest wages (£2.10.0 per week), holidaying at all was 'wonderful'. This was, and was not, family togetherness. Although his labour financed the

---

[18] Grossek, *First movement*, 250–2. One year after publication, the first Holidays with Pay Act (1938) passed.
[19] Stamper, *So long ago*, 115.
[20] James Turner, *Hard up husband: James Turner's diary, Halifax, 1881–2* (Orwell: Ellison's Editions, 1981), 14 and 21.

holiday, Harris's father hardly ever accompanied wife and children on their jollies. Paternal responsibilities then could exclude men from family time on two fronts: working to pay for holidays rendered men absent from everyday life while the impossibility of taking (unpaid) leave barred them from holidays. Imaginatively, however, the holiday epitomised father's involvement in family togetherness: it testified to his labour and 'unselfish' privileging of his children's pleasure. This father was simultaneously in, and out, of family time. Driving home his father's attachment to his children, Harris concluded the story by noting that his father did not smoke or drink.[21] Henry Turner's (born 1902) father had regular work as a lamplighter, which he supplemented in 'leisure' time by cleaning windows. Even then, his wages did not go far with ten children to support. Turner's family never holidayed together. Nevertheless, his father financed holidays for his children through a local subsidised scheme, paying a shilling a week, months in advance, to meet the cost, 6/- per child. His father also paid weekly into a sick club, but at Christmas he could draw one pound for festive goods. If children believed that father's provision held affective significance, then for Turner, these modest saving schemes epitomised his 'happy' family despite limited practices of togetherness. Throughout his memoir, Turner repeatedly expressed gratitude that his father had regular work and was unselfish: he drank very little and smoked, infrequently, roll ups with just a whiff of tobacco in them. In cutting their cloth 'to suit their pocket', both Turner's parents enacted an abstract form of togetherness.[22]

The exclusion of father from family holidays was not uncommon. As a young father and fledgling entrepreneur, T. J. Hunt (born 1854) worried so excessively about money the first time he took his family on holiday that he returned home after three days, leaving his wife and children to enjoy the break without him.[23] Lilian Slater's mother took her children to Blackpool while father stayed at home and worked at the Manchester United pub to supplement earnings.[24] Kathleen Dayus's mother took her offspring on a hop-picking holiday while father remained in work, joshing that he would get 'a bit of peace' in their absence.[25] As with Harris, stories of holidays as fragmented family time reinforced the distinct roles and identities of family members. The domestic incompetence of hapless fathers who stayed at home while wife and children holidayed was a

---

[21] Harris, *Under oars*, 10.   [22] Centreprise, *The Island*, 19–20.
[23] Hunt, *The life story*, 28–9.
[24] Slater does not mention closure of the works but her father worked for large firms in Manchester who probably had annual closures. Slater, *Think on! Said Mam*, 35–37.
[25] Dayus, *Her people*, 101–171.

common device in social commentary and popular fiction.[26] Slater's otherwise dutiful father relaxed in the absence of wife and children: having worked late behind the bar of a pub, he overslept and missed meeting the train on their return. Told with an indulgent wink, Slater could find her father's failure endearing because it highlighted just how sober he was when mother was there to manage him. Kathleen Dayus claimed to have spent her 'holiday' pining for home, even writing to her father to plead for rescue. Dayus's depiction of the holiday as a disaster, precipitated largely by her mother's hot temper and greed (she stole a pig), heightened Dayus's identification of her father as head of household: without his quiet authority, mother and children rapidly slipped into difficulties. That her father had 'missed you all' confirmed Dayus's subtext: family worked best when family stayed together.[27]

Some fragmented holidays worked in reverse, with fathers who were involved in clubs, education or associations taking 'improving' trips with other men.[28] Other fathers took solitary holidays that, despite the absence of family, amplified the significance of men's provider role. When diagnosed with tuberculosis, Joseph Toole's father was advised to holiday by the sea. At the lower end of the socio-economic scale, the cost seemed inconceivable until the family established a neighbourhood fundraising scheme. This father's lonesome trip fragmented the household but, in terms of the family's mobilisation to secure his health, the holiday confirmed the significance of father to the family group. On a more general level, the collective action of neighbours, equally unable to afford holidays, in coming to the family's aid provided the socialist Toole with a powerful allegory for his political agenda.[29] When Joseph Stamper's father was sick with a 'churchyarder' cough, his mother suggested he visit family in mid-Wales to recover, taking his son 'for company'. In a vulnerable trade, Stamper's father was terrified that ill health would precipitate another period of unemployment and he worked through the chest infection, becoming increasingly debilitated, until the factories closed for summer shutdown. Only when he could holiday without damaging his reputation as a worker, did he venture to Wales. That Stamper's story about the holiday culminated in mother delivering another baby in their absence accentuated the importance attached to father's wage.[30]

---

[26] See Chapter 5, pp. 169–72.   [27] Dayus, *Her people*, 157.
[28] See for instance, Beaven, *Leisure, citizenship and working-class men*; and, Melanie Tebbutt, 'Rambling and manly identity in Derbyshire's Dark Peak, 1880s-1920s', *Historical Journal*, 49:4 (2006), 1125–153.
[29] Toole, *Fighting through life*, 31.   [30] Stamper, *So long ago*, 114–7.

Stamper's account of the holiday drew out multiple components of fathering, not least because it was rare that father and son spent time separate from other family members, outside their normative roles. His father navigated (with difficulty) the Welsh language on their behalf, carried his boy's luggage and ensured they were not separated while travelling. It could be that Stamper accompanied his father to ensure the older man did not forget his obligations at home. Less cynically, neither Stamper nor his father knew the relations they were staying with and it is probable that the company of a child smoothed the older man's path in navigating another family's dynamic. In Stamper's memory, the holiday represented exceptional father-son togetherness: 'Father and I had a marvellous time.' Endowing the time with magical properties, Stamper recalled that a shooting star framed his father's silhouette on the journey to the farmhouse. Stamper transformed a few days in Wales into a lifelong imaginative trip: it filled his mind with 'vivid pictures' of a 'glorious sunny' space and time. When it ended, Stamper recalled his 'sluggishness' and 'grief', dawdling behind his father as they headed to the rail station. So potent was this memory, Stamper borrowed it as the setting for one of his novels. That he tried, but failed, in adulthood to find the location added to the ethereal, out-of-time, quality of this experience. The exceptional holiday demonstrated the possibilities of father-child togetherness when removed from the drudgery of everyday commitments. In doing so, it also magnified the devotion of fathers who performed those commitments.

Memories of exceptional family times enabled authors to mark milestones in individual life trajectories. Albert Mainsbridge (born 1876) insisted that children like him, from 'normal' 'decent' working-class homes, derived 'happiness, even exultation' from simple pleasures. An 'outstanding experience' in his memory was a family trip, organised by his father, to the south coast on Good Friday where, for the first time, Mainsbridge saw the sea. The timing of the trip was significant: Easter, laden with symbolism of sacrifice and rebirth, marked the excursion in calendar and spiritual terms. Coming upon the sea, Mainsbridge was overawed by its magnitude and power. For a man whose career was dedicated to adult learning, the sea offered a compelling metaphor for the empowerment of education. Mainsbridge organised his autobiography into three parts: a sketch of generic social, economic and educational conditions; short biographical essays of 'inspirational' public figures; and, an outline of his beliefs, particularly, his Christianity. Although self-contained, the parts were inter-dependent: the 'condition of England' section established a context for Mainsbridge's adult interests and beliefs; his selection of public figures made sense in relation to his childhood and ideals; his beliefs established a postscript on experience and future agenda.

Within this, Mainsbridge's fleeting references to his hardworking, upwardly mobile father, a carpenter who became a general foreman and, later, clerk of works, appears almost incidental. They were, however, quite deliberate: the paternal asides, epitomised by the Good Friday story, signified the son's pride in an exceptional yet ordinary man, his values and influence on Mainsbridge's life course. This is confirmed by the public figures identified in Part Two whose values echoed those of Mainsbridge's childhood and formed a significant part of his beliefs (Part Three). In this sense, the Good Friday trip marked a milestone in Mainsbridge's development from child to man as he experienced new horizons, literally and metaphorically. In an overwhelmingly impersonal autobiography, the almost inconsequential detail that father organised the trip was significant because it identified father as an agent broadening those horizons, aligning the humble father-carpenter with Christ (another carpenter) and exceptional secular personalities.[31] Mainsbridge's autobiography gives no indication that the boy spent much time in the company of his father. As this extract suggests, however, when adult children sought to give meaning to childhood experiences in a public context, it was not always the amount of time spent with fathers that mattered but, rather, the significance of father and his values in the sum of a life story.

Public values, private lives

Public figures like Albert Mainsbridge approached autobiography with a clear agenda. Family experience in this framework carried symbolic importance as narratives moved towards the meat of the story: the author's career. The vast majority of working-class autobiographies studied here were loaded with notions of self-improvement and plebeian independence. In this context, fathers' leisure activities offered a representational framework for readers to gauge the character of men and, by extension, the tone of family life. Fathers who spent their leisure time drinking, gambling, or entirely disengaged from family were readily identifiable as feckless.[32] Fathers who spent leisure time performing

---

[31] Mainsbridge, *The trodden road*, 14–15. One of Mainsbridge's biographical sketches focused on Margaret McMillan, the child development pioneer who advocated fresh air for deprived children. He also published a book about her work, *Margaret McMillan, Prophet and Pioneer* (1932).

[32] See for instance, Martin, *Ups and downs*, 42, 47, 55; May, *Tiger woman*, 20–3.

additional labour, either in a domestic context, for payment or some form of exchange, fell into categories of the conscientious provider.[33] 'Respectable' pastimes generally signified the morality, intelligence and aspiration of men.[34] Some authors portrayed father's high-minded activities as companionable, even though they were not for children. D.R. Davies absorbed his father's passion for music; Fred Gresswell followed his campanologist father to the bell tower; plenty of children listened to fathers debate or accompanied them to hear political and religious speakers.[35] Many families attended church together or had some quasi-religious ritual on Sundays, often with father at the helm, a suitably symbolic enactment of patriarchal authority and duty; other men rooted their leisure in the conviviality of home with wives waiting on.[36] 'Respectable' pastimes were not always incompatible with the less reputable. Joseph Stamper's father saw no incongruity between taking his boy to Liverpool's Walker Art Gallery and treating him to refreshment in a public house.[37]

'Respectability', understood broadly as a motif for the positive attributes of self-improvement and reliance, carried public value. When authors depicted fathers engaged in 'respectable' activities, they staked a claim for macro markers of esteem. For some authors, it was not activities that determined a father's respectability but his innate qualities and values. Henry Jones (born 1852) provided a touching tribute to his father's character that refuted acquired attributes of self-improvement to stake a claim for intrinsic values:

'First pure, then peaceable, gentle, and easy to be entreated, full of mercy and good fruits'; for such, in truth, my father always was. He was not in the least intellectual; he read slowly and with some difficulty and stumbled at the long words, and he read very little; he was not a social leader in any direction, nor sought to be; he was unassuming and unselfish to the last degree.[38]

Jones remembered his father as an energetic man who spent most of his time in the shoemaker's workshop adjoining their house or on

---

[33] For some authors, 'father time' was spent engaged with fathers' absorption in work. See for instance, Brown, *Round the corner*, 14–7.
[34] See for instance, Jonathan Rose, *The intellectual life of the British working classes* (New Haven and London: Yale University Press, 2001); Hewitt, *The emergence of stability* and Vincent, *Bread, knowledge and freedom*.
[35] Davies, *In search of myself*, 19; Gresswell, *Bright boots*, 49.
[36] For the specialness of Sunday see pp. 97, 109; for an example of the convivial home, see Lax, *His book*, 42–3.
[37] Stamper, *So long ago*, 32 and 41.
[38] The first sentence of this quotation was the epitaph inscribed on his father's grave. Henry Jones, *Old memories: autobiography of Sir Henry Jones*, edited by Thomas Jones (London: Hodder & Stoughton Ltd., 1924), 42–5.

humanitarian missions to the sick and the needy. Such were his innate qualities that the typically 'respectable' attributes he lacked, painstakingly listed by Jones, could not obscure his son's depiction of him as 'the most beautiful sample of a gentle humanity in all the land'. The balance of natural and acquired characteristics was especially important because, as an adult, Jones was renowned as an intellectual (Professor of Moral Philosophy, University of Glasgow) and, by extension, a social leader. In socio-economic scales, Jones outstripped his origins but in the micro-hierarchies of everyday life, the professor continued to revere the shoe-maker 'whom I adored'. Of Jones's memories of his father, few were rooted in family space or time. When Jones reflected that his father's 'neighbours hardly knew the depth of their love and respect for him, till he was taken away', he intimated the gravity of his loss too. Laden with social and cultural significance, Jones's depiction of his father's qualities operated as an interface for Jones to articulate intense attachment to his father.

Where fathers did seek improving pastimes, the public-private interface of 'respectability' could have pragmatic and devotional significance. Chester Armstrong's (born 1868) autobiography made clear the rich environment of his parents' household, even if he later rejected their beliefs. As a father, Armstrong also sought to enrich his children's cultural and moral capital and, as he saw it, liberate them from institutional religion by schooling them in free thought and radical socialism. Armstrong's programme of 'enlightened' child rearing was dependent upon his absence from home. His wife worked hard at domestic economy while he pursued intellectual and philosophical development in associational classes and groups. Crucially, Armstrong emphasised that he discussed this element of childrearing extensively with his wife who supported his programme. In Armstrong's reckoning, his leisure apart from family was a form of labour performed on their behalf: his pastimes were the basis of his 'intense' family life in that his external pursuits were pivotal in shaping the family's 'own little world'. As Megan Doolittle suggests in her analysis of fathers' obligation to protect, the desire to transmit beliefs and values could be deeply oppressive. Chester Armstrong was aware of this: his autobiographical depiction of his programme is riddled with anxiety that it amounted to an imposition of his ideas on his dependents, especially as it differentiated his children from their peers. Indeed, this is why he took such pains to emphasise the collaborative dimension with his spouse.[39]

---

[39] Doolittle, 'Fatherhood, religious belief and the protection of children', 31–42.

The masculine world of 'self-improvement' was, in this model, another act of devotion, geared towards the 'mutual improvement' of family members.[40] Not all dependents appreciated such efforts. The labourer James Turner continually agonised in his (1880s) diary over finance. Simultaneously, he recorded his expenditure on improving books (nine pence on *Thoughts for Thoughtful Men* for instance), binding his issues of *Cassell's Popular Educator*, membership fees for the YMCA and assorted evening classes to learn, among other things, shorthand. Like Armstrong, Turner justified his personal expenditure as undertaken on behalf of his dependents, rooting his activities and associated costs with his search for a better job (the unskilled labourer longed to be a clerk), his desire to reduce overall debt in the long term, and his ambition to move the family to better housing. If Chester Armstrong lauded his wife's support for his endeavour, Turner was under no illusions: frequent arguments with his illiterate and perpetually pregnant wife suggested her exasperation with Turner's seemingly skewed priorities.[41]

The majority of autobiographers lauded fathers who undertook rational or improving activities, but to see this in terms of 'respectability' alone is to miss the public and private inter-face of such accounts. In highlighting what we might call 'front stage' values, authors offered insights into the 'back stage' drama of family life. This is not to separate the 'public' from the 'private' father. As Erving Goffman noted, the self is constituted of multiple front and backstage performances.[42] In autobiography, authors appropriated public values and practices to intimate abstract bonds between parents and children. 'Respectability' provided a framework for explaining and outlining the dynamic of domestic life: fathers' pastimes enabled authors to locate him within a social nexus of esteem; sometimes, fathers' leisure facilitated literal togetherness; more often than not, authors invoked fathers' values to indicate imaginative bonds between a man and his child.

William Lax's father was a Methodist lay preacher of 'irresistible attractiveness'. Lax cited numerous examples of time spent with his father, portraying the older man as the epitome of nonconformist respectability. Lax's emphasis on the Evangelical context of his childhood was inextricable from his ongoing attachment to his father: the older man's beliefs, shared by his adult son, forged an abstract bond

---

[40] See Rose, *The intellectual life*, 58–91; and, Vincent, *Bread, knowledge and freedom*, 30–1.
[41] Turner, *Hard-up husband*, 29–32, 34, 42, 53. For marital acrimony generated by husbands' pursuit of learning, see also Rose, *The intellectual life*, 76–7.
[42] Erving Goffman, *The presentation of self in everyday life* (London: Penguin, 1990).

between them across the years. Not only had the son also turned to lay ministry, he identified his father as the agent of his religious conversion (when Lax was eleven). Religion was the glue that bound this family together, literally, in that 'family' time at home, presided over by father, was characterised by spiritual worship and his father's generous persona and, metaphorically, as a family united in Christian belief. Rodney 'Gipsy' Smith (born 1860) was explicit about the affective glue of shared spiritual conviction. On hearing the news of Smith's conversion to Christ, his father 'rejoiced' and 'wept tears of joy'. This mirrored Smith's depiction of his father's conversion whereupon the widower called each of his children to him, embraced and kissed them, before falling to his knees to pray. Intrinsic to Smith's proselytising was the degree to which immersion in the Christian faith made the family respectable, despite their outsider gipsy status, and enhanced family ties. Certainly, Smith portrayed his father's conversion as the motor to better fathering. The older man's beliefs created a 'beautiful' family life for Smith and his siblings.[43]

Men's values provided a framework in which adult offspring could give meaning to father-child ties. Many working-class authors paid tribute to maternal ambition for children's education and occupation. For some, however, father was the agent who quickened their intelligence, advocated heterodoxy and schooled them in politics. Again, this need not depend on men spending time with children. Rather, a man's values could facilitate an abstract bond between father and child. Thomas Bell's (born 1882) father spent weekends reading books from an 'old radical' library, shorthand for his father's 'respectable' status and the intellectual milieu of home. The books bound father with boy in a tangible sense because Bell visited the library on his father's behalf. Retrospectively, the memory of these books formed a figurative bond. Far removed from his father's liberalism at the time of writing his autobiography (Bell was a founder member of the Socialist Labour Party, which merged with the Communist Party in 1920), the radical library provided a bridge between a paternal lineage of 'radicalism' and the son's development into radical political activist.[44] James Griffiths (born 1890), a Labour politician, recalled that his blacksmith father hosted 'parliaments' in his smithy, where local men gathered to debate politics. Recalling his boyish spectatorship, Griffiths established a logical path from his father's village 'parliament' to the House of Commons. In an understated way, Griffiths not

---

[43] Rodney 'Gipsy' Smith, *Gipsy Smith: his life and work* (London: National Council of the Evangelical Free Churches, 1904), 56–7, 72.
[44] Bell, *Pioneering Days*, 15–16.

only marked a cross named 'father' on the map of his life, he portrayed the politically informed and argumentative blacksmith as an unwitting but essential co-cartographer. Griffiths's jocular description of his father's chairmanship of smithy discussion as 'Stalinesque' paid tribute to the older man's passion and demonstrated a pedigree of political conviction: as an MP and cabinet minister, Griffiths was no shrinking violet either.[45]

With hindsight, authors could construe fathers' interests and values as a model of child development. Jack Lawson's father was a sailor before becoming a miner. Possessed of an expansive personality, his father was a first-rate storyteller. For Lawson, these yarns had all the flavour of Captain Marryat's (1792–1848) seafarer novels, with his (illiterate) father cast as narrator and hero. Lawson listened to his father's stories 'so often', but, far from dulling the thrill, familiarity quickened Lawson's imagination and intelligence. Marryat, a phenomenally successful author, fused didactic purpose with cracking adventure; criticised for his sloppy literary style, he was an outstanding storyteller. In drawing comparison between his father and the author, Lawson emphasised his father's narrative gift, sharp wit and virtue. Always entertaining, his father's stories provided moral guidance to his impressionable boy. Many of his father's discourses, whether seafaring stories, accounts of the pit or distillations of Gladstone's latest speech, were told from the tub in the living room where, on returning from work, his father would bathe, sweeping soap across his enormous torso, emblazoned with a tattoo of a ship. That Lawson liked his father 'best' at such moments encapsulated his esteem for the older man's multiple masculine qualities: as a brave young sailor, family breadwinner, political and social commentator and as a hulking mass of corporeal manliness.

The real Captain Marryat here, perhaps, was Lawson who doubly transformed the account of his father's storytelling into, first, a valorisation of the generic labouring man and second, an allegory on his illiterate father's vital role in nurturing Lawson towards his destiny as a politician. Seated in his tub, his father adopted the attributes of a ship in full sail carrying his boy on the stormy seas of life, from the relatively narrow dock of Lawson's plebeian childhood to drop anchor at the House of Commons. The gratification of public recital of personal memory echoed the swelling pride of Lawson the boy who took great pleasure in neighbours witnessing his father's chronicles: this magnificent specimen of labouring masculinity was *his* father. For Lawson, the generic qualities

---

[45] James Griffiths, *Pages from memory* (London: J.M. Dent and Sons, 1969), 5.

and responsibilities that constituted the older man's heroic identity emphasised his unique significance for his boy: Lawson Senior was a 'first rank' pitman, a fine sailor but, after all, 'a better father than anything else'.[46] Lawson recalled that his mother nourished him with calories, ranking her among a 'class' of heroic women. His father, however, was 'exceptional' for his nourishment fed Lawson's heart and imagination, his intelligence and ambition.

Thomas Jackson's father was 'very informative' about Fenianism and had taken his young son to see Charles Parnell at a rally. Jackson's father never told fairy tales or fables. He was a political storyteller with a repertoire that ranged from Irish nationalism and dire warnings about blacklegs to American civil war and transported convict songs. In adulthood, Jackson repudiated his father's brand of (Gladstonian) liberalism to become a founder member of the Communist Party (Great Britain). Nonetheless, the paternal politics of his formative years was as pivotal to Jackson's development as the excellent food his mother cooked. Jackson's wry comment that, had his father lived just a little longer, he might have succeeded in completing the older man's slide towards socialism suggested that father and son had sustained a pleasure in political repartee. Even if not united as communist comrades, everything that Jackson held dear, he 'got' from his father.[47] Mick Burke's (born 1898) stepfather was a 'red-hot Communist'. Although no communist, an adult Burke was clearly proud of his stepfather: he was a strong union man, well informed and valued honesty. Most of all, he 'talked to us kids more than most fathers did in those days', sharing his politics, stories from his exotic past as a championship dancer and soldier and snippets of subversive local and national history. There is little sense of how Burke measured his stepfather's talk against that of other fathers but the accuracy of this statement is not what makes it interesting. Rather, it is Burke's desire to claim his stepfather's talk as evidence of his exceptional fathering, despite bearing no biological connection to Burke and his younger brother.[48]

Fostering children's political and intellectual interest was by no means the preserve of fathers but autobiographical stories of paternal encouragement offered authors a medium for communicating men's abstract and affective legacy.[49] Pride in paternal politics or fathers' encouragement towards education facilitated a positive language of attachment and

---

[46] Lawson, *A man's life*, 12–32.   [47] Jackson, *Solo trumpet*, 35–9.
[48] Mick Burke, *Ancoats lad: the recollections of Mick Burke* (Manchester: Neil Richardson, 1985).
[49] Many mothers were, of course, fiercely ambitious for their children. See for example, Bob Stewart, *Breaking the fetters* (London: Lawrence and Wishart, 1967), 21–2; Ross, *Love and toil*, 158–165.

gratitude without veering into sentimental territory. Guy Aldred's grandfather had a minimal early-Victorian education. The older man poured all his regret for this limited learning into ambition for his dependents. Aldred knew no man who 'loved' learning more than his grandfather: he 'believed in scholarship', challenging convention and questioning orthodoxy. Every day, Aldred's grandfather rose at six to prepare breakfast for the family of five and complete 'all kinds' of domestic chores before going to work. The boy Aldred also rose at six. His grandfather's insistence that the boy use the time for study thwarted Aldred's instinct to help the older man.[50] In retrospect, this exclusive time was a moment of literal and abstract togetherness where grandfather and author proclaimed the value of learning. Indeed, Aldred's chapter, entitled 'My Grandfather's influence', traced the root of all Aldred's political interest to his grandfather's beliefs and encouragement. In telling this story, Aldred confirmed his grandfather's respectability while paying tribute to the older man for his sacrifice and support.

One of the first women in Scotland to qualify as a medical practitioner, much of Elizabeth Bryson's biography concerned education and women's career opportunities. Bryson paid tribute to the sacrifice and intelligence of her mother in facilitating her (and her siblings') career, but, it was her father that, in memoir at least, she identified as pivotal to her professional success. Bookishness and intellectual awakening had intimate as well as aspirational meaning. Bryson remembered her father as a literary man gifted with imaginative creativity. She printed some of her father's verse, noting especially his capacity to engage small children with limericks: 'Then the humpy old man/ Who lives in the cave/ Will take you and chain you/ And make you his slave.'[51] Following his financial collapse, her father contributed occasional pieces to *People's Friend* magazine, and collated some of his stories and poems, 'a little nonsense' as he called it in the preface, into a published volume paid for by subscriptions from friends.[52] Buffering the family's privation, father's poetry had economic 'value' but Bryson's memories of the verse operated at a public and personal interface. Reproduction of his verse alongside statements of childish delight in his rhymes confirmed Bryson's pride in her father to suggest the affective value of his authorship. Recounting her father's literary interests enabled Bryson to knit his values tightly with her ambition. She recalled picking Thomas Carlyle's *Sartor Resartus* (1837) from the bookshelves when she was fourteen, knowing it was one of her

---

[50] Aldred, *No traitor's gait!*, 18, 29, 36.   [51] Bryson, *Look back in wonder*, 36–8.
[52] Donald MacDonald, *Will o' the wisp flashes: a selection of stories, sketches, poems and c.* (Dundee: J. Leng & Co., 1890).

father's favourite books. After several false starts, the 'miracle' of understanding and recognition came: Carlyle, a surrogate intellectual father, became the 'kindling' to her thought and self-realisation. That this particular book germinated Bryson's cerebral maturity located her, and her father, within a powerful culture of autodidactism. Working-class readers typically found the book challenging but life changing.[53] The note that her father was the agent for disseminating Carlyle mattered because it identified father and daughter as matching bookends around the revelatory Carlyle to suggest how Bryson's intellectual maturity brought her closer to her father.[54]

At the age of ten, Bryson won a bursary that enabled her to continue education at a superior school. 'The Bursary', her chapter title, demonstrated the significance of this grant to her career and she opened the chapter with the affirmation 'I'm going to be a doctor' in place of her usual poetic epigraph. Her father spotted the bursary and encouraged his daughter to enter. That this was a bursary donated by another father in memory of his dead child was beautifully poignant, creating an uncanny dynamic between fond fathers, education and their children.[55] In Part Two of the autobiography, 'Growing up', a chapter called 'My Father' combined a brief account of his financial ruin with lengthy recollection of Bryson's entry to university. Much of this narrative did not relate to Bryson's father at all beyond acknowledging his support for her ambition. In juxtaposing father's shortcomings as a provider with his commitment to her education, Bryson elevated her father's status beyond material obligation. Naming the chapter 'My Father' dedicated Bryson's achievement to his memory. During her first summer holiday from university, Bryson reflected that she began to know her father 'as a man', suggesting a time of enriched father-daughter intimacy on shifting terms. Like Aldred's homage to his grandfather, Bryson's depiction of her father as an intellectual comrade suggested that his support was vital to her achievement. Sustaining the tangled history of father and daughter, the chapter concluded with her father's death, just at the point Bryson began her medical career. In selecting lines from T. S. Eliot's 'Little Gidding' (1942), a poem that addresses the relationship between the timeless and time-bound, for the epigraph to this chapter, Bryson confirmed the degree to which her career, and her memoir, enabled her father to transcend the limits of mortality.[56]

Attaching value to children's education provided a model for men, and children, to talk about relationships. Bryson's father, potentially

---

[53] Rose, *The intellectual life*, 41–8. [54] Bryson, *Look back in wonder*, 80–1
[55] Ibid, 53 [56] Ibid, 88–94.

intimidated by the stiff academic at St. Andrew's University, found his feet talking with pride over his children's achievements.[57] M. E. Loane noted that it was not uncommon for fathers to assist children with learning. She gave an example of one father who, before his daily departure for work, had taught his five children to read and write until they were eight years old. His relaxed approach, to encourage them to learn only when they wanted to, proved successful: when the children went to school, they were considered advanced.[58] Such anecdotes supported Loane's claim that negative stereotypes of working-class fathers were misplaced. They also suggested how pride in children enabled men to stake a claim to the fulfilment and pleasure of fathering tasks, in work and outside it. This father's child talk was shot through with indicators of intimacy: he was sensitive to his children's foibles and sought to encourage rather than chastise, he sacrificed his leisure time for his children and boasted about their quick wits to distinguish them from children in general.

Fathers who developed habitual practices associated with instruction routinized their time with, and for, children. This could be tiresome when children wanted to play but it also legitimated father-child togetherness in a context of multiple demands. Louise Jermy (born 1877) loathed her abusive stepmother and chided her father for his weakness in the face of a domineering wife. Within a narrative of family detachment, one story of father-child togetherness stood out. When she failed to progress at school, her father bought a spelling book and made time to teach Jermy new words each day. The useful and necessary purpose of this father-daughter togetherness justified the activity in the face of a jealous wife. Jermy's inclusion of the anecdote denoted her trauma: her inability to learn was symptomatic of the abuse she suffered at the hands of her stepmother. That this was one occasion when her father challenged his wife simultaneously acknowledged his weakness (he should not have let things come to such a pass) and his care (here, he took action). Jermy's praise for her father's teaching skills (she 'soon learned' with him), suggested the pragmatic value of his instruction but also the emotive significance of the lessons as a balm to her searing unhappiness. The story heralded a small victory in the affective battle of family life: for once, father made a stand and prioritised his daughter over his wife.[59]

Utility might appear to be the antithesis of sentiment but, as with respectability, a public story of pragmatism could provide a language of

---

[57] *Ibid*, 91.
[58] Margaret Loane, *An Englishman's castle* (London: Edward Arnold, 1909), 138–142.
[59] Louise Jermy, *The memories of a working woman* (Norwich: Goose and Son, 1934), 18.

personal esteem. The 'usefulness' of father's instruction to an adult Thomas Jackson, writing Irish history, confirmed his father as a reliable teacher and identified the memory of his father taking him to see Parnell as a moment of political socialisation to embed his father firmly in the formation of Jackson's adult identity.[60] Henry Hawker (born 1870) declared that 'no one could have had a better father' than his: he was kind, eager to help his son or give him pleasure, and spent time teaching him things, such as carpentry.[61] That his father was 'useful' was testimony to his attachment, and enabled Hawker to appropriate masculine practice and invest it with significance in child rearing terms. The effectiveness of father's instruction distinguished *my* father from fathers *en masse*.

Instruction, however extraneous in the outcome of life, indicated a desire to do something for one's child. Loane noted that 'fond fathers' liked to teach toddler boys to kick, an activity with a high casualty rate of infants falling over.[62] For all Loane's bewilderment, she tacitly conceded that such practices depended upon fathers taking interest in their children and seeking to socialise little boys in the rough and tumble of masculine life. Rather more comprehensible, perhaps, was the 'family man' who spent evenings with children engaged in rational instruction. One report on the occupants of London tenement dwellings drew attention to 'Mr A.', a cabman at a railway depot, who 'made a point' of doing gymnastics with his boys each evening and putting them to bed.[63] Teaching children skills enabled men to engage in a masculine form of childcare that, retrospectively, was freighted with symbolic significance. One woman's (born 1905) father purchased rabbits, guinea pigs, mice and fish for his children, teaching them to care for the animals. This had an instructive element but was a source of togetherness, too; time marked out for pets was time with father. As the children tended the animals, father told stories and teased his offspring. His pet-keeping scheme, in terms of responsibilities and pleasure, also provided a metaphor for fathering: the pets were dependent on the children for food, shelter and wellbeing; this placed an obligation on the children but one that brought satisfaction.[64]

Inevitably, men's efforts to engage children were not always successful. One Bolton (born 1903) man recalled that his father, an 'avid reader', encouraged his children to share the books he brought home. None of his

---

[60] Jackson, *Solo trumpet*, 37.
[61] Henry Hawker, *Notes of my life, 1870–1918* (Stonehouse: W. G. Davis, 1919), 17.
[62] Loane, *From their point of view*, 54.
[63] 'A lady resident' in Ross, *Slum travellers*, 40–4.   [64] BALS, Tape 60b, AL/JW/1a/003.

children took advantage of this opportunity and the story was less about respectability than a father's personality, domestic pastimes and, perhaps, retrospective awareness that the invitation to read had been a paternal attempt to communicate.[65] Indeed, children's rejection of paternal overtures could represent a powerful rejection of the man. Joseph Keating (born 1871) acknowledged his father's good intentions and devotion. An unskilled labourer, his father worked on Cardiff docks and sent money to his wife in the South Wales valleys. When he visited, he brought books for his children on 'all conceivable subjects'. The books ought to have symbolised self-improvement and attachment, but Keating scorned his father's indiscriminate choices: the profusion of texts symbolised the older man's ignorance of literature and his children. Keating's aside that his father thought the mere sight of books improving differentiated Keating, the writer with cultural capital and discernment, from the unskilled labourer. It also mirrored the affective chasm between father and son.

In Keating's retrospective, his father was an idealist who lacked rationale; he worked hard in jobs that took him away from home but his sentimental attachment meant he never sustained them; he made all the right gestures as a father-provider but they fell short of his son's (high) expectations. Keating's sneer at his father's book buying came immediately after an account of his schoolteacher's contempt for the older man's occupation (just what was a 'hobbler'?) to compound Keating's irritation with his father's manifold deficiencies, a theme he periodically returned to throughout the autobiography. Keating resented his mother for marrying such a poor prospect, musing that she had fallen for good looks and vibrant personality over breadwinning potential. Certainly, his resentment towards his father sprang from the complex nexus of obligations rooted in male breadwinning. On the cusp of literary success, Keating was temporarily thwarted when his father sustained an injury at work and Keating had to take his place to provide financial support to his family.[66]

As a child, Tom Barclay delighted in his father's cachet of myths, legends and prayer. In retrospect, he disdained childish pleasure in such poor fare: his recollection that 'we arose [from father's discourse] feeling good and comforted and strengthened for the morrow's work' was distinctly sarcastic. His father substituted storytelling for material provision and even the stories proved hollow. In adulthood, Barclay renounced the older man's Catholicism and nationalism in favour of secular socialism.

---

[65] BALS, Tape 71b, AL JW/1a/006.
[66] Keating, *My struggle for life*, 23. Hobbler refers to a casually labourer on the docks, traditionally, to tow boats in or out of the quay.

Like Keating's rejection of his father's books, Barclay's renunciation of father's stories echoed his rejection of the man over his strong attachment to his mother. If Guy Aldred and Elizabeth Bryson wrote their life stories because of fathers, Barclay and Keating appeared to write in spite of them.

For some authors, youth's burgeoning intellectual, political or confessional independence created barriers between them and their parents. Harry Burton had an ambivalent relationship with his father but regretted that, for so many of his peers, education and social mobility had driven a wedge between children and their origins.[67] Many authors of published autobiography were labour activists and freethinkers who rejected the mild liberalism, conservatism or religious belief of their parents, although this frequently was cited as a marker of 'generation'.[68] Slippage of childhood appreciation of father's values, whether cultural or political, into condescension was sometimes intrinsic to personal development, but this did not always diminish children's attachment to their father. As a boy, Edwin Muir stood in awe of his father's journal collection, *The Scots Worthies*. So enamoured was Muir's father with these 'sacred' volumes that when the family moved from the Isle of Sanday to Garth, the *Worthies* travelled with them. The removal left the volumes in 'hopeless confusion' and Muir set about repairing them for his father. Muir Senior reciprocated by having the volumes bound as a gift to his son. Impressed as a child by the *Worthies*, Muir distanced his adult literary persona from this 'poor stuff'. Yet the *Worthies* retained implicit value to the author Muir who continued to venerate his father and recalled with pride the older man's wonderful capacity to tell stories and legends, many of which were probably culled from the 'poor' journal.[69] Memories of fathers' values and his attempts to impart them to his children enabled authors to narrate stories about the increasing divergence between paternal and child identities over time, while, simultaneously, sketching continuities in inter-personal relations.

Will my real father please stand up?

In his essay, 'Will the real Bill Banks please stand up?', Peter Bailey persuasively demonstrated the multiple 'fronts' one man knowingly adopted in a single day depending on context, purpose and audience.[70] Autobiographical accounts of fathers also navigated men's shifts and

---

[67] Burton, *There was a young man*, 187. [68] See Chapter 6.
[69] Muir, *An autobiography*, 11, 64.
[70] Peter Bailey, 'Will the real Bill Banks please stand up? Towards a role analysis of mid-Victorian working-class respectability', *Journal of Social History*, 12 (1979) 336–53.

continuities between roles at work, leisure and home to mediate insight into father's different 'fronts'. For some authors, 'Father at Leisure' provided a narrative frame which not only suggested multiple, situational fathers, but, which also enabled them to distinguish an authentic individual nestling beneath the manifold roles men performed. The revelation of the man behind the breadwinner was not always welcome. V. W. Garrett lauded his father's performance as a worker but despised the 'real' man whose inveterate gambling taxed financial and affective resources. In a flat sentence that mirrored the domestic atmosphere of father at leisure, Garrett observed that '[t]here was little laughter and happiness in the home'. Garrett preferred to obscure his 'real' father, resorting to obstructive noise ('thumping' piano keys to drown his father's voice) or total silence in his presence.[71] Jack Martin's father was an excellent miner, 'too conscientious' even in the 'working man' role, but the public provider masked a belligerent, unpleasant man about the house. When Father returned from work, a 'hush which could almost be felt' descended over home. When their father absconded for a time, Martin reflected that, despite losing his wage, none of his children had the 'slightest regret' at his absence. Like his older brothers, Martin left home as soon as he could.[72] In these cases, men's public semblance of 'good' providing was a blind to obscure the uncomfortable truth of their domestic character.

For others, anecdotes about father in his unpaid time confirmed his status as provider while simultaneously distinguishing individual men from the proletariat at large. T. A. Westwater (born 1888) presented his signalman father's formidable personal qualities: he was free, jovial, cultured, alert, quick, cool and reliable in judgement, diligent, skilled and intelligent. The benefit of these qualities was twofold. His father was an excellent workman, as evidenced by the older man's progressive promotion through Westwater's youth. He was also a pleasure to be with. Westwater accompanied his father 'wherever he went' and all their jollies, even mundane chores, were 'happy'. In memory, Westwater eschewed his peers, declaring that he went about 'a good deal with my Dad': 'I was his constant companion'.[73] Joseph Stamper's father, an iron moulder, made extra income moulding ornaments on the kitchen fire to sell. With an infant Stamper as audience, his father's prosaic trade became fantastic as he transformed molten metal into pretty artefacts. Family practice around this 'hobby' replicated the sexual division of labour: father made goods to sell while mother protected the boy from the fire and scalding

---

[71] Garrett, *A man in the* street, 4 and 117.   [72] Martin, *Ups and downs*, 42–47.
[73] Westwater, *The early life*, 1–6; 18–20.

metal. For Stamper, the scenario transformed more than metal: his father's dexterity, creativity and aesthetic sensibilities worked alchemy to turn the unskilled (and often unemployed) iron moulder into a gifted craftsman.[74] His everyday identity as a labourer trapped, or concealed, the artistic individual he would be.

Mimicry between pastimes and paid work underpins cultural critics' disdain for the 'hobby'. For children, however, men's 'work' activities at home, with children as spectators, separated their father from the 'masses' of workers to facilitate insight into the enigma that was 'Dad'. For skilled men, work could give expression to creative sensibilities. John Eldred's father had little charisma but his craftsmanship as a waged stonemason and, in his spare time, as a carpenter who made elaborate pieces of furniture to sell to neighbours, suggested hidden depths. Eldred's tribute to the skill trapped inside the silent, menacing figure of his father, offered a presentiment to Eldred's revelation of his father's interiority whereby the foreboding stonemason of his boyhood gave way to an adult appreciation of a frustrated man who longed for love.[75]

Father's leisure reinforced and separated men's work identity. Michael Llewelyn turned to his father's pastimes to illustrate the depth and intelligence of his father's character. A blacksmith, his father wrote a column collating folklore and historical stories for a newspaper in his spare time. While Father the Writer was inextricable from Father the Blacksmith, not least because his column was called 'Sparks from the anvil', Llewelyn depicted reading and writing as his father's antidote to labour: intellectual creativity restored his father to 'himself' after the day's wage labour. This acquired added significance when, in an economic downturn, his father surrendered skilled labour for quarry work. For Llewelyn, his father inhabited twin personae, as worker and scholar, both of which carried affective value. Although the chapter Llewelyn dedicated to his father focused largely on his writing, he titled it 'The Blacksmith'. The pride Llewelyn expressed in his father's literary output identified his esteem for the unique qualities of the older man among 'hands'. That his father incorporated his offspring into both identities illustrated the attachments inherent in them: Llewelyn accompanied his father to the quarry to play or hung about his smithy; his father often trialled or adapted stories destined for publication on his offspring. As a provider, his father worked hard to support his family. As a 'father at home', he provided a 'rare' atmosphere that set his home apart and, of course, above others.

[74] Stamper, *So long ago*, 20–1.   [75] Eldred. *I love the brooks*, 41–2.

Although the labourer and author were both meaningful, Llewelyn clung to the memory of the author as the authentic, inner father. Twenty-five years after his father died, Llewelyn continued to locate the essence, and presence, of his father in the memory of his study:

> I can see him now in that little room with shelves and cabinets all round the walls, filled right up to the ceiling with books and papers of all kinds. He wore on his nose little steel pince-nez spectacles. He smoked a pipe. There were steel engravings of Welsh subjects on the few blank spots on the walls...

In the field guide to Llewelyn's childhood, the study, constructed of culture and national pride, was his manual worker father's natural habitat. The *momento mori* that Llewelyn treasured was not an anvil, but, rather, the local history book his father published. Like Elizabeth Bryson's appraisal of her father's publication, Llewelyn validated the personal value of his father's writing by situating it in relation to public esteem. The book received favourable reviews and he 'cherish[ed] my copy and still feel as I handle it the pride I felt as a boy that my father had written a book which people spoke well of and read with joy'.[76] Father's breadwinning was intrinsic to paternal identity but it was in his leisure labour, the tasks father selected for himself, that the 'real' man emerged.

Llewelyn's father was fortunate in securing sequestered household space for personal use. For many authors, the individuality and authenticity of fathers was imagined best in the outdoors, especially when dwellings were, imaginatively, 'woman's place'. Outdoor recreation probably reflects a degree of father-child practice. Elizabeth Bryson recalled that the municipal park of her childhood was dotted at weekends with fathers and children flying kites.[77] Many children went fishing or walking with fathers, especially in families with dogs.[78] Other fathers indulged children's desire for nonsense and larks in outdoor amusement and played catch or chased 'bogies'.[79] Bryson's walks with her father as a young woman were characterised by discussions of social problems but small children who walked with father probably prattled. James Turner, Halifax labourer, frequently took his children for walks at weekends. When his daughter died, Turner reflected how much he missed his 'chatterbox'; she had 'always something to tell me'.[80] Turner's regret for the loss of this chatter suggests the easy familiarity of childish prattle and play that is missing from the earnest autobiographer's account, with its emphasis on worthy values and political objectives.

---

[76] Llewelyn, *Sand in the glass*, 80–84.   [77] Bryson, *Look back in wonder*, 13.
[78] BALS, Ref: AB/SP/1/023, Tape 1B and BALS, Tape 60b, AL/JW/1a/003.
[79] Bourne, *Change in the* Village, 188.   [80] Turner, *Halifax labourer*, 37–8.

Social surveys and popular fiction suggests that fathers made good playmates.[81] The district nurse M. E. Loane noted that babies became fathers 'plaything' from about six weeks old. Indeed, until reaching ten to twelve years of age, children liked to 'be hanging around their daddy' in the evenings.[82] Even the sober man of business enjoyed high jinks with his children at home while popular culture depicted Prince Albert making merry with his little ones.[83] Some working-class authors were keen to highlight the playful dimensions of fatherhood, although this was not necessarily in time set aside for children.[84] Most published working-class autobiographers wrote with an agenda. Laughter and games were not incompatible with moral or intellectual improvement but they did not necessarily serve the political (or Political) object of a life story. This is not to suggest that there was no 'fun' father in these autobiographies, but rather that stories of fun were subjugated to the ideological ends of autobiography. Guy Aldred described his grandfather as 'my pal', although much of their togetherness revolved around the older man's furthering of Aldred's 'heresies of outlook'. Walter Southgate's father had a wicked sense of humour about political matters; Jack Lawson's father entertained his son with lively, informative stories about different cultures and climes; Edwin Muir's father had a stock of exciting stories that drew on Scots heritage.[85]

Published life-story accounts that were positive about father's leisure tended to vindicate the working-class man more generally. Joseph Stamper's recollection of his father's ardent defence of farm animal welfare on their country rambles conveyed the working man's compassion for the weak and vulnerable. Such anecdotes provided a tender foil to the social prejudices that imagined working men as rough and made Stamper so cross.[86] Recollections of fathers at large could also work in reverse to illustrate a father's innate self. Authors' dislocation of men from an industrial environment provided an alternative imaginary in

---

[81] The many publications of M. E. Loane staked a claim for seeing fathers as (not always responsible) playmates. See also Economic Club, *Family budgets*, 17–22. Laura King suggests this became an increasingly important facet of fathering after the First World War. King, 'Fatherhood and masculinity', 77–84.

[82] Loane, *The Queen's poor*, 20–21; Loane, *From their point of view*, 146.

[83] Tosh, *A man's place*, 87–9. Valerie Sanders showed how the century's cleverest men indulged in whimsy and nonsense. See, for instance, Sanders, *The tragi-comedy*, 23–4, 37–41. The illustration on Sanders' book jacket shows Prince Albert on the floor being pulled about by his offspring.

[84] See Chapter 5 and for example, Slater, *Think on! Said Mam*, 62–3.

[85] Aldred, *No traitor's gait!*, 32; Southgate, *That's the way it was*, 20, 32, 53; Lawson, *A man's life*, 12–32; Muir, *An autobiography*, 3–4.

[86] Stamper, *So long ago*, 30–79.

which to narrate the 'natural' character of labouring masculinity. The idea of leisure as separate to work gives the illusion that leisure time is exceptional, precious and the antithesis to the everyday.[87] Although this dichotomy can be crude, autobiographers could appropriate a bifurcated leisure-work model to convey a father's identity outside, or beyond, work. In this context, fathers took waged labour seriously because they performed it for their children; at the same time, they were alienated by that labour. Only in leisure could men's 'authentic' selves emerge. When leisure took place in the outdoors, the vista of natural space could provide an ideological and affective canvas to liberate men from work and worldly care. For Alfred Coppard, the 'sweet hours' of childhood summers when his father hoisted the boy aloft his shoulders to go rambling provided a landscape for imagining a harmonious father who contrasted to the troubled, consumptive, underpaid tailor working in cramped conditions at home, and who died when Coppard was just nine.[88]

David Kirkwood introduced his chapter, 'My father', with reflection on his father's seriousness of spirit, his self-reliance, austerity and conviction. Certainly, the photograph of his parents that Kirkwood included in his autobiography pictured his soft-faced mother and her stiff, unsmiling spouse. As Kirkwood acknowledged, this character sketch, accompanied by the conventions of the formal portrait, represented the archetypal 'front stage' self that was characteristic of his father's generation. Other elements of his father's self emerged 'occasionally': as a husband and lover when he took a dram in the evening and sang to his wife and, on Saturday afternoons, when he took young Kirkwood walking in the countryside. Like much of Kirkwood's story, the personal was inextricable from the political. The introduction to his father at leisure was via his alienation in labour: 'He was a strange creature. He was a labourer. He should have been a farmer.' This clipped narrative with its shifting cadence from what his father 'was' to what he 'should have been' was inflected with sadness. As rural children would readily concede, agricultural life was hardly idyllic. But the realities of farming were not the point: the urban writer's rural imaginary enabled Kirkwood to give birth to an 'authentic' father. Only in the fields, amongst wildlife and agricultural technology, did the 'real' man trapped inside the Glasgow labourer emerge. The 'strangeness' of this man was in his ethereal quality, his ability to see the rural everyday as something of beauty and power. That his father spoke 'Doric' (northern Scots dialect) when talking 'of the soil' aligned him with a pre-industrial world to echo

---

[87] Henri Lefebvre, *Critique of everyday life*, trans. John Moore (London: Verso, 2008).
[88] Coppard, *It's me O Lord!*, 14–15.

common cultural bifurcations between the traditional and modern, the rural and industrial, the natural and artificial.

Father and son were at their happiest in the countryside: rural walks were one of the older man's 'great joys', and for Kirkwood the privilege of pastoral father-child companionship was so great (the 'most joyous experience') that he preferred it to other children's society. At large in Nature, liberated from industrial capitalism, Kirkwood and his father were 'monarchs of the world'. In this sphere, his father was equal to the minister, doctor, ploughman and dairymaid, for all were levelled by their affinity with nature. Kirkwood sought to reproduce some of his father's eloquence, his lines of poetry, knowledge of natural and national history but his apologies for the poor impersonation served to emphasise the inimitable quality of his father's voice. His father was alienated by work, for sure, but not entirely suffocated by it, and Kirkwood pointed to evidence of the 'natural' man inside the labourer during the working week. In springtime, his father's homecoming was characterised by a search for daisies, a practice that, integrated with his father's fondness for reciting Burns's *Ode to a Daisy*, further identified the romantic ensnared in prosaic obligation. Coupled with this 'natural' man, Kirkwood's introduction to his father emphasised his love of reading, his quick mathematical brain, his religion and politics and, Kirkwood implies, his temperamental alignment with great Scottish heroes. In a seventeen-page chapter dedicated to his father, Kirkwood assigned a mere seven and a half lines to detailing his father's paid work. That his father, bursting with all the vitality of springtime, performed his obligation to labour in industrial capitalism augmented the affective significance of that sacrifice.[89]

The rupture between the working man and work, the industrial and rural, provided authors with a model for representing the man behind the breadwinner. Indeed, the authenticity of the natural world could be deployed to highlight sham fathering. Alice Foley frequently went walking with her father but recalled little conversation or interaction with him: their walks symbolised two subjects inhabiting parallel worlds, a useful device for conveying the affective ambivalence between father and daughter. Foley Senior was not 'at home' in the natural world, craving fresh air and exercise only when recovering from drinking bouts. He punctuated their walk with pit stops at the public house. Foley reflected that she had been too young to 'revere' the countryside and there is no suggestion that her father encouraged her to do so. Foley's father

[89] Kirwood, *My life of revolt*, 11–27.

approached the natural world as utility; his ambivalence to nature amplified his wider shortcomings and mirrored Foley's confusion over his interiority. He could be entertaining, but only in 'happier moods'; he was committed to politics, but at the expense of family; he was heavy handed with discipline and possessed of a murderous temper, his rage against capitalism kept Foley in school long after her peers. She might have been friends with this radical, passionate, brooding man but his volatility and selfishness, epitomised in his inability to embrace the natural world on its terms, precluded it. Foley's father was not simply alienated from work but also from the 'natural' ties that should have bound.[90]

Even apolitical autobiographies could advance stories of fathers' mundane leisure activity as mild but barbed social commentary, while distinguishing individual fathers from fathers *en masse*. When Harry Watkin's dad wrote a letter, the event was a 'special occasion' with rules and established patterns of behaviour: he must not be disturbed and no one must knock the table. Watkin transformed this banal, potentially exclusionary, activity into evidence of his father's qualities, executed with elaborate ritual for the gratification of offspring. The climax of this performance was addressing the envelope. Filched from an employer, the envelope was embossed with the firm's name, prompting Watkin's father to alter the employer's logo into a pint of beer and add the words 'A pint of the best'. This subterfuge transformed the banal into something spectacular and, in his children's eyes, repositioned father the lackey as father the hero. 'Every time' his father engaged in this ritual, his children 'admired his ability and cunning'.[91] Father's 'hidden' defiance, paradoxically, became a public narrative of Watkin's esteem.

At a more explicitly affective level, Lilian Slater recalled the 'times' she stood at her father's side 'just' to watch him write his name. Spectatorship could imply detachment but, Slater configured watching as pleasurable consumption, ostensibly of father's skill, but more intimately, of her father's essential self. His 'really beautiful' handwriting marked him as unique. The memoir's transcription of his signature in full, Alfred Ernest Barrington, confirmed his status as an individual. The distinction between the name printed in typeface and the remembered copperplate underscored the intimacy of recall. Slater's inability to convey the particular quality of her father's handwriting in a printed medium reflected the difficulty of articulating profound internal feeling to a public audience in anything other than cliché. Stories of writing clearly carried

---

[90] Foley, *A Bolton childhood*, 29.   [91] Watkin, *From Hulme*, 57.

ideological or 'respectable' significance. Guy Aldred also recalled the 'excellent' quality of his grandfather's 'good, clear handwriting'. A symbol of education, the written subject matter, transcribed trade union meeting minutes, highlighted Aldred's political lineage.[92] In Slater's account, memory of her father's writing developed into a reflection of his favourite 'quotations', most of which were proverbs or maxims. Despite the commonplace character of these phrases, they enabled Slater to intimate something of her father's interiority. 'It's the environment that counts' staked a claim for her father's cognisance of his role in socialising offspring and the seriousness with which he took this responsibility. 'Smile in the face of adversity!' was a particular favourite of Slater and her dad. This was far removed from the literary life of Llewelyn, Bryson or Kirkwood's fathers, but the esteem and intimacy Slater invested in the cliché was hardly less. Again, the publication of the phrase could only partially convey the feeling with which it was said: her father would ruffle her hair, cup her chin and lift her face to meet his gaze.[93] The juxtaposition between the banality of the maxim and the tenderness with which it was expressed underscored the intimacy of the words in memory.

The seamless shift in Slater's narrative, from her father's handwriting to his favourite quotations, is typical of this genre of life story where apparently random memories stack up in a stream of consciousness. Yet the narrative has logic when read as an account of Slater's attachment to her father whereby his writing and quotes were intrinsic to a story of intimacy, authenticity and attachment. Likewise, it is easy to dismiss the bright optimism of memoirs like Slater's, but nostalgia can have a political edge.[94] Slater's determined portrayal of a happy, secure childhood staked a claim for positive values in working-class culture generally and her father in particular. 'Smile in the face of adversity' did not imply that her childhood, or adulthood, was without difficulties. If anything, it drew attention to working people's adversities, but declaimed whinging as weak and disloyal. In the context of Slater's memoir, smiling in the face of adversity positioned her father's strength of character and fortitude at the kernel of her everyday life, long after he died.

For some authors, father's 'real' self remained forever inscrutable. Grace Foakes was never fond of her father. The one mellow memory she held of him related to weekly church attendance where he delighted

---

[92] Aldred, *No traitor's gait*, 18.   [93] Slater, *Think on! Said Mam*, 7.
[94] See Ben Jones, 'The uses of nostalgia: autobiography, community publishing and working-class neighbourhoods in post-war England', *Cultural and Social History*, 7:3 (2010) 355–74.

in singing stirring hymns: the surly, tired man Foakes knew became 'cheerful and happy' until he retreated 'back into his shell', becoming 'tired and grumpy again'.[95] In this memoir, it is unclear who was the 'real' father was, although this glimpse of a different kind of man supported her assertion that, had he allowed it, she could and would have loved him. For Foakes, confusion over her father's character emphasised the constancy and assurance of her mother. For others, father's obligations to provide eclipsed the opportunity to know any other kind of man. Men's leisure hours spent in sleep highlighted the extent to which exhausting labour precluded the emergence of a 'real', potentially more interesting, father. During summer, Richard Hillyer's father worked such long hours that he only had an hour to himself before retiring to bed and he spent this asleep. His father 'didn't talk much' and probably did not have 'much to say anyway'.[96] This was not a criticism but, rather, bore testimony to the incompatibility of father the exhausted labourer and a father with personal dynamism.

Conclusion

Respectability was (and is) an elastic concept typically related to specific questions about working-class leisure: were activities rational, reactionary or conformist; where did the plebeian desire for self-improvement originate; and how far did the working classes adopt or resist bourgeois moral imperialism? In life stories, 'respectability' provided a macro language of esteem through which authors could articulate intimate dimensions of family life and intersubjectivities. Respectability matters here because it suggests a dynamic concept that had the potential to be about far more than working-class conservatism, consumerism or ambition.[97] Working-class authors trying to make sense of fatherhood in a public context could appropriate shared markers of regard to illuminate and explain hidden or private facets of life. The tasks father self-selected enabled adult children to narrate men's interiority and distinguish individual fathers from father-providers in general. While children may not have recalled spending quantities of time with fathers, some at least focused on the quality of father time, even when this did not entail time set aside for children.

---

[95] Foakes, *Four meals for fourpence*, 92–3.
[96] Richard Hillyer, *Country boy: the autobiography of Richard Hillyer* (London: Hodder and Stoughton, 1966), 25.
[97] See also Lawrence on 'affluence' in constructing class identities. Jon Lawrence, 'Class, 'Affluence' and the Study of Everyday Life in Britain, c. 1930–64', *Cultural and social history*, 10:2 (2013) 273–299.

Provided fathers were not engaged in 'feckless' activities, such as gambling or drinking the week's food, adult children writing in the mid-twentieth century seemed to accept the lack of father time in their childhood as normative. What mattered was to explain how attachment to fathers, and knowledge of who father *really* was, did not depend on father dedicating time to his children. Father Dolling, with whom this chapter began, thought that everyday maternal care for children rendered mothers responsible for moral training. To a point, this was true. Yet his disregard of fathers was more problematic, not least in its echo of many 'slum' or temperance narratives that identified fathers as agents of detachment or decline in family life. In a retrospective context at least, working-class life stories suggest that, however indistinct in temporal terms, father time carried enormous significance in imaginative contexts. This was especially important, first, because autobiographies produced in the mid-twentieth century were published in a context where social expectations of fathering had expanded to include domesticated togetherness and, in a way, underscored Dolling's correlation between attachment and father-child time. Second, the majority of autobiographers here were male; many were fathers and most of them were committed political activists or enjoyed busy careers. Despite the emergence of 'fun dad' in their adulthood, most of these men probably spent relatively little time with their children. In this sense, authorial efforts to construct meaningful father-child relationships that were not typified by togetherness reflected a desire not only to credit their fathers with affective significance but, also, to stake a claim as fathers to being attached to their children.

5 Funny talk: laughter, family and fathering

"Come up to my house Martin and hear my baby talk. It's the most wonderful-"

"You forget," said Martin, with dignity, "that I am a father myself".

WIFE: "It's the little things that worry."
HUSBAND: "Especially when there are six of them."

Tommy (who has just had a scolding): "Father, don't you wish we hadn't never married mother?"

A man about to be executed refused to let his children see him hang. "That's just like you" said his wife, "for you never wanted the children to have any enjoyment."[1]

Poor fathers: hen-pecked by wives, beleaguered by paternal obligations, and made comical by blustering pride. At least children, also subject to the rule of Mother, might prove sympathetic allies. No pity at all for the feckless father; just grim satisfaction that the last laugh might yet be on his downtrodden dependents. Such were the parameters of popular jokes about fathers in the cheap press in the 1890s. The tone of such gags resonates throughout autobiography to suggest that, for some families at least, comedic stereotypes provided a framework in which to position family life. As Lucy Delap observes with reference to jokes about domestic servants and their employers, analysis of humour illuminates the emotional range of social dynamics.[2]

This chapter examines how laughter and comedy operated within family stories to identify roles and responsibilities, affective allegiances and tensions, moments of conflict and resolution: who laughed, when, with whom and at what, indicates parenting practices, attachment and ambivalence in the working-class family. Autobiographers' identification

---

[1] *Penny Illustrated Paper*, 1 June 1895, 347; 28 December 1895, 417; 23 July 1898, 6; 28 December 1895, 410.
[2] Lucy Delap, 'Kitchen sink laughter: domestic service humour in twentieth century Britain', *Journal of British Studies*, 49:3 (2010), 623–54.

and manipulation of laughter, in its many forms, in the narration of childhood put the emotional housekeeping of family life in order. Sometimes, humour enabled authors to retrospectively divest fathers of power, neutralise the sting of humiliation and reorder emotional hierarchies. Laughter with fathers, or that enabled authors to relate sympathetic qualities in fathers, highlighted attachments. This sometimes conflicted with loyalty to mothers, resulting in a kind of guilty laughter. Similarly, a particular kind of masculine humour that made light of being a father suggests the ways in which comedy could function as a form of 'baby talk', allowing men to relate parenting tasks and attachments in a non-sentimental way.

While few wrote their autobiographies as comedy, it was rare for authors to omit any laughter. Mostly, humour is discernible in wry smiles rather than belly laughs, exclamation marks that intimate incredulity or, through anecdotes about events that seemed humorous at the time. Often, humour is far from obvious and readers are not meant to laugh alongside the author but rather to recognise a capacity for fun or laughter in contexts different to the authorial present. Autobiographies that lack lightness usually relate stories of unresolved trauma, while a distinct form of grim comedy could relate what was sober and sad. As the cultural studies critic Andy Medhurst notes, humour that created space for the working classes to laugh at life's cruelties was not reactionary but, rather, facilitated a knowing language of observation on hardship: 'life's like that'.[3] Taking laughter seriously matters because what at first seems trivial or, in some cases, trivialisation, is suggestive of how individuals give meaning to relationships and experience. Given the scholarly assumption that working-class autobiography gave little insight into private life beyond cliché and proselytising, the turn to comedy can generate insight into alternative languages of feeling.

Emotional housekeeping

Scholarship on humour has emphasised that laughter is often a weapon of the weak: it can ameliorate suffering and provide a medium for expressing complaint. Humorous anecdotes can operate as a site for the navigation and negotiation of power; and as Lucy Delap demonstrated, humour can suggest the ambiguities of identity and social relationships. To laugh at someone is to gain authority over them or to resist the indignity they would inflict. Laughter can cement or rupture social

---

[3] Andy Medhurst, *A national joke: popular comedy and English cultural identities* (London: Routledge, 2007), 65.

scripts, boundaries and broader social identities.⁴ In the joke about the condemned man above, a downtrodden wife laments her husband's objection to allowing his children watch him hang. The last laugh is, of course, with the mother and children who are liberated by Pater's execution. We know we should treat neither capital punishment nor domestic oppression with levity. But the muted triumph of the dependents is irresistible, even while offering poor consolation for life's inequalities.

Historians and anthropologists have long pointed to laughter as a discourse that facilitated the subversion of power hierarchies and enabled those at the bottom, temporarily at least, to triumph over those above them.⁵ Often, the laughter turns on an ambiguous subject, not readily associated with humour. Robert Darnton's study of a 'joke' about a cat massacre in early modern France advances a gruesome but illuminating analysis of how seemingly inappropriate laughter can generate a powerful critique of power relations.⁶ In his study of music hall humour, Medhurst considers how historians have damned laughter among the oppressed as a culture of consolation. Far more useful, Medhurst contends, to see it as survival laughter, that is, laughter that is 'communal, collective, resigned, blunt, basic, a way of getting by, of alleviating the depressing limitations of low horizons'. For Medhurst, music hall was a place where working-class punters and performers could articulate alternative values and thumb their noses at middle-class attempts to inveigle everyone into constricted codes of 'decency' and propriety.⁷

Medhurst and Darnton examined survival laughter as a group activity that criticised the status quo and cemented a sense of belonging for those who laughed. Such laughter operates at a more fractured level, too. The anthropologist Donna Goldstein examined humour in the context of poverty and violence in a Rio shantytown. As the title of her book readily acknowledges, humour in grim contexts is often 'laughter out of place'. Yet, Goldstein illustrates how such humour operates as a powerful device to articulate the concerns of the weak and consolidate group sympathies. When told a 'funny' story about rape by two victims and their family, Goldstein was unable to 'get the joke'. That victims of sexual violence

---

⁴ Delap, 'Kitchen sink laughter.
⁵ Mikhail Bakhtin, *Rabelais and his world* (Bloomington: Indiana University Press, 1984), trans. Helène Iswolsky; Stedman Jones, 'Working-class culture'; Peter Bailey, *Popular culture and performance in the Victorian city* (Cambridge University Press, 1998), Dagmar Kift, *The Victorian music hall: culture, class and conflict* (Cambridge University Press, 1996).
⁶ Robert Darnton, *The great cat massacre: and other episodes in French cultural history* (London: Allen Lane, 1984), 75–106.
⁷ Medhurst, *A national joke*, 63–86.

could laugh about it was repulsive to Goldstein's, and her readers', sensibilities. Nevertheless, Goldstein unpacks the humour to explain how comedy supported the victims' recovery and enabled them, paradoxically, to express anger. The women reconfigured the trauma and shame of sexual violence as a terrible experience that they survived, that informed their relations with men and sharpened their critique of socio-economic conditions. The story also enabled the women's mother to express disapproval of 'premature' sex, teenage pregnancy and men's inability to provide economic support (or protection) to their families. In relating their ordeal, the women's flippancy advanced a 'thinly veiled account of the troubled nature of male-female relations and of everyday life'.[8]

Goldstein's thesis makes for deeply uncomfortable reading, not least because the association between laughter and violence raises the possibility that humour might absolve the perpetrators of brutality. She acknowledges this possibility, but argues that, if anything, the laughter here amplifies women's vehement protest against violence and sociolegal structures. Goldstein does not share the women's laughter but, by understanding the context and function of their decision to communicate the story in a particular way, argues that it is possible to recognise how humour, far from trivialising trauma, can express survival and anger. The women's laughter advanced critical insight into how Brazilian legal codes of communication that privilege formal, articulate and rational discourses, mirror macro power structures and preclude alternative ways of talking about crime, violence and their consequences. Humour in 'bad taste' offers the oppressed a legitimate language to challenge a moral and legal system that marginalises them. One may construe this contained form of laughter as conservative and consolatory, but it was hardly reactionary or merely flippant.

For some autobiographers discussed here, humour was entirely the wrong genre for purpose. Impassioned political narratives drew authority from memories of distress and the author's desire to right injustices. (Lord) Henry Snell (born 1865), recalling the poverty and malnourishment of his childhood among the agricultural labouring classes, noted that he could 'scarcely bear to write about' some experiences. Snell positioned the intense sorrow of his childhood memories, which he explicitly linked to a lack of laughter and frivolity, as the motor to his stellar political career.[9] Of course, the mere mention of what was difficult to express intimated the profundity of feeling. Edwin Muir, despite

---

[8] Donna Goldstein, *Laughter out of place: race, class, violence, and sexuality in a Rio shantytown* (Berkeley, Calif.; London: University of California Press, 2003), 259–74.
[9] Henry Snell, *Men, movements and myself* (London: J. M. Dent and Sons, 1936), 11.

psychoanalysis, struggled to write about the trauma of his childhood.[10] Some autobiographers probably censored their account to omit difficult experiences altogether; much depended on authors' motives for writing and their sense of audience. For others, the trauma of the past was pivotal to telling their story but remained difficult to articulate in any form.

Emma Smith, sexually abused by her foster father, relied on euphemism to relate the harrowing story of her life. There was little indication that Smith had recovered from the trauma of childhood and her autobiography is the most depressing in all the life stories featured in this book. Encouraged by her friendship with a sociologist, Smith wrote a story that, although restrained, was a damning critique of welfare services for children and the doubly oppressive consequences of sexual taboo and supposed social niceties.[11] Although located in the past, the publication of her story in the 1950s resonated powerfully in a context where child sexual abuse remained a shameful secret.[12] Louise Jermy's stepmother physically abused her in childhood. As an adult, Jermy appeared partially reconciled to her father, whom she held accountable for failing to protect her in childhood, but bitter resentment remained the keynote of her 1930s memoir. That Smith and Jermy told their stories at all represents a monumental act of bravery and resolve. Their stories continue to operate as critiques of domestic and sexual abuse, welfare services and the powerlessness of children. Notably, as female authors writing in the 1930s and 1950s, they exposed the gender politics surrounding sexual violence and domestic abuse that continued (and continue) to belittle and disempower women.[13]

When authors did relate childhood trauma with humour, they were (here, at least) exclusively men. As a professional actor, Charlie Chaplin (born 1889) excelled at tragicomedy and it is unsurprising that his autobiography scanned his youth for signs of skill in this genre. The pivotal moment he lighted upon related to a sheep's slaughterhouse break: careering about the streets on a dash for freedom, chased by members of the pubic, the ovine flight evoked Chaplin's laughter. Yet the dawning realisation that the sheep was running for its life inflected the comedy with unbearable melancholy.[14] Chaplin's identification with the tragicomedy of the sheep served as a presentiment to his acting genius. It also held an implicit mirror on Chaplin's construction of his childhood as

---

[10] Muir, *An autobiography*, 90–3.   [11] Smith, *A Cornish waif's story*.
[12] Louise Jackson, *Child sexual abuse in Victorian England* (London: Routledge, 2000).
[13] For a provocative essay on memory, truth and the politics of trauma see Janet Walker, 'The traumatic paradox: documentary films, historical fictions, and cataclysmic Past Events', *Signs*, 22:4 (1997), 803–825.
[14] Charles Chaplin, *My early years* (London: Bodley Head, 1979), 35.

marked by incongruity: light-hearted laughter (his parents' world of vaudeville) contrasted with his father's abandonment of wife and children; his comic, handsome father who broke hearts and left his estranged wife penniless; his beautiful, singing mother who lost her reason; the smart suburban house his father kept with his mistress contrasted with the slum of the abandoned family. Chaplin did not need the sheep anecdote as the marker for his career: he told his family story in the frame of tragicomedy. As in the best narratives in this genre, the poignancy of misfortune was offset by the quirks, foibles and eventual triumph of the hero.

Chaplin's autobiography ordered the messy dynamics of his family story into a meaningful structure. He chastised his father while, nevertheless, drawing parallels between man and boy to identify connectedness (such as Chaplin's recognition of his unknown father and his unwitting presentiment of his death) that cut across the older man's betrayal and acknowledged the Chaplin legacy of talent. His heartbreaking account of his mother's struggle against poverty and her periodic admission to the asylum positioned Chaplin and his brother as boy-men who sought to adopt the mantle of heads of house. Emotional housekeeping was usually the task of maternity. As Chaplin's organisation of his childhood sympathies attests, autobiography could facilitate retrospective emotional housekeeping where adults gave meaning and coherence to the affective disorder of childhood. This carried particular significance for authors whose stories suggested that mothers' suffering at the hands of their spouses had precluded their fulfilment of emotional management obligations. Autobiography enabled a rebalancing of scales.

As Lucy Delap notes, stories of abuse can be reassuringly funny, not least because they create emotional affinities.[15] Tragicomedy provided one genre for acknowledging the calamities of family life while staking a claim for survival and, paradoxically, dignity; it could also advance a searing critique of sexual politics whereby economic dependency and social disapproval hamstrung women who should have left violent or abusive men. For autobiographers, writing trauma as humour relegated suffering to the contained past, and, for most, highlighted the subsequent distance between authors and their childhoods. Indeed, Emma Smith could not be 'funny' about her past because she had no resolution in her adult life; her continued misery and disempowerment made it impossible to dislocate the past from her present.

The tension between violence and laughter was evident in authors' choice of 'grim' comedy or 'farce', modes which tend to exploit the

---

[15] Delap, 'Kitchen sink laughter', 629.

friction between comedy and calamity. For some, this device amplified the trauma and inequalities of the past. William Bowyer (born 1889) described his childhood as 'grim comedy', dominated by the violent mood swings of his father: his family story was a 'sordid and tragic farce' whereby his father exerted a 'paralysing' influence. His mother, sometimes locked in the damp scullery by her husband, reminded Bowyer of a 'trapped animal'. His father, likewise, was a 'thwarted, injured animal'. The bestial characteristics of both parents reflected the contrast between ideals of family, that bastion of Victorian civilisation, and the brutal struggle for survival in a context of despair. Indeed, the contradiction between ideal and experience made Bowyer's story farcical. It also underpinned the tension between Bowyer's criticism and sympathy: like animals, his parents behaved in ways that were predetermined by environment rather than reason. Imagining his father's behaviour as farce stressed the gross exaggeration of normative masculine attributes, notably authority and virility, into an improbable and extreme characterization that, like farce, had no intrinsic meaning and distinguished the older man's behaviour from other forms of violence, such as playground fights, that had rules.[16] The classic structure of farce is episodic which, again, mirrored the unpredictability of Bowyer's father in his random outbursts of aggression.[17]

Six months after her children finally persuaded their mother to leave him, Bowyer's father committed suicide. The 'comedy' in Bowyer's reminiscences is in the cruel irony of fate: after years of indecision about her marriage, his mother's eventual bid for independence appeared to trigger the bully husband's absolute collapse. There is a rueful, albeit unspoken, suggestion in Bowyer's account that if only she had struck out sooner, father might have done himself in long ago and saved a lot of trouble. Farce, here, rested on Bowyer's portrayal of his father as a preposterous figure: he was 'fantastic', 'absurd', 'ridiculous'. Bowyer spent pages of his autobiography trying to map possible psychological origins or explanations for his father's behaviour without any clear solution: unsatisfied sexual desires, the fear of poverty, some dreadful event in his past or a great betrayal. That Bowyer constructed his childhood as farce heightened his survival, but also his continued bafflement with those experiences.[18] While emphasising his powerlessness as a child who wanted to protect

---

[16] Jacob Middleton, 'The cock of the school: a cultural history of playground violence in Britain, 1880–1940', *Journal of British Studies*, 52: 4 (2013), 1–21.

[17] On mid-twentieth conceptions of farce as comedy with the meaning left out, see Leonard Potts, *Comedy*, (London: Hutchinson's University Library, 1949), 37 and Jessica Milner Davis, *Farce* (London: Methuen and co., 1978).

[18] Bowyer, *Brought out in evidence*, 68–72; 92–99; 109–12; 121–2; 125.

his mother, the autobiographical mapping of childhood enabled Bowyer the author to neutralise the impotency of Bowyer the boy.

Pat O'Mara (born 1902) also turned to farce to recount his violent childhood. O'Mara's family story was one of downward mobility precipitated by his dock labourer father's heavy drinking and periodic spells in prison for assaulting his wife. O'Mara began his parents' story with their first meeting in a pub. His mother had held out for a husband until the age of thirty and, on meeting his father, felt gratified to find a man who, although currently down on his luck, apparently hailed from a wealthy family. As O'Mara wryly noted, his mother's social ambition, gullibility and self-satisfaction in being rewarded for her patience made her easy prey. O'Mara took grim consolation in reassurance that his mother's kin at least had the insight to 'hate' his father on first sight. O'Mara's mocking tone rested on the benefit of hindsight: exclamation marks indicated incredulity at his mother's naivety while sneering at his father's pretension. That O'Mara could relate so much about his parents' courtship and early marriage gave the semblance of an oft-rehearsed story of bitter regret and exasperated resignation tempered by a sense of the absurd. Throughout his story, comic asides about his 'bellicose father' and mimicry of the older man's hectoring indicated O'Mara's contempt for his father. His flummoxed approach to his parents' relationship, much of which predated O'Mara's birth, identified his sympathy with his mother but also established O'Mara as a detached narrator for whom such human calamities were a sad but, for all that, distant fact.

Three older siblings had died by the time Alice, O'Mara's older sister, and the author were born. Their father was anything but funny: he beat his wife, tried to set her on fire and, on one occasion, attempted to throw her from a third-floor window. The comedy of these scenes rested on the incongruity of small children, O'Mara and his sister, seeking to protect their mother. O'Mara joined his father in cursing his mother as a 'slummy' while urging him that his wife was not worth the effort of beating; Alice stood in front of her mother with her hand over the older woman's mouth, begging her to ignore the stream of insults issuing from her spouse. O'Mara acknowledges that this is no laughing matter: they only 'might have seemed humorous', but through the very suggestion of laughter, O'Mara confirmed the pathos of their family tragedy, especially as the siblings were rarely successful in averting violence. In imagining the children's efforts as valiantly absurd against a powerful but equally ludicrous father, O'Mara drew on melodrama with exaggerated characteristics of good and evil locked in a tug of war.[19]

---

[19] O'Mara, *The autobiography of a Liverpool Irish slummy*, 30–3; 36–7; 42–7; 50–3.

O'Mara's narrative was inflected with didactic undertones that extended beyond the confines of family to implicate readers. The danger of family sagas like this was the very real possibility, without external support and conscious resistance, of perpetuation, with the boy child socialised into violent contempt for women while his sister advocated refuge in the classic emblems of female oppression, silence and stillness. O'Mara's rendering of his childhood advanced a particular critique of the predicament of Catholic women whose obedience to church authority consigned them to the body bag of marriage to pathologically violent men. As O'Mara was quick to note, although economic structures meant life without a male breadwinner, however feckless, was tough, families could survive materially without men. His father's spells in prison were financially fraught but harsh economies were compensated by the calm, regular rhythm of life and reconciliation with his mother's kinfolk. In a sense, O'Mara's depiction of his mother and her children echoed farce's celebration of human failure. As Jessica Davis notes, such failures touch the audience because the gruesome joke is on humanity rather than individuals.[20] O'Mara drew his reader into sympathetic alignment with the victims of his father's abuse, especially the little children who tried so hard to protect their mother. Simultaneously, their failure to prevent the father's violence becomes, through O'Mara's retelling, his audience's failure for their absurd, if unwitting, collusion with the invisibility of 'everyday' violence.[21]

Punctuating O'Mara's account is his father's oft-repeated criticism of his wife and her family: 'You're all bloody slummies and were raised in S--houses!' As the reader knows, the real 'slummy' in this show is the father, for all his pretensions to an ancestral estate and noble heritage. Indeed, this irony carries through to the title of the book, *Liverpool Irish Slummy*, which purportedly refers to the autobiographical subject. In appropriating the insult, O'Mara effectively celebrates all that the 'slummy' son achieved. The adult O'Mara migrated to America where he thrived as a taxi-driver and was able to finance passages for his mother and sister. His wry authorial voice mimicked the narrative style of the Baltimore taxi-driver he became to give a chatty but authoritative tone to a story that, even while gruesome, was entertaining and ultimately uplifting. Comedy, like the Atlantic, separated O'Mara, Alice and their

---

[20] Davis, *Farce*.
[21] Shani D'Cruze 'Unguarded passions: violence, history and the everyday' in *Everyday violence in Britain, 1850–1950: gender and class*, ed. Shani D'Cruze (Harlow: Longman, 2000), 1–26; Anna Clark, "Domesticity and the problem of wife beating in nineteenth-century Britain: working-class culture, law and politics' in *Everyday violence in Britain*, ed. D'Cruze, 27–40.

mother from their violent past to emphasise just how far they had travelled, literally and emotionally, from their Liverpool slummy.

Bowyer's farce, in contrast, was darker, not least because Bowyer did not give narrative closure to his family story. The contempt he expressed for his father was shot through with sympathy for a 'frightened man' whose ghost hovered at the corner of his son's eye. In a plot directed by 'treacherous' love, Bowyer's marriage repeated the failure of his father's experience: like his father, Bowyer was unfulfilled and uncontrollably temperamental. Farce, as far as it went, referenced the cruel mockery of fate that made nonsense of individual aspirations. Bowyer's identification of father and son as victims of a sinister predetermined plot implicitly let both men off the hook while apportioning some blame to female characters in his and his father's drama. Bowyer railed against possessive and ruthless parental love, especially the 'masochistic "unselfishness" of mothers' who took a 'queer pleasure' in 'indulgent' self-sacrifice. The conflict between Bowyer's sympathy and resentment reflected the larger object of his story: to weigh the inherent principle of evil running through the world against the potential of human reason for goodness. The philosophical conflict at the heart of his book played out in microcosm in the name Bowyer attached to the text. In his adult career as a museum curator, Bowyer published under the name William Bowyer Honey. Bowyer was his mother's name. In publishing his autobiography, he dropped the patronymic 'Honey' altogether. In rejecting his father's name, Bowyer made a powerful gesture of rejecting his father and, for all his unresolved bitterness against women, aligned his core identity with that of his mother.[22]

Bowyer's autobiography was, as his publisher noted, 'unusual' in tackling a philosophy of conflict through the medium of personal history. The technique, however, of presenting a 'comic obverse' to tragic themes was not uncommon, and mockery or irony provided the keynote of authorial contempt for volatile or feckless fathers in a number of autobiographies studied here. Making paterfamilias the butt of the family joke facilitated a kind of insolence that children probably dreamed of but lacked the audacity to deliver. In this light, autobiography offered scope for venting years of indignation and exacting retrospective justice through ridicule. Mockery was especially effective as a form of imaginative patricide given the public esteem invested in paternal authority.

If the title 'Father' resounded with solemnity and decorum, one of the easiest ways to subvert paternal stateliness was to assign an alternative

---

[22] Bowyer, *Brought out in evidence*, 11; 15–17; 266–7; 333–6.

appellation to the head of household. Throughout his memoir, Albert Jasper (born 1905) referred to his father interchangeably as 'my father' and 'the old man'. The 'old man' is qualitatively different from 'my father', which, in all its formality, rang with respect for the dignity of paternity.[23] 'My father' could indicate the stiffness of a relationship but more usually invoked a degree of generational regard, as might be expected in accounts of working-class respectability, and mirrored the formal convention of published texts. A few authors used 'Dad' to intimate the less formal boundaries of a relationship and, in some cases, the genre of autobiography too. 'Old man' was not automatically impertinent: much depended on context. Fred Bower's colloquial style lent his memoir a chatty, confidential tone. In just three pages, the appellations for his father ranged from the formal to the affectionate. As a just-married man, his father was 'young Joe'. In his guise as head of family who took a brave stand against blackleg labour, the older man became 'my father'. Bower's endorsement of his father's politics was embedded in his turn to the more informal 'my old Dad'. In the final shift, his father became 'the dear old Dad', an endearment that suffused pride in his father with affection.[24] In Jasper's case, the definite article denoted the impersonal character of the kinship relationship to divest the potentially fond 'my old man' of positive meaning.

'The old man' laid verbal stress on the 'o' to emphasise 'old' in the phrase ('my old man' places stress on 'my'), implicitly contrasting the declining manhood of fathers with youthful vitality. This had particular resonance when authors reimagined relations with fathers from the perspective of their juvenile selves: in a social and economic context where work was pivotal to masculine identity and labouring men experienced increasing difficulties finding employment over the age of forty, 'old' manhood implied dwindling manliness. It is notable that Albert Jasper and Robert Roberts, two autobiographers who habitually referred to 'the old man' throughout their memoirs, were scathing about their fathers' material contributions to family life. Robert Roberts's *The Classic Slum* used autobiography as a framework for social commentary on poverty in the industrial city at the turn of the twentieth century. Roberts's disparaging asides about his 'old man' were given added momentum by appearing mostly as footnotes to suggest that his father did not warrant the 'serious' attention of the main text.[25]

---

[23] Albert S. Jasper, *A Hoxton childhood* (Slough: Barrie & Rockliff, 1971).
[24] Bower, *Rolling stonemason*, 17–20.
[25] See for example, Roberts, *The classic slum*, 34.

Thomas Barclay (born 1852) introduced his father into his life story by asserting that he was too antiquated in notions of showing older generations respect to use the term 'the old man'. This was a neat narrative trick: Barclay knew the term rang with insolence, but in declaring that politeness prohibited its use, he conveniently signalled that the term was, nonetheless, apposite.[26] Indeed, Jasper's use of 'the old man' was knowingly disrespectful, not least because he used it in scenes where his father was a ludicrous figure; his attempts to establish governance at home through swearing and hectoring underlined how far removed his father was from the dignified authority of Victorian Paterfamilias.[27] The incongruity between the paternal ideal and Jasper's experience completed his characterisation of 'the old man's' status: Jasper Senior was a joke.

Such examples demonstrate how authors might deploy narrative devices to signal shifting scales of feeling. As a child, Albert Jasper was probably intimidated (at best) by his hectoring father. In adulthood, with his father long dead, Jasper could renegotiate his father's status at home. 'The old man' divested his father of fear and his capacity to humiliate. Notably, where Jasper's memoir did register resentment at his father's fecklessness, the jeering tone of 'the old man' was replaced by the more potent 'the old sod' or 'the old swine', terms that lacked humour to convey distress.[28] Likewise, in pretending to discount the phrase, 'the old man', Thomas Barclay winked at its impertinence to assert his superiority in favouring a more thoughtful impudence: the rejection of his father's beliefs in nationalism, politics and religion.

Laughing at belligerent or arrogant fathers retrospectively modified the mortification of childhood to reorder the hierarchies of a remembered past. In many autobiographies, the material culture of home was a staple signifier of respectability that demonstrated thrift, household management and pleasure in domesticity. Robert Roberts's account of his father's pride in the material clutter of home, as Chapter 3 demonstrated, entirely subverted this 'respectable' reading to develop a riotous puncturing of his father's pomposity that illustrates just how detached his father was from family life. In a similar vein, Albert Jasper drew on key moments of supposed paternal dignity to expose his father's empty vanity. Jasper's autobiography set the tone of paternal indignity with an opening anecdote about his unmarried sister copulating under her father's roof while hapless dad lay sleeping. A shotgun wedding followed. One might expect, given contemporary codes of respectability, the

---

[26] Barclay, *Memoirs and medleys*, 38.
[27] Jasper sets the tone in the first chapter. Jasper, *A Hoxton childhood*, 7–33.
[28] *Ibid*, 33.

pregnant bride to be the object of shame in this story but, through mockery of his father's attempt to simulate a dignified Paterfamilias, Jasper established his 'old man' as the family outsider.

With striped trousers and a bob tailcoat purchased for the occasion, Jasper's father assembled the sartorial props to support paternal dignity but his performance lacked authenticity: 'My sisters just could not keep a straight face. I thought they were going in hysterics when he started to put on a collar and tie; he had never worn one in his life. They eventually got it on for him after a lot of swearing and blinding. The coach was going green with age.' The family's complicity in assisting father to dress might confirm his worth were it not for his daughters' laughter and Jasper's tittering verdict: 'He did look a sight.' That his father was 'quite pleased with himself' and believed he was imitating 'gentry' added further humour by juxtaposing the old man's vanity with the ridicule of his family. The second-hand status of the wedding clothes might have suggested thrift but, instead, Jasper implied they were second rate and, in that sense, a metaphor for low-grade fathering. Indeed, the humour in this account provided a foil against which to measure the family's wretchedness at the end of the wedding day when Jasper's father's drunken, obnoxious behaviour ruined the celebration.[29]

The hackneyed tone of Jasper's wedding anecdote suggested that this story had been told many times and operated within family life to delineate the roles and expectations of family members. Not all humour directed at puncturing masculine vanity was deliberately malicious or, even, personal. Grace Foakes related an anecdote from her childhood concerning the compromised dignity of a neighbour, which she, and other children, told with riotous glee. A man in pursuit of privacy decided to take his weekly bath in the bedroom, removed from the hullabaloo of living-room life. A miscalculation between bath water and the volume of his body resulted in water seeping through the floor into the tenement below. The humour in this narrative rested on the naked father rushing into the kitchen to alert his wife to the catastrophe. Foakes and her peers laughed 'so much' at this story, relishing that it took the father a long time to live it down. Her inclusion of the poor man's embarrassment in her life story suggested that she continued to be tickled by the incident.[30] As Foakes acknowledged, there was no sophisticated humour here. But, in a memoir that charted her father's sombre and sometimes harsh reserve, Foakes's literal exposure of another father as a

---

[29] *Ibid*, 26–35.   [30] Foakes, *Four meals*, 45.

figure of laughter indulged a fantasy about subverting paternal dignity in the most corporeal fashion.[31]

Other autobiographers' comedies were more subtle. Alice Foley described her father as a loud-mouthed, belligerent fellow, fond of drink. As much of Foley's memoir made clear, this coarse man was out of kilter with her gentle mother and, ostensibly, had little in common with his earnest daughter. To explain the incongruity between father and family, Foley rehearsed a favourite childhood fantasy: that her father was 'not my proper parent'. Denying her father to her school friends, Foley replaced him, and his kin, with exotic characters: more affluent, more interesting, much less embarrassing.[32] This gentle mischief, epitomised in Foley's note that, when rumbled, the fantasy caused her family some consternation, nevertheless emphasised Foley's deep-seated frustration with her depressing father. Notably, the fantasy did not displace her mother. In retelling the comedy, Foley advanced a serious story of the way her father's personality oppressed his dependents. Yet, by treating father as a family joke, Foley was able to contain and survive him. Humour fortified bonds of sympathy between those on the receiving end of his foul temper and readjusted the scales of authority.

Comedy, conflict and affective loyalties

If some authors used grim comedy to subvert domestic conflict, others deployed fun and laughter as signifiers of positive family dynamics: laughing with father denoted bonds of attachment. At a simple level, portraits of the 'fun' father could indicate the fond father. Lilian Slater presented her family dynamic within a context of fast-talking banter that elevated the banality of everyday life to signal affectionate and easy ties. Slater's dominant memory of her father was of a handsome, smiling man who sang ditties and told jokes, laughing through life and persuading his wife and children to laugh with him. When her father jokingly referred to a shoe last as 'what the cobbler threw at his wife', Slater and her siblings understood this as a comic foil between the everyday violence that might characterise other families and the easy-going, good-natured ambience of the Slater home. Her father invoked the same phrase when handing out pennies to his children on Saturdays. Again, the incongruity between his warm generosity and an imagined callous father was so extreme as to

---

[31] See Vic Gatrell, *City of laughter: sex and satire in eighteenth-century London* (London: Atlantic Books, 2006), 178–209.
[32] Foley, *A Bolton Childhood*, 32.

be funny. In Slater's memory, his 'pulling their leg' cushioned even father's discipline.[33]

Laughter as a signifier of Slater family togetherness included father's complicity in being the butt of the joke: his elaborate moustache presented a source of family comedy about his vanity. As Slater's mother observed: 'I moustache you not to mention it.'[34] Unlike the humour of Jasper and Roberts, which they directed at their fathers, Slater's laughter was congenial because father was in on the joke. Dolly Scannell did not share Slater's paternal effusiveness, being rather more sympathetic to her self-sacrificing mother. To the prim Scannell, her father was coarse and always lowered the tone with his smart comments. Even here, however, father's potentially divisive humour was offset by the jocularity of Scannell's authorial voice to suggest that her criticisms should not be taken too seriously. Her father's description of his offspring as a 'winkle-eyed lot' might aggravate a fastidious child, but Scannell's narrative acknowledged that such insults bound family members together in light hearted, curmudgeonly realism about each other's shortcomings.[35]

It would be a mistake to think all high spirits denoted conviviality. William Brown's (born 1894) father alternated between 'boisterous exaltation' and 'brooding melancholy'. His periods of despondency frightened his children, but as Brown notes, his extreme animation was hardly less terrifying.[36] Nonetheless, comedy and laughter could bring Father into a child's realm to stake a claim for affection and attachment, especially when set against the order and rigour of maternal domestic authority or, indeed, as a foil to the absent man engaged in breadwinning responsibilities. Walter Southgate recollected that his parents sometimes hosted evening entertainments for friends and relatives. Invariably, his father would sing an old ditty 'Medicine Jack'. The refrain, 'Quack, quack, quack', encouraged much arm flapping and audience participation. His father dressed for the part with a battered high hat, carried props (a pail and sack on his back), and 'did slapstick' with ladies corsets which 'never failed to raise a great deal of laughter and applause'.[37]

For Southgate, this 'unsophisticated fun' demonstrated the inclusiveness of diversions that did not depend on wit or contextual knowledge but was 'silliness' for its own sake. The hackneyed character of his father's performance was partly what made it funny, in the anticipation of father's usual turn, the comfort of familiarity and group participation.

---

[33] Slater, *Think on! Said Mam*, 13, 64   [34] *Ibid*, 6.
[35] Scannell, *Mother knew best*, 65.
[36] W. J. Brown, *So far* (London: George Allen and Unwin Ltd., 1943), 17.
[37] Southgate, *That's the way it was*, 69

As Andy Medhurst notes of popular television sitcoms in the mid-twentieth century, there is something reassuring about repetition, not least because it fosters a sense of belonging.[38] Southgate Senior's slapstick mirrored his consistency in other dimensions too, whether it was pontificating on politics, interrupting Southgate's homework or never quite earning enough. The wry tone adopted throughout his memoir enabled Southgate to illuminate the complex dynamic between the frustrations and comforts of family life. In smiling with, rather than laughing at, his father's shortcomings, Southgate was able to identify the financial and specifically marital strains within his family while acknowledging affection for the quirks and foibles of his father. The story of 'Medicine Jack' rang with an echo of the family groan as his father began his predictable turn, but, in playing along, Southgate suggested the ways in which family ties weathered disappointments.

Southgate's celebration of comedy that referenced body parts or functions considered taboo by 'respectable' working-class families (father in women's corsets) was rare in political memoir. Many published working-class autobiographies strove to emphasise an autodidactic culture of self-improvement and rational recreation. Even authors whose texts presented a ragbag of anecdotes were sensitive to the dangers of fun and liveliness being mistaken for stupidity. A. V. Christie recalled many of his father's amusing or entertaining anecdotes but was quick to point out his political and religious commitments, too.[39] At the start of the twenty-first century, comedy taste retains symbolic power to communicate distinction and cultural superiority.[40] Perhaps it was indicative of Southgate's self-fashioning as a radical that he could annexe silliness to a broader programme of political heterodoxy. Unapologetic rejoicing in 'unsophisticated fun' enabled Southgate to suggest the vitality of working-class culture, but also to highlight the ongoing bond between his adult status and the memory of childhood experience. Sociologists have pointed to the ways in which humour and laughter are pivotal in 'everyday interaction rituals' as individuals form 'durable bonds' with others to 'create positive emotional energy'. Shared laughter signifies similarity, which in turn 'breeds emotional closeness and trust'.[41] Southgate's father in drag, in this context, was a positive commemoration of attachments forged through shared laughter.

[38] Medhurst, *A national joke*, 146. [39] Christie, *Brass tacks and a fiddle*, 11–17.
[40] Sam Friedman and Giselinde Kuipers, 'The divisive power of humour: comedy, taste and symbolic boundaries', *Cultural Sociology*, 7:2 (2013), 179–195.
[41] Friedman and Kuipers, 'The divisive power of humour', 187. See also R. Collins, *Interaction Ritual Chains* (Princeton: Princeton University Press, 2004); and Medhurst, *A national joke*, 187–203.

As head of household and family, men were legally and politically invested with dignity and authority. Slapstick and silliness, temporarily at least, subverted this dignity. Joseph Stamper's father liked to attend 'men only' potato and pie suppers in the function room above his local pub. Stamper recalled his childish fascination with this mysterious homosocial world, detailing that his mother took him to watch the entertainment from the street where, among other things, he witnessed the men dancing in a chain, singing 'Our Sally's britches'. Stamper's enthralment is suggestive of the subversive quality of grown men behaving with such vulgarity. The comedy continued as Stamper recollected his father's homecoming whereupon he sat in his chair, the font of paternal authority, and tipped his head back seemingly unable to open his eyelids. Father's dignity was finally shot as his hat rolled off his head. The evening ended with Stamper's mother pretending disapproval and his father's elaboration of meek obedience.[42] The teasing patter on these nights, apparently exaggerated for the benefit of wide-eyed children, illuminated how father's excursions were sanctioned within the boundaries of family life and, in a subversion of the temperance narrative where such indulgences always ended in tears, underscored normative roles and responsibilities in family.

The comic interludes described by Southgate and Stamper were, perhaps, examples of a working-class 'culture of consolation', whereby brief carnival moments provided men with a safety valve of release from onerous responsibilities. For Stamper, the men's potato and pie nights fortified their identities as male breadwinners. His father may have simulated tipsiness but he still rose at 4.30 AM for work, a note that located these excursions within periods of employment and demonstrated the regulated character of release. Likewise, although the 'domestic' character of plebeian pubs is debatable, they could act as proxy for family space in providing masculine space for father-son interaction. Since boyhood, Stamper had accompanied his father on occasional jaunts to the pub, where father and son appear to have sat mostly in companionable silence. Although the adult Stamper had no taste for beer, the ritual of going to the pub with his father forged the habit of father-son sociability.[43] Jack Jones's father also liked a beer. As his boys grew older, the pub became the locus of father-son space outside of work. This was especially important after Jones left mining, his father's trade.[44] Like Stamper, Jones did not much care for beer but the pub was his father's place and being taken by older sons for a pint gave the older man

---

[42] Stamper, *So long ago*, 106–7.   [43] *Ibid*, 41–2.
[44] Jones, *Unfinished journey*, 118–120; 173.

great pleasure. Sons who took fathers to the pub signified their willingness to make time for father while the homosocial character of taprooms facilitated the inclusion, albeit temporary, of upwardly mobile sons into their fathers' labouring domains.

Laughter and silliness enabled the serious breadwinner to engage with family life on a frivolous and tactile level, even where this acknowledged men's specific duties as fathers. Cataloguing rural life before the First World War, George Bourne noted 'delightful' routines where smaller children played with father, taking components of fathering and exaggerating them for playful effect. A 'happy' hour could slip by in games where father pretended to discipline offspring who played at defiance: they shouted 'Old Father Smithers!' and leapt out of reach as their father chased them, the shouts interspersed with peals of hilarity. Even where fun appeared largely one-sided, the compliance of tired or irritable men in play suggested paternal tolerance for childish amusement. A father drawing water was accompanied by his four or five children, who were pretending to be afraid of 'bogies'. Although the man irritably told his offspring to be quiet, the children would resume play after a minute or so. Indeed, this father's curmudgeonly griping was sufficiently ritualised to have become part of the game, and Bourne characterised the saga as punctured with 'tittering and squeals of excitement'.[45]

Laughter was tactile and drew individuals together in a corporeal sensation. John Paton's (born 1886) mother remarried in his boyhood. Paton recalled that he liked his stepfather 'immensely': the older man 'gurgled' with laughter, had 'merry twinkling eyes', and allowed the boy to climb all over him, tugging at his tufty beard.[46] These were clichés of affectionate paternity but, in the context of telling his story, they enabled an adult Paton to depict the priorities of a small child who could not comprehend the complexity of his mother's first marriage and subsequent abandonment but who could fully embrace a new 'father' who was so warmly tangible. In reconstructing the pleasure of his stepfather's laughter, Paton identified his affection for, and attachment to, the man who stepped in to fulfil the absent father's obligations.

For older children, laughter with fathers could provide a bridge to cordiality in an otherwise fraught relationship. George Acorn's (born 1885) autobiography fumed at his parents' shortcomings: he was angry at their ignorance, their demands for money as he got older and their failure to love him. Even here, Acorn's rage was shot through with flashes of togetherness that suggested how family ties might have played out

---

[45] Bourne, *Change in the village*, 188–9; see also 28.
[46] Paton, *Proletarian pilgrimage*, 61–2.

differently. Of these moments of unity, predominantly with his father (his mother was too preoccupied with work and childcare to afford such luxuries), Acorn emphasised how shared emotions raised the prospect of mutual sympathy: first, when reading Dickens aloud and shedding sentimental tears for the suffering of their favourite characters and, second, when attending Music Hall and laughing at 'gags' together.[47] As Jonathan Rose notes, Acorn's autobiographical style probably borrowed heavily from his favourite literature (Dickens) but this does not diminish Acorn's narrative; if anything, it shows how important the consumption of cultural texts was in working-class authors' attempts to give meaning to their life stories. For Rose, Acorn's style suggests the influence Dickens exerted.[48] Here, Acorn's decision to include anecdotes of laughing and crying with his father in an otherwise bleak relationship matters because it illustrates the power of shared sensation to create (temporary) bonds between individuals.

Laughter moves people: they shake, show teeth, throw their heads back, clap hands, slap objects (or people), close their eyes and make noise, from ringing laughs to indecorous cackles and inelegant snorting (although, as Delap notes, such physicality is overwhelmingly coded with class).[49] Laughter sometimes hurts and can feel indecently intimate. It is easy to see why men who moved women with their laughter were successful in forming romantic attachments when they had little else to offer; as Joseph Keating noted of his father, his capacity for laughter transformed him from a hopeless marriage prospect into a 'Lady killer'. Jean Rennie (born 1906) loved her father's rich laughter. She claimed the inheritance of his fun and loved to recall laughing with him. Yet the laughter that bound Rennie to her father presented a conundrum, for this laughing man caused her mother so much heartache with his unreliable income and fondness for whisky. Rennie recalled the childhood conflict of being 'torn' between being 'in love with' her father and ready to forgive him most things, and awareness that she needed her mother (a woman who sacrificed much to keep Rennie in school for as long as possible). Although laughing with her father was a source of guilt, in real time and recollection, it also provided a window of resolution to her suspicion that this amounted to a betrayal of her loyal and long-suffering mother. After all, father's humour was precisely what had attracted his wife in the first

---

[47] George Acorn, *One of the multitude* (London: William Heinemann, 1911), 13.
[48] Rose, *The intellectual life*, 111–2.
[49] Delap compares servants with their robust, full laughter in contrast to the smirks and half smiles of bourgeois employers. See Delap, 'Kitchen sink laughter', 623–54.

place: he sang, laughed and danced his way into her heart.[50] However much Rennie's mother might rue the day she laughed alongside this man, in Rennie's implicit reckoning, she should at least have understood the appeal of his laughter to their daughter. Shared laughter drew an emotional alignment between father and daughter and mirrored other similarities: if her father disappointed his wife with his insobriety, Rennie proved a disappointment to her mother by leaving school to work in a mill, followed by domestic service.

Matters of who laughed, when and with whom emphasised the fluidity and tensions in the emotional dynamics of a household. As adults writing of childhoods, authors were cognisant of the complex allocation of family sympathies and loyalties. Comic anecdotes helped map the nuance of childhood relationships. Kathleen Dayus told amusing anecdotes about her parents to convey the affective loyalties of family life. In one prolonged anecdote, Dayus recounted laughing with her sister over the sentimental value their mother invested in father's decrepit billycock hat (a crowned and brimmed hat of felt). The humour here was multilayered: the incongruity between the dilapidated hat and its pristine condition in their parents' marriage photograph; and, the contrast between their parents in an everyday context and the wedding image that pictured a proud man with his adoring wife. The decline of the billycock mirrored Dayus's sympathetic rendering of the bridegroom's diminishing status into the beleaguered fellow of her autobiography. That their mother had a sentimental attachment to the hat provoked hilarity because it raised the prospect that mother, portrayed by Dayus as a termagant, was romantic. Even here, there is a degree of ambiguity that extends the mileage of Dayus's anecdote. It is entirely possible that her mother prized the hat not because of sentimental association but because it turned out to be the finest thing about her man.

The joke developed another layer when Dayus's sister suggested that the hat was a vital prop in familial rites of passage, notably christenings. The potentially solemn significance of this was transformed by the sister's revelation that father kept a dry nappy stuffed in the crown of the hat so that, as their parents left church, nappies could be changed to facilitate immediate repair to the pub, the soiled nappy tucked neatly in father's hat.[51] Dayus's reproduction of the story in her memoir suggests her sustained pleasure in this comedy: the ingenuity of her father; the subversive contrast between Sunday best for church and bodily

---

[50] Jean Rennie, *Every other Sunday: the autobiography of a kitchen maid* (London: Arthur Barker, 1955), 7–13.
[51] Dayus, *Her people*, 77–8.

functions; and the juxtaposition between religious ritual and speedy repair to the pub. The anecdote also demonstrated Dayus's sympathetic alignment in family loyalties. Her mother's attachment to the hat suggested her capacity for feeling while, slyly, intimating the limits of her sensibilities: she might hold a hat in great esteem but Dayus depicted her mother as a coarse, impetuous, hot tempered woman with little affection for daughter or husband. In contrast, while the nappy headdress might have encouraged laughter at father, in Dayus's rendering, the joke was on those who failed to realise what this smartly attired man had concealed in his hat. Father's complicity in facilitating the nappy exchange established his pragmatism and easy affability.

In another story, Dayus and her brother fled the house as dumplings they made for a stew exploded and rolled across the kitchen floor. In haste to escape maternal fury, they collided at the back gate with their father. The farcical crash, bang, dollop of this episode enabled Dayus to present a neat foil between her parents' temperaments and her different relationships with them. Father colluded with the children's escape and viewed the exploding dumplings in a humorous light. The conclusion to the story, that Mother made the children eat the blasted suet remains, underlined the older woman's austere domestic authority and the latent antipathy between Dayus and her mother.[52] Scholars may despair at the frivolous banalities of working-class autobiography but, in examples like this, the trivial, seemingly inane elements of plebeian lives were richly revealing of family ties.

In a similar vein, refusal to laugh along with father could confirm children's loyalty to mother. James Royce's (born c.1890) verdict on his father was that he was a 'rover' who refused to take responsibility for his family. If John Paton's twinkle-eyed stepfather epitomised affability, the 'merry' face of Royce's father signified incorrigible recklessness. Absent for most of Royce's childhood, his father's return to the homestead when Royce was around twelve was marked by gaiety and laughter as Royce's elder siblings and mother greeted the prodigal father with glee. In an overwhelmingly solemn household prior to his father' arrival, the unaccustomed festivity of home boded ill in retrospect, as Royce deployed his father's laughter as the key motif for his hollow character. When Royce needed new boots, his father stole some for him. His father's lack of sympathy to his sensitivity amplified Royce's indignation at the theft: his father 'chuckle[d] to himself' at Royce's naiveté. Royce's protests that his mother would be mortified by the robbery merely

---

[52] *Ibid*, 36–8.

elicited a 'quick glance of amusement' from his father. When his mother wept at news of the theft, his father made jest of her shame, taking all 'good-humouredly'. The older man's humour, at the expense of Royce and his mother's integrity, symbolised his detachment from the family and their moral framework. Even in death, when Royce looked upon the countenance of his father for insight into the man, he saw only his father's smile. As with Rennie's and Keating's fathers, the elder Royce had the 'gift of the gab' and could 'charm blood from a stone'. The initial appeal of his father's hearty laugh and jaunty whistle explained for Royce how his mother had chosen such a mate. Yet, in the sum of Royce's life story, the sheer inappropriateness of his father's laughter, in life and death, especially juxtaposed with his mother's tears, affirmed Royce's assertion that his father 'didn't count'; his laughter marked his insubstantiality.[53] Autobiographers used laughter or comic anecdotes to identify appropriate components of parenting and loyalty within families. In Royce's case, the lack of laughter in his father's absence signified the family's struggle to survive without a paternal breadwinner, but contrasted with his father's unseemly laughter, it also denoted their decency.

Sometimes, failure to laugh alongside father highlighted that father and child were on different wavelengths. When Harry Watkin was told to bring an empty (broken) eggshell to school, his father thought it great sport to blow an intact eggshell so that the teacher would think Watkin had an egg in its slippery entirety. Caught between reluctance to disobey his father by breaking the eggshell and fear of his teacher's disapproval, the joke made Watkin 'miserable'. His father's failure to appreciate his son's anxiety highlighted the conflicted relationship between man and boy: his father could cut a heroic figure to the growing lad, but sometimes the bravado that gave a veneer of manly glamour also inhibited sympathy with his sensitive son.[54]

Thomas Burke (born 1886) wrote many versions of his autobiography throughout his lifetime and his stories function primarily as a narrative frame for imagining the East End of London, especially the Chinese community. He is also interesting for his description of the relationship between an orphan boy (Burke) and the uncle who raised him. Burke used humour and fun to convey the general contentedness of childhood ('ours was a jolly little home') and to stake a claim for working-class self-determination against the 'hands of the Interferers' (social workers). The difficulty of focusing on jollity was that the serious slipped out of view: 'I loved Uncle Frank and it hurts me today that I can only

---

[53] Royce, *I stand nude*, 9–10; 41–7.   [54] Watkin, *From Hulme*, 7.

remember him as a shiftless figure of fun whom nobody took seriously. The farcical gestures alone remain – the nods, winks, the finger at the nose, the rude words, the schoolboy foolery...' It took conscious effort to recall his 'service and companionship, the self-denial', his 'care and thought'. Even then, images of slapstick clumsiness intruded on Burke's will to revere. Yet the 'hurt' of remembering the ludicrous was a reflection on cultural norms that valued the 'solemn requiem'. There was no doubt that the boy 'loved' his Uncle Frank. Perhaps, Burke reflected, 'laughing remembrance' counted as 'high' on interpersonal terms as the unsmiling obsequies of public commemoration.[55]

Laughter, parenting and funny talk

Most laughter within and about families highlighted the disparity between maternal and paternal approaches to family. The jokes at the beginning of this chapter about men's 'baby talk' and the competing priorities of mothers and fathers illustrate cultural assumptions about mothers' preoccupation with children and domestic life while fathers prioritised selfish concerns and misjudged childcare matters. As with the little boy who quipped to his father that he wished they 'hadn't never married mother', paternal haplessness nevertheless could forge bonds of sympathy between father and children. For some autobiographers, funny stories about parenting could facilitate masculine navigation of 'baby' or 'child talk'. Humorous stories concerning babies confirmed the sex segregation of parenting tasks to affirm a father's masculinity in relation to his infant. As Walter Southgate noted in his memoir, babies compromised men's dignity: fathers did not push perambulators or go to christenings.[56] For 'old hand' fathers, humour directed at the new father confirmed the superior experience and knowledge of the practiced Pater.[57]

This mirrored men's dislocation from childbirth and childrearing tasks more generally. It is notable that most autobiographical reconstructions of the author's birth imagined fathers either returning from, or departing for, waged work to establish the sexed spheres of parenting. Jack Jones began his autobiography with his mother in labour and his father

---

[55] Thomas Burke, *The wind and the rain: a book of confessions* (London: Thornton Butterworth Ltd., 1924), 15–17; 20.

[56] Southgate, *That's the way it was*, 12. See also Laura King, '"Now you see a great many men pushing their pram proudly": Family-orientated masculinity represented and experienced in mid-twentieth-century Britain', *Cultural and Social History* 10:4 (2013), 599–617.

[57] Loane, *From their point of view*, 147.

discussing miners' wages, working conditions and industrial change.[58] In T. A. Westwater's story, his mother laboured through the night as his father sat fully clothed in the kitchen, waiting to depart for work at 3 AM.[59] Reader Bullard and William Lax began their birth stories with their mothers' pregnancies and their fathers' desperate search for work.[60] Adult children's humorous anecdotes about fathers and babies both confirmed and complicated this narrative. When Sidney Campion's father was asked to state his contribution to his wife's newborn babe, he reputedly smiled and retorted, 'Just influence'.[61] Walter Southgate related his father's faux-belligerent riposte of 'He'd better be' to neighbours who commented that baby Walter was the 'dead spit of his farver'.[62] Harry Harris's father discovered his wife had given birth to twins when his mates lined the street on his return home and made exaggerated cradle movements with their arms, gesturing the number two at him.[63]

On one level, the stories underscored authors' depiction of a working-class culture that celebrated resilience in a harsh world: births were perilous affairs for mothers and added to men's breadwinner responsibilities. The stories also outlined the differing tasks and meanings attached to parental roles, acknowledging father's lack of involvement in childbirth, not least Harris's father who was at Epsom for the Derby, to highlight the physical and emotional 'labour' of mothers. Simultaneously, the anecdotes above stated men's contribution to babies by asserting paternity, through referencing masculine virility or provision. Campion Senior's smiling 'Just influence' was deceptively casual in staking a claim for what it was to father. It made explicit men's minimal role in pregnancy and childbirth but the laughter also depended on Campion and his reader knowing that his father's real contribution was rooted in his provision. Campion Senior sent his heavily pregnant wife to relatives while he worked at his labouring job in readiness for the arrival of their first baby. There is also an implicit pride in the claim to paternal influence; the fake modesty of the 'just' is funny because the 'influence' references the very necessary male contribution to making babies. Given that the baby was a boy, Campion's father was also responsible for socialising his son in masculine identity and obligation. Indeed, Campion's autobiography made clear how seriously his father took this role, citing the recurring clashes between father and son over the adolescent Campion's occupational choices.

---

[58] Jones, *Unfinished journey*, 9–15.   [59] Westwater, *The early life*, 1.
[60] Bullard, *The camels must go*, 17–8; and, William Lax, *His book*, 19.
[61] Campion, *Sunlight on the foothills*, 4–5.   [62] Southgate, *That's the way it was*, 12.
[63] Harris, *Under oars*, 9–10.

Southgate's memory, located in the context of his christening, is strikingly similar. His father's claim to paternity and faux outrage that there would 'be ructions' if baby Walter resembled anyone else made play of men's anxiety about wifely fidelity. Harry Harris's anecdote about his father's friends miming the news of twins depended upon his father's absence from home. That his father missed the birth because he was at the racecourse further emphasised the gap in parenting roles. As with Campion and Southgate, there was an element of masculine bravado in Harris Senior's friends congratulating his virility in fathering twins and joshing him in sympathy for the presumed chaos multiple births heralded. While these anecdotes emphasised father's literal distance from childbirth and babies, their comedy nevertheless highlighted a masculine kind of 'baby' talk.

As popular comic portrayals of men and babies made clear, typical baby talk, that is, talk to and about babies, was reserved for women. This is what made the confusion in the 'come and hear my baby talk' joke above so funny; men supposedly were excluded from *doing* baby talk. Music hall and print depictions of fathers caring for babies rested on the assumed incongruity of men imitating mothers.[64] Imagined communications between fathers and babies identified men as ludicrous imitators of maternal 'baby talk': 'Did'em, did'em, wake 'em up, pretty ickle chap/ Want a tiddy-iddy bit till papa gets the pop.' Any astute infant could spot a fraud and knew that men's attempts at baby talk were appalling: 'The more I kitched, kitched – So – and walked about, up, to and fro/And gave him everything you know, the *more* the darling roar'd.'[65] In this formulaic scenario, only when mother returned was order restored and baby satisfied. That the father usually relayed these narratives heightened the comic effect as performers, on stage or at home, indulged in slapstick performances of men's inappropriate handling of babies, their exaggerated baby talk and the general chaos that ensued when men tried their hand at childcare duties. One comic song that promoted a brand of baby food exploited this set-up to emphasise that where mothers were lazy (probably exhausted), baby's hopes rested on Dr. Ridge's infant food rather than Father who will 'nurse the bacon and Frizzle the baby, at the least, I don't mean that, I mean boil the baby and nurse the kettle, at least not that, you know what I mean...'[66]

---

[64] See the range of comic songs about matrimony and parenthood in *Howard & Co.'s comic annual* (London: Howard & Co., 1892–1903). This is quite different to the nonsense talk of Edward Lear, Lewis Carroll (or Thomas Hood). See Sanders, *The tragi-comedy*, 23–4, 37–41.
[65] Thomas S. Lonsdale, *A night with the baby* (London: C. Sheard, 1884).
[66] H. Hunter and Walter Redmond, *The beautiful baby, or Dr. Ridge's food* (London: Unknown, 1876).

One print version of this situation, *A Night with Baby* (1873), related the appropriately named Jeremiah Smallpeace's 'speechless terror' at being left with 'a bald-headed, and toothless, but nonetheless terrible individual', his 'deceitful little baggage' of a nine-month-old son.[67] In these scenarios, male narrators principally addressed their bachelor friends to exaggerate the chasm between masculinity and baby care. Such humorous routines underscored the 'natural' affinity of mothers with baby work, and the ineptitude of paternal imposters. Indeed, while men were the fictional narrators, the author of *A Night with Baby* was 'Julia' Chandler and the book was promoted as suitable for reading aloud at family occasions, thereby confirming and legitimating the components of maternity, ostensibly at men's expense, for the gratification of family members.

Jokes about men's haplessness at 'mothering' acknowledged and approved the gendering of parenting tasks. Edwin Pugh, the comic novelist, put gender stereotypes at the keystone of his domestic dramas. One short story focused on bath night for the six children of Dick Swann. As the children take turns being bathed by efficient Mrs. Swann, each child is despatched from the tub to its father for towelling under Mrs. Swann's critical eye and vicious tongue: do not 'dab at the poor child as if she was a punchin' machine'. Swann has invited his mate Foy to call for him on bath night, intending to embarrass the bachelor. In the event, it is Swann who is the butt of the joke, as his wife and Foy make it clear that in performing this task so poorly, Swann is a man out of place. Evidently, bath night was a weekly ritual in which all family members participated. Foy's presence rendered Swann's involvement uncomfortable, because it exposed his domestic ineptitude instead of allowing him to boast about paternity. That Swann had not anticipated this implied his conventional acceptance of his wife's rule over childcare matters. His exposure to the gaze of another man makes Swann aware of his incompetence in the domestic sphere and the apparent tensions in paternal dignity. The camaraderie between Swann and Foy is restored with the superficial reinstatement of patriarchal order. As Mrs. Swann puts the children to bed, Swann and Foy deftly steal out for beer leaving instructions for the harassed woman to lay a cloth for their supper.[68]

These jokes were integral to imagining marital harmony: only when spouses fulfilled their appropriate roles could couples be happy. Pugh played upon this joke numerous times in his short stories. One story

---

[67] Julia Chandler, *A night with baby* (Stourbridge: J Thomas Ford, 1873), 4.
[68] Edwin Pugh, *The Cockney at home: stories and studies of London life and character* (London: Chapman & Hall Ltd., 1914), 45–9.

hinged upon the chaos that ensued when two couples swapped wives: one couple had an orthodox division of labour; the other had 'progressive' notions of men helping in domestic labour.[69] The narrator's sympathy was aligned firmly to suggest that participating in domesticity diminished masculinity, with attendant implications for marital romance. In 'Women's Work', a father boasted that women exaggerated their domestic tasks: childcare and housework simply needed the application of masculine logic and method. After one night of testing this theory, hapless dad is pooped, the house is in disarray and children run riot. When his wife returns early, anticipating that he would be in 'trouble enough', his gratitude is expressed in the conflation of female tasks with feminine appeal: 'never had she seemed so beautiful in his eyes'.

For audiences, the premise of such comedies confirmed female parenting expertise whilst locating fathering firmly in the realm of paid labour. Domestic comedy traded on men's contempt for 'women's work'. The district nurse M. E. Loane thought some men played up the role of hapless dad as a form of self-serving flattery: in praising women's superior skill in childcare, men emphatically rejected the suggestion that they should acquire the skills to perform 'mothering' tasks.[70] Such prejudices were ameliorated (albeit slightly) by the joke's reliance on masculine incompetence that enabled female audiences, who were stuck with such tasks, to lay claim to the very particular nurturing relationship endorsed in wider culture and social policy between mother and child. The power dynamics of such comedies are intrinsic to understanding their popularity and reproduction at a familial level.

Laughter at sexed parenting also facilitated ways of talking about men and babies that was light hearted, inclusive and affectionate while acknowledging the sacrifices made by mothers. Chandler's story about Jeremiah Smallpeace paid tribute to maternal superiority but was an extended discourse by a married man to his bachelor friends about the unique cleverness of his baby. Similarly, the comedy of Edwin Pugh's character Dick Swann rested on the father's desire to show off *as a father* to his bachelor friend. Jokes that made fun of beleaguered or inept fathers tended to imagine children as precociously astute. When a son asked his father 'What is a King?' and his father responded that 'A King, my child, is a person whose authority is practically unlimited, whose word is law, and whom everybody must obey,' it was a savvy child that applied this directly to the domestic: 'Papa, is Mamma a King?'[71] Men did not *do* 'baby talk' in a feminine sense but by indulging in

---

[69] Ibid, 70–8.   [70] Loane, *From their point of view*, 148.
[71] *Penny Illustrated Paper*, 11 May 1901, 318.

'funny talk', they certainly did talk, sometimes extensively and repeatedly, about their children.

For autobiographers, humorous anecdotes demonstrated a particular form of 'baby talk' that confirmed rather than compromised masculinity, even when men were the butt of the joke. Despite claiming that men never attended christenings, Southgate situated the anecdote about his father's paternity at his christening. He noted that female neighbours' attention to the likeness between baby Walter and his father was intended as a compliment; his father's robust riposte acknowledged this and playfully asserted his claim to fatherhood. Campion portrayed his father's cocky claim to 'influence' as well rehearsed. In its very repetition, it had the potential to intimate pride in abstract and biological ties between father and son. When Harris's father returned home to his new twins, his mates explicitly 'talked' about his new babies in a congratulatory and knowing way. These men, to facilitate talking to each other and to women about their new offspring, appropriated baby banter. Rodney Smith's memoir teemed with affection and pride in his children as he related anecdotes from family life that he found amusing or 'quaint'. Invariably, the stories enabled Smith to boast about just how clever his little ones were.[72] Even baby habits that might seem unattractive could be transformed through baby banter into markers of pride. One father grinned as he told the district nurse Loane that he generally took baby for a 'trot' on his return from work as it was the little one's 'cross' time. How many middle-class fathers, asked Loane, would 'see any joke in such a reception' after ten hours labour?[73]

Of course, domestic humour could be misunderstood, and much depended upon context. Loane noted that working-class men's humorous diffidence towards children was apt to be misconstrued by external observers unfamiliar with popular forms of comedy or, for that matter, working-class expressions of attachment. As an example, Loane recalled sitting with a man in his kitchen when his two noisy little girls burst into the kitchen. Commenting that she had not seen the girls before, the father's 'sullen' reply had the ghastly whiff of parental indifference: 'And I wish I hadn't neither!' For the earnest social worker, such comments were evidence of men's disaffection from family life. When read in context, Loane cited this as an example of masculine 'showing off', whereby straight-faced statements signalled the antithesis of sentiment: 'Certainly no little girls would have burst with such a joyous and confident air into a presence where they were habitually unwelcome.'[74]

---

[72] Smith, *Gipsy Smith*, 221–38.　[73] Loane, *From their point of view*, 145.
[74] Loane *An Englishman's castle*, 153.

Taken at face value, some 'humorous' reminiscences can seem ambiguous. James Griffiths made fun of his father's domineering qualities by likening him to Stalin: his father's 'iron grip' of debate in his blacksmith's workshop poked light-hearted fun at the older man's dislike of contradiction in his domain. Far from suggesting that Griffiths found his father overbearing, the joshing tone of the comparison suggested a familiar family joke about father's bluster that subtly chastised the older man while, nevertheless, underscoring familial tolerance.[75] Mark Grossek's father was an Eastern European migrant who worked hard to learn English. He moved through phases of favourite words, especially words of invective, but sometimes confused them, thus, a penchant for 'despicable' and 'unspeakable' morphed into 'despeakable'.[76] Grossek's chaffing of his father's earnestness coupled with self-ridicule in taking his father's word as law as a child, was not malicious but suggested nostalgia for evenings spent with his father and regret for the passing of childish certainties, whereby hero fathers staggered under the weight of expectation to eventually topple from their pedestals.

Importantly, comic stories enabled authors, particularly sons who presumably were similarly hamstrung in 'baby talk', to locate fathers in a domestic or 'babyish' context to evoke the significance of fathers in a family dynamic. Harry Watkin related with some glee that his father had dressed him, aged one, in Manchester United colours for the FA Cup and taken him on a tour of beer houses with his mates.[77] Joseph Stamper used his birth story to establish the affectionate dynamic between his parents while the tasks he assigned them in marking his entry to the world established their personalities and responsibilities. As his lively mother sought to ignore the pain of imminent childbirth, his loyal father went shopping to purchase a gift for his wife. This was practical in that female neighbours attending the birth excluded his father from the scene but it also represented Stamper's sense that father wanted to give thanks to his wife for delivery of their child. The potential sentimentality of this was tempered by Stamper's jocular ribbing of his father's 'softness' through the medium of neighbours' teasing incomprehension of such a gesture.[78] For all the gentle mockery of Stamper Senior here, the story confirmed his status as a feeling man. For Southgate, Campion and Harris, their 'birth' anecdotes played upon men's tangential role at childbirth while drawing their fathers into the birth narrative to the extent that the stories became, paradoxically, about fathers. The light-hearted comments of Campion and Southgate's fathers enabled the older men to stake a

---

[75] Griffiths, *Pages from memory*, 5. [76] Grossek, *First movement*, 119.
[77] Watkin, *From Hulme*, 4. [78] Stamper, *So long ago*, 7–18.

powerful claim to the baby at the centre of attention, albeit in a way that cemented and referenced their masculinity.

In Harris's account, his mother disappeared entirely from the story of the twins' birth, despite his father's absence from home at the time, to place paternity at the centre of the narrative. Harris's reference to the winner of the Derby that year was potentially significant, too: Sainfoin, the bookies' underdog, won against the favourite, Surefoot. This could be a metaphor for Harris's life story. Born amongst the working classes, Harris's memoir paid tribute to his parents' hard work for their children. In particular, Harris bookended his life story with his father's labour, concluding with the son's pride in the father's rise from underdog to foreman of his trade. Given that Harris's anecdote was probably told to the twins as they grew older, it marked their birth as an exceptional moment in time, and their father's celebration of their birth within a masculine world. All three anecdotes have a stock quality to them, suggesting they had been rehearsed many times. Even if Southgate and Campion Senior's remarks meant little at the time, the retelling of the anecdotes to the extent that the babies concerned incorporated the stories into their adult patter, suggests that the stories held some significance in personal histories beyond simply highlighting the sexed roles of parents.

Good-humoured banter provided a medium for talking about relationships long into a baby's adulthood. Jack Jones's embarrassment as an adult at his father boasting of his son's achievements in the pub was softened by acceptance that light-hearted repartee provided a language in which his father could express satisfaction in his son and, although they teased Jones and his father, other men's confirmation of paternal pride.[79] Likewise, adult authors deployed memories of fathers' fooling as a means of talking about pleasure in fathers' personality. Like many autobiographers, Ernest Ambrose (born 1878) paid heartfelt tribute to maternal care and 'good management'. His father appears in his narrative as a breadwinner, an agent of political awareness and in anecdotes charting his 'great sense of humour'. This ranged from father's lively accounts of his escapades abroad, to playing pranks in public and to 'clowning' around on the football field for the benefit of spectators. This could have the effect of rendering Ambrose's father a remote figure from the intimacies of family life. Instead, in a memoir that recounts Ambrose's 'many schoolboy adventures', the agile tomfoolery of father bound man and boy in cheeky camaraderie. Even when a horse kicked Ambrose in the head,

---

[79] Jones, *Unfinished journey*, 165–8.

the dramatic panic of his father's dash to fetch the doctor had an element of slapstick, as his father took a flying leap over the railings of the practitioner's garden. The jocularity of such reminiscences should not obscure the seriousness underscoring them. From Ambrose's perspective, his father's furious race to the doctor was pivotal to the positive conclusion of a narrative that might have ended fatally. That Ambrose still bore the scars from the horse's hoof embedded the memory of his father's protective instinct into an ageing Ambrose's everyday life.[80]

Conclusion

The deployment and celebration of humour in autobiography is far from conservative or trivial. For most autobiographers, the ability to be 'daft' was a skill and had serious implications, both in terms of survival and as a language for articulating what was significant. Harry Gosling concluded his memoir by recounting his experiences as a councillor for St George's and Wapping on London County Council. Charting the 'twofold horror' of hunger and hopelessness that characterised these districts, he found no contradiction in describing residents as 'gay'. This seemingly anachronistic adjective did not mean that slum dwellers were gurning idiots. Rather, Gosling's depiction paid tribute to their bravery and lack of selfishness.[81] Despite all the grief his father caused, Albert Jasper concluded his story with relief and congratulation that his family had a sense of humour: 'I will say this for my family, however sad the occasion, there was always someone who would try to raise a laugh.' Even in 'terrible times', he and his kin made time for laughter, taking pleasures where they could find them.[82] For Jasper, humour was neither reactionary nor apolitical. It functioned as a reminder to seize the day. Jasper, having become an 'old man', closed his memoir by pleading with younger generations to be tolerant towards their parents' failings. Humour did not let his father off the hook for the misery he caused, but it did provide a way of demonstrating everyday unhappiness while simultaneously commemorating the resilience of his mother and siblings in containing and surviving father. For others, laughter and humour provided a medium for tactile engagement, corporeal sensations and expressions of sentiment or meaning that were otherwise just awkward or embarrassing.

[80] Ernest Ambrose, *Melford memories. Recollections of 94 years by Ernest Ambrose* (Long Melford: Long Melford Historical and Archaeological Society, 1972), 31–2; 23; 51; 108.
[81] Gosling, *Up and down stream*, 88–91.
[82] Jasper, *A Hoxton childhood*, 122, 127.

The place of humour as a marker of personhood and a symbolic boundary of distinction probably made some authors cautious of including what seemed superfluous or silly. It would be a pity, however, to dismiss memoirs that appear to trade in mockery, inanity or sun-kissed nostalgia. Andy Medhurst closes his book on national humour with a case study of Roy 'Chubby' Brown, one of the most vilified British comedians of the late twentieth and early twenty-first centuries. Medhurst's conundrum is to navigate a path between the 'we', liberal and educated commentators who find Brown sexist, racist and homophobic, and his audience, mostly a white working class, to determine what Brown means to those who pay to see him. Brown makes Medhurst uncomfortable in much the same way Goldstein found her interviewees' laughter in bad taste. Nevertheless, Medhurst identifies how Brown's humour offers a familiar worldview and, crucially, a voice to a class of people who, during the late twentieth century, increasingly became marginalised, deskilled and politically invisible. Medhurst's conclusion is that, however distasteful or juvenile we find some forms of humour, we ignore them at our peril. The complex dynamics of laughing at or with others is integral to telling stories of who we are, what matters to us and how we relate to others.[83] There is little humour that is offensive in working-class autobiography; mostly, it appears merely inane. Yet for working-class autobiographers, remembering fathers with and through laughter could provide a vital framework for articulating awkward facets of the past, putting disorder in place and explaining the conflicts and pleasures of family ties.

---

[83] Medhurst, *A national joke*, 194–203.

6   The fond father: protection, authority, reconciliation

Sidney Campion's autobiography opened with three scenes from the summer of 1891: his birth, an infant girl and her father and Ramsay MacDonald making his way to London.[1] The scenes introduced the key players in Campion's life story: his parents, wife and mentor. They also suggest the multiple dimensions of paternal obligation: providing, protection and authority. The first scene, Campion's birth at his maternal relations' home, noted father's absence: he stayed home to work.[2] Campion extolled his father's manly qualities: as a soldier in Egypt, he was 'devilishly' brave;[3] despite war wounds, he boasted superb physical fitness; though just a labourer, he had 'quite a bit of brain'. His commitment to wife and children was evident in his deeds. Not only did he labour for the new babe, he also fashioned a cradle from orange boxes, and painted it white, a useful motif for the extra-utilitarian facets of paternal protection. The second scene pictured Campion's future wife, aged two, walking with her father, Horatio Armitage: the silent countryside punctuated by the little girl's prattle and the 'klip klop' of her father's wooden leg. Armitage had lost his leg in an industrial accident (crushed by two tonnes of stone), an injury that subsequently limited his capacity to earn. This constraint threw other components of fatherhood into relief. The affection between father and daughter here was explicit: they held hands, chattered and he called her 'love'. When she whimpered, Armitage carried her 'determinedly', despite pain in his amputated limb. When the wooden leg struck a pothole, Armitage stumbled but protected his child from the fall, sealing his character as father *par excellence*.

In the final story, Campion imagined a youthful Ramsay MacDonald, would-be father figure of the labour movement, struggling along the path to Westminster. This had particular resonance for Campion who, as a

---

[1] Campion, *Sunlight on foothills*, 3–8.
[2] As a young married man, Campion repeated this pattern, dispatching his pregnant wife to the fresh air of Knutsford while he stayed in industrial Chorley for work. *Ibid*, 94–96.
[3] Britain invaded in 1882.

youth, approached MacDonald at the Houses of Parliament for advice on becoming a journalist. MacDonald became a key mentor in Campion's career. Having clashed so much with his biological father over his occupational future, one might read this as the juvenile Campion's rejection of the labourer in favour of the politician. Yet, it also highlighted just how far Campion's father tried to fulfil this obligation and the limits of his experience in understanding, let alone facilitating, the kind of future his son craved. Father and son clashed precisely because the labourer felt his responsibility to help the boy find a job (he obtained Campion an apprenticeship); his son resented the imposition of fatherly authority.

Campion's opening chapter emphasises key sites for understanding the significance of fathers' obligations, sites that he reiterated in his account of becoming a father and that, with hindsight, he knew could be bitter.[4] Provision, protection and authority were not the preserve of fathers but, as numerous scholars demonstrate, legal, social and cultural discourse overwhelmingly identified these obligations as the chief components of fatherhood, well into the twentieth century. The resonances of paternal authority and protection were different to the nurturing connotations of maternal care, not least because they were inextricable in law from patriarchal power.[5] The authority of men made wives economically and politically dependent and denied women custody of their children in cases of marital separation. The obligation to protect presupposed power, as Megan Doolittle outlines so convincingly in her study of fathers and religious belief; it also assumed that children should, and would, obey the authority vested in fathers. Throughout the nineteenth century, protection also defined affective dimensions of fathering: men were supposed to care *about* their children while women cared *for* them. As Doolittle notes, this could lead to conflict within families where mothers sought to protect children from unreasonable or excessive paternal authority.[6]

This chapter focuses on men's obligation to protect, guide and discipline children. These elements of paternity could be overbearing and oppressive; they frequently led to conflict as children cantered towards juvenile independence. In hindsight, when autobiographers sought to explain relationships with fathers, paternal protection and authority could indicate a man's detachment or tyranny. For others, fathers' efforts

---

[4] For example, he and his wife's first babies, twins, died at birth and their third child was so frail she had to undergo surgery shortly after birth. *Ibid*, 3–8, 29–38.
[5] King, 'Fatherhood and masculinity', 85–118. Davidoff et al, *The family story*, 135–57; Broughton and Rogers, 'Introduction', 8–12.
[6] Doolittle, 'The protection of children', 31–2.

to discipline, guide and protect were caring components of parenting, enabling children to identify the generic features of fathering and distinguish *my* father within that model. As with providing and respectability, authors' sense of how seriously fathers took their responsibilities could provide an interface for giving meaning to intimate dimensions of family life. The authoritative and protective obligations of fatherhood were sometimes a burden on men as well as their children. Men's desire to mould children in their values and beliefs could represent an intended gift, potentially loaded with affective significance: the degree of adult children's acceptance or rejection of this gift was equally charged.

Spare the rod: authority and discipline

The abuse of paternal authority or, failure to protect offspring, operated as key signifiers in autobiography and social commentary of father-child detachment, rejection and failure. Jack Martin, George Acorn and Vero Garratt depicted their fathers as self-centred brutes, careless of their offspring's welfare. They enjoyed the advantages of paternal power but accepted none of its responsibilities.[7] Garratt was acutely sensitive to his father's shortcomings. When he left home, he adopted financial responsibility for his younger siblings and reported his father to a medical authority for child neglect.[8] For some autobiographers, dissipated fathers could be forced, in print, to take responsibility for unorthodox, potentially wayward, life choices. The actress Betty May, known exotically in the inter-war period as 'Tiger Woman', traced her bohemian persona, associated with orientalism, sex, and occultism, to her father who took his children to live in a brothel.[9]

Fathers' legal authority over dependents could prove disastrous, especially where fathers were ignorant, obstinate and bigoted. Alice Foley fumed that her brother died after their father refused consent for medical surgery, an operation that would almost certainly have saved the boy's life and which their mother desperately wanted.[10] Other autobiographers emphasised that paternal authority took place in a context of discussion between spouses and, where appropriate, older children, although this sometimes amounted to little more than lip service. Harry Lauder's (born 1870) father called a 'Counsel of Ways and Means and Future Prospects' when offered a job in Derbyshire that necessitated the family

---

[7] Martin, *Ups and downs*, 42, 47, 55; Acorn, *One of the multitude*, 5–8, 37; 84; Garratt, *A man in the street*, 4–7.
[8] Garratt, *A man in the street*, 121–2.   [9] May, *Tiger woman*, 20–3.
[10] Foley, *A Bolton childhood*, 38.

leaving their Highland home. His mother expressed reluctance but father's enthusiasm, backed by arguments about better wages, inevitably won out.[11] In some families, mother readily was acknowledged as the 'real' decision maker. Fred Gresswell's mother ruled aspects of material, social and economic life. Her motivation and drive manoeuvred the family from rural hardship to relative comfort and her spouse unhesitatingly conceded her superior intelligence.[12] To acknowledge women's supremacy did not always sit easily. Richard Hillyer contrasted his mother's agile, sharp-wittedness to his father's lumbering intelligence. Where external agents were concerned, however, it 'wouldn't have looked right' if his mother represented the family. Instead, his mother 'drilled' father to perform her instructions so the couple could preserve the myth of masculine authority.[13]

Intrinsic to paternal authority was the duty, and right, to discipline children. By the second half of the nineteenth century, prescriptive literature advocated moral training and guidance as the source of discipline, although confessional debates over the God-given responsibility to discipline offspring continued on both sides of the Atlantic. For most, however, corporal punishment, if considered at all, was a last resort.[14] As Claudia Nelson and John Tosh point out, this reflects the increasing transformation throughout the nineteenth century of childrearing as something that demanded guidance from experts who, in turn, identified mothers as the market for advice. Combined with men's habitual absence from home, fathers were sidelined in terms of everyday authority.[15] This could provoke men to excessive displays of authority in a bid to assert their position but, as Tosh says, this was more an issue of individual personality than a common model of paternity. 'Tyrannical' fathers expose the legal system's failings towards women and children but, despite their popularity as the archetypal 'Victorian paterfamilias', they were hardly representative.[16] Advice for working-class families reiterated the importance of moral over physical authority. The explosion of infant care and nutrition programmes aimed at working-class mothers in the late-nineteenth and early-twentieth centuries demarcated parental ideals clearly: mothers nurtured goodness; fathers provided and did not drink.

---

[11] Harry Lauder, *Roamin' in the Gloamin'* (London: Hutchinson and Co., 1928), 35.
[12] Gresswell, *Bright boots*, 19–21; 26.   [13] Hillyer, *Country boy*, 16–17.
[14] Linda Pollock, *Forgotten children: parent-child relations from 1500–1900* (Cambridge University Press, 1983), 173–87; Philip Greven, *Spare the child: the religious roots of physical punishment and the psychological impact of physical abuse* (New York: Alfred Knopf, 1990).
[15] Nelson, *Invisible men*, 62–7 and Tosh, *A man's place*, 85.
[16] Tosh, *A man's place*, 95–7.

As heads of household, fathers carried chief responsibility for protecting children from vice but advice writers increasingly urged them to exert authority through moral example.[17]

Certainly, few autobiographers wrote about corporal punishment. To a point, children may have deemed a degree of physical reprimand sufficiently normative to render it unimportant in relating life stories, corroborating the invisibility of everyday violence. Nevertheless, several authors surveyed here were keen to emphasise that their fathers rebuffed physical chastisement (including that enacted by mothers or schoolteachers).[18] For Guy Aldred, reared by his mother and grandparents, his grandfather's opposition to 'all corporal punishment' underlined the depiction of the older man as 'patient, thoughtful and understanding': the repudiation of violence sealed his 'calm', 'warm' consideration. This did not make grandfather a sop; indeed, his displeasure was expressed through 'kindly and loving coolness' that expressed 'tremendous' authority.[19] Edwin Muir portrayed his father as 'a gentle man' who 'never beat us'. The closest he came was a rare clip across the ear with his soft cap. Even then, he would 'look ashamed', the reprimand causing him more pain than his children.[20]

A. V. Christie noted that he 'was punished only once by my father'. Even then, this 'unprecedented' treatment stemmed from his mother, who insisted that her spouse man up and punish the boy. Despite his 'fiery nervous temperament', Christie's father had 'never laid a finger on any us'. In the event, the idea of physically assaulting his boy proved too traumatic and father and son colluded in a noisy fake thrashing for mother's benefit.[21] As Lynn Abrams notes of Scottish working-class fathers, their bark was often worse than their bite.[22] Neville Cardus recalled his grandfather's indignation at the racy clothing and bold behaviour of his daughters, warning them of 'wrath to come'. Yet for all the older man's ire, his daughters changed nothing and if they cried, their father crumpled in horror.[23]

---

[17] See for instance, Thomas Legh Claughton, *The duty of fathers concerning the education of their children. A [short, plain] sermon addressed to the working classes* (Oxford: J. Henry and J. Parker, 1864) and Robert Ainslie, *The rod and its uses, or Thomas Dodd and Bill Collins* (London: S. W. Partridge, 1865).

[18] John McGovern, *Neither fear nor favour* (London: Blandford Press, 1960), 19 and Dayus, *Her people*, 36–8. See also Jacob Middleton, 'The experience of corporal punishment in schools, 1890–1940', *History of education* 37:2 (2008), 253–75.

[19] Aldred, *No traitor's gait!*, 10.   [20] Muir, *An autobiography*, 16–7.

[21] Christie, *Brass tacks*, 43.

[22] Abrams, 'There was nobody like my daddy', 228–9.

[23] Cardus, *Autobiography*, 26–7.

As Joanna Bourke's study of working-class culture demonstrated, men's authority was frequently nominal: mothers exercised dominion over everyday life, many took chief responsibility for discipline, some wives were skilled in manipulation and covert control.[24] Some authors realised their fathers' discomfort in the role of disciplinarian long after childhood. As a child, Dorothy Scannell accepted her mother's assertion that Father was master of the house. In retrospect, she suspected her mother created a 'paper tiger' for reasons of her own. Indeed, father had complained that his wife made him an 'ogre' to their children. Scannell suspected that, left to his own devices, father would probably have left his children alone, just the kind of parenting that wives running a tight ship deplored.[25]

The move away from corporal punishment towards moral training at the end of the nineteenth century also made talking about physical chastisement problematic. Walter Southgate asserted with pride that 'My father never laid a rough hand on his children.'[26] Does that mean he never struck his children or, that he never went beyond a 'reasonable' hand? Impossible to know and, of course, the legal definition of 'reasonable' discipline was ambiguous. What we do know is that Southgate's statement buoys his depiction of the older man as a progressive, of his childhood home as genial and of the abiding affection he held for his father. Southgate's suggestion that his mother took charge of discipline reflected the different parenting styles of mother and father: she ran the household with precision while Southgate's father was far more ambivalent. The anecdote also tells something of the norms and expectations of Southgate's audience. Despite paternal discipline regaining prominence in popular and professional literature during the First World War, Laura King has shown how corporal punishment became increasingly controversial after the War: if the rod fell out of fashion at the end of the nineteenth century, the 'smack' was contentious by the middle of the twentieth.[27] When autobiographers publishing in the twentieth century talked about corporal punishment in the home, then, they had to think carefully about how to present it.

Physical violence could be presented as evidence of men's innate brutality and detachment. Vero Garratt suspected his father had a

---

[24] Bourke, *Working-class cultures*, 74–81. For an example of unbending maternal discipline, see George Reakes, *Man of the Mersey* (London: Christopher Johnson, 1956), 10.
[25] Scannell, *Mother knew best*, 101–2.   [26] Southgate, *That's the way it was*, 44.
[27] For the resurgence of interest in paternal discipline during the Great War, see Tim Fisher, 'Fatherhood and the experience of working-class fathers in Britain, 1900–1939', Unpublished PhD thesis, University of Edinburgh, 157–8; King, 'Fatherhood and masculinity', 95–105.

sadistic streak, slapping his children when they were in bed for no apparent reason.[28] Sam Shaw's father boxed his ears for the 'least fault'. This violence had an eruptive, unpredictable quality. The only motor Shaw could assign to his father's aggression was that he despised his son.[29] For others, physical chastisement operated within a framework of responsibility and reason that could be understood as good fathering in different social, economic and cultural contexts. Henry Turner's father was 'very strict' with his ten children. Turner placed this within a moral and material context. His father, a lamplighter, gave him a new pair of boots with instructions to look after them. When his father left the room, Turner put the ugly boots out of the window. Furious, his father gave Turner the strap. In reflection, Turner sanctioned the violence as an instructive component of paternal authority that taught him the value of the boots for sure, but, more to the point, the value of his father's labour.

The story was inextricable from a wider narrative of his father's many part-time jobs with which he supplemented his regular income. His father 'had to be' strict. Not only did his violence have a rationale, it was performed in a rational way: just enough for his sons to be able to 'take' it and never applied to daughters. A father who chastised with discrimination and logic was, in this reckoning, a caring father.[30] Minnie Ferris's (born 1907) father, a builder, never allowed his children to be 'saucy' or answer back. His austerity operated within a framework of moral training and there was no contradiction between her father's discipline and his status as 'the nicest' man. Like Turner, Ferris proffered paternal discipline as evidence of good fathering: none of Ferris's siblings, seven brothers and a sister, ever got into trouble and all her brothers made excellent family men in their turn.[31] For Turner and Ferris, there was something unseemly in fathers applying physical discipline to daughters, partly because violence to women was unchivalrous (and even more taboo in a public context) and, partly, because sons' burgeoning masculinity represented more of a challenge to paternal authority.[32] The district nurse M.E. Loane lamented that fathers were far too indulgent of small children and then got frustrated when boys approaching ten refused to learn obedience; on balance, girls were far more biddable.[33] Turner and Ferris's memoirs also derive from a group memory project; their willingness to broach this subject and the similarities in their narrative imply a response to a question posed by a facilitator.

---

[28] Garratt, *A man in the street*, 14. [29] Shaw, *Guttersnipe*, 5–6.
[30] Centreprise, *The Island*, 17–18. [31] *Ibid*, 30.
[32] See King, 'Fatherhood and masculinity', 95–105.
[33] Loane, *From their point of view*, 154–5.

Corporal punishment did not necessarily diminish children's loyalty or affection to the parent. Loane noted that adult children whose fathers gave them the strap for misdemeanours articulated just as much filial gratitude as those whose parents indulged their whims.[34] Some children took the 'good' father model of corporal punishment further to explain disciplinary violence as a mode of attachment. William Lax's childhood home ran on the 'patriarchal system': as 'head of the house', his father was responsible for discipline. Mother, the figure of nurture, monitored the severity of reprimand. Acknowledging shifting values of parenting, Lax located his father's discipline as normative within a 'Victorian' evangelical context: 'Spare the rod and spoil the child.' As he wryly observed, his father 'certainly did not spoil' his children. Anticipating his readers' arched brow, Lax asserted that the violence was never excessive (falling within legal notions of 'reasonable' and 'moderate' discipline) and, more importantly, that it was necessary: when father punished his children, it was with due cause. The final endorsement for this 'patriarchal system' was Lax's correlation between the Holy Father's insistence on obedience, his biological father, the rod and attachment: 'We loved him.'[35]

Gipsy Smith's opening gambit to his father's chastisement was ambiguous: father was 'a very fatherly man'. Far from indicating 'softness', Smith also played up notions of the strict, evangelical, Victorian paterfamilias. Father thrashed his children, an action that Smith endorsed: 'they all did me good'.[36] Smith returned to this theme later in his book. As a young father whose 'heart was full of tenderness' towards his sons, Smith faced the dilemma of punishing the boys for truanting from school. Smith knew his obligation was to discipline them but 'I loved my boys' and 'did not well know how to begin'. Eschewing violence, Smith sent them to separate rooms for the afternoon, allowing only bread and water at teatime. Even so, the punishment was 'more to me than to them' and his equivocation (he kept going to check they were all right) limited the success of reprimand: the elder boy affected complete immunity whilst the younger son's desire for his 'real' supper motivated a display of contrition. Although violence was counterintuitive to the loving father, Smith's emphasis on the ineffectuality of gentle authority underscored his earlier approbation of his father's decisive action.[37] As Lax and Smith were

---

[34] Loane *Englishman's castle*, 60. This was different, however, to fathers who used indiscriminate violence to spouses or children. Loane, *The Queen's poor*, 18–19.
[35] Lax, *His book*, 57–62.
[36] Smith, *Gipsy Smith*, 29–30.
[37] *Ibid*, 221–8. It is worth noting that Smith first published his autobiography in 1911.

active nonconformist missionaries, their narratives were not necessarily straightforward accounts of corporal punishment. Rather, their stories also provided allegories to the lamentation of God the Father, both Old and New Testament, who demanded obedience or, at least, contrition for wrongdoing and who was pained by humanity's sinfulness.

Recounting paternal violence was, for some authors, a device to highlight the sheer complexity of family relationships, especially in retrospect. As he aged, Alice Foley's father became increasingly alienated from his political associates (Sinn Feiners) and sensed his household authority waning. He always was an unpredictable man, and his temper grew murderous.[38] It is unclear from her autobiography how far her father inflicted violence on Foley. Rather, she asserts that 'Father was not usually unkind to me'. When she received a heavy blow (she notes only one), she was 'stunned and bewildered'. Foley recalls the shock of violence as rupture: she felt 'wholly rejected and dejected'. Simultaneously, she acknowledges that this was temporary, for although her dynamic with her father was conflicted, it was never unequivocally rotten. Indeed, she notes how quickly, 'in happier moods', her father could please her. Foley's recollection highlights the messiness of family dynamics, not least for children whose fear of an adult was inextricable from their desperation to please.[39] Likewise, Foley's youthful desire to propitiate brought her into conflict with an older sister who flagrantly despised the old man (and her mother for marrying him in the first place), a conflict that Pat O'Mara, who despised his father's feckless and violent antics, also experienced.[40] Although he loved his sister 'intensely', O'Mara could not comprehend her readiness to forgive their father.[41]

George Baldry's father, a Norfolk bootmaker, had a robust approach to moral guidance. Injuries his sons incurred in everyday play would 'learn them a thing or two'.[42] When his boys erred, he beat them. Baldry's pathos for the thrashed little boy was evident in the description of his 'poor thin little behind', a 'mass of bruises'. Baldry gestures towards explaining this brutality as rational fathering: 'So there was one lesson learned, and we did not forget that dose of strap oil nor what it were given for, and maybe 'twas the better for us as the lesson was sharp.'[43] It is not entirely convincing; that 'maybe' lacks conviction. There is also a sense in which his father's beatings, some of which clearly exceeded his wife's sense of proportion, were sufficiently frequent to have become,

---

[38] Foley, *A Bolton childhood*, 43.   [39] *Ibid*, 10–11, 67.   [40] *Ibid*, 44–7.
[41] O'Mara, *Liverpool Irish slummy*, 105; 182.   [42] Baldry, *The rabbit skin cap*, 27
[43] *Ibid*, 190.

paradoxically, almost banal. Indeed, Baldry paid far more narrative detail to a punishment that struck his heart, not his body.

Baldry and his brother had taken some of their father's work materials to make a boat, of which they were inordinately proud. Alas, their father was enraged for they used his things without permission. Aside from the hiding he delivered, their father smashed the boat and made the boys throw the wood on the fire. This 'nearly broke our hearts'. Even here, however, Baldry refused to admonish his father's discipline: he taught them a harsh but necessary lesson. Certainly, they never took their father's work materials again. More importantly, in Baldry's reconstruction, the experience was an allegory on men's lot: the smouldering boat mimicked 'much of a man's labour during his life's work'. Baldry continued to build boats late in life and reflected ruefully that 'each one teaches me summat'.[44] In this light, the 'nearly' but not quite broken heart demonstrated the need to learn survival in a harsh world.

Baldry's memoir epitomised the ambivalence of some father-child attachments: he longed to emulate his father, loved to spend time with him, wanted his approval, was wounded by rejection and feared him. His random stack of memories (even with editorial intervention) mirrored the peaks and troughs of everyday family life. Thrashings when children misbehaved were but one element of Baldry Senior's fathering. Violence did not define his father all the time. Baldry blithely noted that although his father's 'black tempers' were common, he was 'as happy as a sandpiper' otherwise.[45] Hard on the heels of the boat anecdote, Baldry recounted a story of companionate togetherness with his father on a Saturday jaunt into town, recalled 'as if it were yesterday'. In his old age, Baldry had a souvenir from the outing still, a clock his father gifted to him. That this timepiece still ticked in the elderly Baldry's bedroom denoted its value, in terms of quality and sentiment.[46] Far from denouncing his father's violence, Baldry partially normalised it to suggest how children, even in adulthood, sought to manage the power inequities of family life and present the conflicted loyalties of the past in a framework that resisted neat categories of contented or miserable childhoods.

In the reverse of father-child power relations, autobiographers were in control of the meanings inscribed on the past. Reflecting the twentieth-century move towards psychological models of behaviour, some authors groped around for explanations of paternal violence. Authors did not always find adequate answers, as William Bowyer's (Chapter 5) anguished account of his father shows. Likewise, explanation

[44] *Ibid*, 113   [45] *Ibid*, 142   [46] *Ibid*, 113.

did not always cancel the sting of humiliation or the confusion of childhood. Walking with his father one night, the myopic John Eldred was unable to read text on a poster at his father's behest. Explaining that he could not see, his father accused him of lying and knocked him to the floor. In Eldred's reconstruction, this violence was '*apparently* insane' (my emphasis). Eldred located his father's violence in his personal unhappiness (he was 'sorely tried'), ill health, and paradoxically, concern for his son's vision and, by extension, his future. Eldred even drew father and son together in corporeal sympathy: the older man's absolute terror that his son was losing his sight made him 'blind' with rage.

To a point, this echoed Eldred's earlier construction of his father's care: 'gruff' instructions to stay safe offered some approximation of solicitude.[47] Yet it is worth noting that Eldred followed the explanation of his father's violence with reflection on how obtaining glasses marked a turning point in his life. With clear vision, he embraced sport and, having inherited his father's physique, his boyish frame quickly grew muscular: he was able to 'assert my claim to equality with my world' by 'cracking its ribs'. There came a point in most young men's lives when they could return, blow for blow, the violence visited upon them (or their mothers) by fathers. Placed within the overall context of Eldred's memoir, where he deliberately sought to revise his childhood bifurcation between loving mother and problem father, it was inevitable that he would seek to understand both their flaws: attachment incorporates ambivalences. Despite Eldred's attempt to make his father's 'insanity' logical, the structural connection between paternal violence and the boy's transformation into an equally powerful man highlighted, possibly unintentionally, the ongoing damage of father-child violence: just months after the incident, Eldred's narrative suggests, he could have retaliated.[48]

The tenderness of authority

Eldred's reconstruction of his father's violence as rational located it within a context of men's obligation to protect offspring. Tosh points to men's twin obligations of provision and protection as the defining features of fatherhood in the nineteenth century.[49] Discipline was intrinsic to notions of protection. Muir's gentle father lost his temper with his son just once. Having caught Muir skating on a frozen milldam, against paternal instructions, his father threatened to thrash him if he did it again. Muir recalled his outrage at being threatened thus (his father *never*

---

[47] Eldred, *I love the brooks*, 14.   [48] Ibid, 52–55.   [49] Tosh, *A man's place*, 85.

threatened violence). Retrospectively, Muir interpreted the unprecedented anger as evidence of his father's intense protectiveness: he 'was terrified' his boy would drown. The sympathy of hindsight enabled Muir to make the leap in imagination to understanding (if not condoning) parents who did deliver physical chastisement. Registering distaste for a distant relation who thrashed his children, Muir speculated that his violence was driven by sheer panic for the consequences of indiscipline.[50] Mary and Cissie Elliott (born 1898 and 1904) did not recall their father as a violent man, but he was strict. A well-rehearsed story about their father's severity stood as a proud testament to his attachment. Like Muir, the girls disobeyed paternal instructions not to skate on a pond where a boy had drowned some days before. Their father threw their ice skates on the fire. As the irons twisted in the heat, their father rejoiced that his daughters would 'never be drowned'.[51] Barnabas Britten's autobiography rang out with affection and esteem for his father. Within this context, Britten related the 'tongue lacings' his father dispensed. Discipline symbolised paternal obligation and reciprocal father-child love: '*I knew Dad. Bless him. I didn't know myself*' (Britten's italics). Britten's emphasis on these words underscored his father's care as a mode of intimacy: 'Dear old Dad!' Although 'strict and stern', Britten's father was 'fair and square to the last button'.[52] In blessing his father, Britten claimed that his affective bond with his father was because, not in spite, of discipline.

Paternal authority and the obligation to protect were never simply about discipline. As Tosh notes of bourgeois fathers, paternal protection was largely figurative. Fathers' duty was to protect his offspring from 'unpalatable' knowledge and experience, a role that had specific sentimental mileage in relation to the protection of daughters' virtue.[53] Working-class fathers similarly, were charged with protecting children from harm, in literal and abstract forms. According to M. E. Loane, men's protectiveness towards their children had a practical value in keeping careless mothers on their toes.[54] Children whom employers or teachers mistreated commonly were said to 'feel the need of a father'.[55] George Baldry's father was a strict disciplinarian, but he would not tolerate other men chastising his offspring: his boys were 'as proud as fighting cocks' when he defended them.[56] When a fireman kicked Sidney Campion's backside, his father 'flared up' and dragged Campion out to

[50] Muir, *An autobiography*, 16–17. [51] Kightly, *Country voices*, 175
[52] Britten, *Woodyard to palace*, 113; 196. [53] Tosh, *A man's place*, 85
[54] Loane, *From their point of view*, 24. [55] Hillyer, *Country boy*, 48.
[56] Baldry, *The rabbit-skin cap*, 40–1.

try to identify the culprit.[57] William Brown thought his father heroic for putting the headmaster who caned his son in his place. He related with pride the sound of his father's booming voice and the 'thwack' of his stick across the headmaster's desk as he took 'superb' command of the situation. Brown Senior was 'as authoritative, as unquestionable' as Jehovah in Genesis.[58]

There is a distinct element of masculine bravado in these stories, for fathers and sons. Many fathers probably resented other men's discipline of their children as a personal affront. Yet paternal protection could also be located in affective frameworks. A 'delicate' child, George Meek was left behind when his parents migrated to America. Meek's grandfather provided for his grandson; did not get drunk; read stories to him; and let the boy accompany him on assorted jobs and errands. In this, his 'too kind' grandfather 'more than filled the place of my father'. Meek was born with myopia, and his eyesight worsened whenever he had a cold. This disability failed to prevent a schoolmaster caning Meek for inattention. When Meek related this 'injustice' to his grandfather, the older man was 'so angry' that he confronted the school master, 'threatened to thrash him', and prohibited Meek from attending school until the intervention of the school attendance officer months later. Meek's grandpa may well have resented the schoolmaster's punishment as an infringement on his paternal rights. In Meek's reconstruction, however, the story formed part of a larger narrative concerning his 'very great attachment' to his grandfather. The grandfather's stand against authority also situated him at the core of the socialist Meek's adult selfhood, despite the older man's death (a 'great blow') when Meek was ten.[59]

Memories of father as a bulwark against the world functioned as a device to intimate the affective dimensions of paternal duty, enabling offspring to locate men in a framework of macro ideals of fatherhood while simultaneously extrapolating the unique significance of their father. Even in play, Elizabeth Bryson's father's warmth, size and security embodied the protective qualities of paternity:

> He is the best father in the world. He is full of fun. He has the warmest hands in the world; on the very coldest day if you can slip your hand inside your father's and both inside his big pocket, you are as warm as toast. He plays with you, gives you high swings, catches you when you take a flying leap down the stairs...

Putting his children to bed each night, Bryson's father told 'endless' stories and rhymes. One verse belonged specifically to her: 'Liz'beth

---

[57] Campion, *Sunlight on foothills*, 5–6   [58] Brown, *So far*, 32–35.
[59] George Meek, *Bath chair man; by himself* (London: Constable, 1910), 19–31.

Macdonald will be there/ Sitting in the rocking chair/ On her daddy's knee/ O, that will be joyful.' As father and daughter repeated this, Bryson seated on father's knee, their tactility mimicked the joy of the verse. Father then tucked his children in bed and led them in the prayer 'Gentle Jesus, meek and mild'. The ritual represented 'security from danger'. This was a double layer of protection: the prayer beseeched Christ to take the child's soul should they 'die before I wake', but, with the fortress of her father's protection, Death seemed an unlikely assailant.[60] In an echo of children's transformation of breadwinning *for* me into profound signs of what father meant *to me*, recollections of father's protective duties located men within a generic framework of fathering to intimate the affective significance of one father in particular. In many ways, the ritual of prayers led by father epitomised notions of the biological father as proxy for Godly authority. But Bryson's insistence that here was the 'best' and 'warmest' of fathers underscored the intimacy she invested in his exceptional status as *her* father.

Margaret Penn's adoptive father was a man of few words who wore his authority lightly. Memories that threw his authority into relief enabled Penn to pay tribute to his tender sensibility: he determined that the family would adopt Penn and, later on, resolved that she should know the truth about her birth. These stories held major significance in the drama of Penn's life story but, even in seemingly trivial anecdotes, father's authority could provide a meaningful framework through which to relate the emotive dynamic at work in this family. One such story recounted the death of the family cat. Penn's account of father's complicity with his children's request to oversee the cat funeral demonstrated how, in real time and reflection, children might appropriate the solemn dignity of paternal authority to invest domestic ritual with significance. That he undertook this responsibility with 'heavy' heart and 'gulping' sadness signalled how far he shared, and validated, his children's sorrow.[61]

Penn marshalled anecdotes about her father's protection and authority to demonstrate that he treated her equally with his biological children. Although fulfilment of parenting obligations did not necessarily correlate to attachment,[62] it is notable that authors' attempts to describe affective dynamics often emphasised deeds undertaken or promised. David

---

[60] Bryson, *Look back in wonder*, 7–8.
[61] Penn, *Manchester fourteen miles*, 155–56.
[62] Francis Anthony was raised in the boarding out system: he called his foster parents 'Mum and Dad', cried when he left their home, but was adamant that their dynamic had no affective attachment. Francis Anthony, *A man's a man* (London, 1932), 7–43.

Kirkwood's family expressed emotion through frugal statements or actions. Kirkwood's sister, Lizzie, was adopted as a baby: she was his 'father's darling'. Kirkwood realised how much their father loved Lizzie when she left home for domestic service: he announced that he would go 'to the uttermost parts o' the earth' should she need him. Spoken with 'tremendous sincerity', the simple promise to protect, even after the girl had left home, rang with devotion.[63] More casually, his father's pet name for the young Kirkwood was 'my cullan', meaning cub, a term that evoked the boy's youthful vitality but, also, the cub's dependence on its provider-protector parent.[64]

If appellations such as 'the old man' (Chapter 5) echoed with insolence, simple terms of endearment could evoke fathers' protectiveness and, in turn, respect for their authority. Joseph Stamper deemed 'Daddy' and 'Dad' suitable words for small children; the formality of 'Father' denoted respect for the Pater in relation to older children.[65] Barnabas Britten paid heartfelt tribute to his 'lovable' father through dialogue. The phrases 'Right-O! Dad!', 'Right you are, Dad!', 'Dear old Dad!' punctuate Britten's narrative, complemented by his father's responses, 'My boy', 'My son!' and 'Laddie'.[66] The terms underscored the authority of Britten Senior while his son's enthusiastic approbation invested it with intimate significance. A middle-aged Rodney Smith continued to call his father 'Daddy', kneeling at his feet each night to declare abiding love for him. The humility of this acknowledged the adult son's respect for father's authority through the life cycle: 'all that I am', Smith concluded, stemmed from the 'beautiful life' his father had given him.[67]

Few male autobiographers portrayed their fathers as explicitly affectionate. Rather, they turned to their deeds to infer the complex nuances of paternal obligation. Jack Jones's miner father was a man of few words but his solicitude for the sons he took into the pit suggested his protective qualities. Notably, their father took the everyday risks. When a broken pit shaft forced the miners to find their way to the surface through old workings, most of which had collapsed or rotted, Jones's father tried to protect his thirteen-year-old son. Jones recollected the foul, menacing stink of stale air and fear: one false move would bury the miners. Throughout their slow ascent, his father offered reassurance and, like a coal-dusted St. Christopher, carried his son on his back through chest-

---

[63] Kirkwood, *My life of revolt*, 24–25.   [64] Ibid, 28–9.
[65] Stamper, *So long ago*, 31.
[66] Britten, *Woodyard to palace*, see for example 89, 149, 150, 160, 162, 223.
[67] Smith, *Gispy Smith*, 310.

deep water.[68] This, like making Jones a member of their trade union, was probably indicative of his father's pragmatism. What matters though is that, in a book that took pains to demonstrate the multifaceted dynamic between men's obligations and family attachments, Jones deemed these details worthy of inclusion.

In one of the few autobiographies to explicitly address the issue of love, Kathleen Dayus reflected in recreated dialogue with her brother that she believed their father loved his children, albeit in a 'funny kind of way'. Dayus, well versed in twentieth-century expectations of parental affection, meant that her father might not have expressed his feelings in neat, explicit statements but that it was possible to read love into his actions. For instance, Dayus and two siblings had filched free samples of 'Ex-Lax', a chocolate-flavoured laxative and, ignorant of its medicinal properties, consumed the lot. The explosive consequence precipitated their hurried departure from school, and was matched by their mother's rage: caning and no supper. When father returned from work, he took the children bread and cocoa, warning his wife not to beat them again, or 'you'll answer to me!'[69] In his desire to protect his children, Dayus thought she recognised 'love'. Other evidence supported this: father dispensed treats, choked up when singing a soldier's lament for his children and, when his son was taken into hospital with scarlet fever, called daily to inquire after the boy's health.

In life stories where fathers were remote and relationships ambivalent, gestures of protection stood out against everyday paternal insouciance. Dorothy Scannell's lively account of growing up in East London unashamedly celebrated her mother, often at the expense of her oafish father. Even so, the older man was not entirely disengaged from affective ties. Careless for his personal safety in the Great War, Scannell's soldier father was frantic with worry when he learned his fifteen-year-old son had enlisted. He worked to get the boy discharged as soon as possible.[70] Seemingly heroic examples of fathers' protectiveness towards children could have particular significance to boys who had less tactile interaction with men. Goaded by an older brother, a seven-year-old Harry Watkin jumped from a height of around seven feet. He hit the ground hard, injured his ankles and fell onto his face in pain. A crowd gathered when, from the commotion, Watkin's father emerged, 'clouted' the older brother and scooped up his tearful son. His father's entry to the scene of Watkin's mortification sealed this as a 'never-to-be-forgotten', 'delightful', 'unbelievable' act of paternal heroism. Watkin 'loved' his

---

[68] Jones, *Unfinished journey*, 76–7.   [69] Dayus, *Her people*, 57–60.
[70] Scannell, *Mother knew best*, 55–56.

father in this moment: he rescued the boy's dignity and reassured him. Most of all, cradled against his father's chest, Watkin inhaled his distinctive 'Dad's smell', confirmation that this hero was *his* father.

Set against the enigmatic man who characterised Watkin's everyday childhood, this rescue was a peculiar moment of tender intimacy. At seven, Watkin was moving towards the fledgling masculinity of older boys. Whereas daughters might enjoy tactility with father throughout adulthood, it was less common for sons to sustain (or acknowledge) demonstrative contact with men (although they did with mothers). To a point, Watkin's rescue marked the epitome and end of boyish fear and awe in relation to his father. When his soldier father called home for an hour's leave in the midst of the First World War, Watkin could not even recall speaking to him: his weeping mother claimed the moment. The inclusion of this memory in his life story suggested the sting of diffidence. Perhaps his father felt it too, for upon reaching his next posting in Ireland, he sent his boys a postcard with some Shamrock seeds.[71] Paradoxically, for adults seeking to give meaning to the past, the smallest acts of paternal devotion adopted extra significance to complicate narratives of blanket detachment. Watkin adored his mother, seemingly without complication. His account of his father, in contrast, pointed to the ambiguities of 'love' as a set of practices, attachments and ambivalences: Watkin's father was heroic, benevolent, proud, caring, indifferent, a provider, selfish and, sometimes, distant.

Watkin's narrative implied that the small child's 'need' for fatherly protection gave way in youthful adulthood to a more critical, distant dynamic. By the time most children left school, their desire for independence created a source of conflict with paternal authority. Unexpected moments of paternal protection in adulthood then could remind children of the caring facets of fatherhood. In his youth, Jack Jones joined the Army, despite his father's opposition to the Boer war and his son's abandonment of their trade.[72] In August 1914, Jones was married with three children, and had returned to coal mining. With the declaration of war, he was recalled to his regiment and sent to France. Jones reproduced his letters home in his autobiography. Correspondence with his wife gave instruction regarding financial management and carried his 'best love' and kisses for their children.[73] Looking back at the letters, Jones was struck by their silences: he made no mention of carrying the corpse of his friend back to the trench, the shrapnel wounds to his head

---

[71] Watkin, *From Hulme*, 8–9. [72] Jones, *Unfinished journey*, 94.
[73] See Tim Fisher, 'Fatherhood and the experience of working-class fathers', 157–8.

or, being right-handed, the two fingers amputated from his left hand. These were communications from the head of household that preserved the fiction of normative protection and authority, even (maybe especially) in father's absence. In contrast, Jones's letters to his parents were missives from a son: he told them of his fears, wounds and the death of his friends; he beseeched them to care for his dependents should he die or become incapacitated; and littered his letters with endearments, gratitude and blessings.

Jones said little about letters received, making an exception for a 'wonderful' response to a particularly fraught letter Jones dispatched from hospital. It was the first and only letter of his father's life; written, as the older man exclaimed 'by my own hand'. Jones emphasised his gratitude: the letter was 'splendid', he could not write better, he would love such letters every week. His father undertook the role of scribe because his wife was illiterate. But, as Jones made clear in an earlier anecdote about his father's literacy, reading and writing did not come easy to the miner.[74] Indeed, Jones spent much of his adult career devoted to adult education. His autobiography made clear the obstacle of literacy to working-class improvement; it also emphasised just how momentous the task of composing a letter was when literacy could not be taken for granted. Crucially, in attempting to allay his adult son's anxieties, Jones's father, a man approaching sixty, enacted a long-forgotten role of protector and guide.

Literacy bound father and son together in Jones's memoir as much as work and their respective responsibilities as fathers: from his boyish admiration for his father's ability to read a little English and Welsh and his willingness to make time, despite exhaustion and difficulty with text, to read to his sick boy; to the wounded soldier's gratitude for his father's letter; to the aftermath of war when remembrance of that letter induced Jones to make time for his ageing father. It traced a lineage of fathers protecting children through ambition for them: from Jones Senior remembering with gratitude his father's determination that his children should have some education, to Jones the author's ambitions for his sons' education, to his desire for his first grandchild (named after Jones's father) to call him 'Granser'.[75] Like other narratives here, Jones's memoir confirmed the social norms of fathering but, in relating how these mapped onto personal experiences, Jones invested *his* father's fulfilment of these norms (and, indeed, his own) with intimate meaning.

---

[74] Jones, *Unfinished journey*, 150–62. [75] *Ibid*, 34–5, 160–1, 168, 296–302.

The burden of obligation

The tenderness of protection could also prove a source of oppression for dependents, as outlined by Megan Doolittle.[76] Famously, (Sir) Edmund Gosse's scorching memoir *Father and Son* (1907) castigated his marine zoologist father's religion (he was a pastor for the Plymouth Brethren) and childrearing.[77] Gosse's rejection of his father's faith was a potent rejection of his father, Philip (especially if, as the biographer of father and son suggests, Edmund's claims about Philip's fathering were exaggerated).[78] For parents whom we have no reason to doubt firmly believed in the importance of Christian salvation, familial commitment to Christ was deeply emotional and enabled family ties to transcend the limits of mortality. The evangelical Gipsy Smith, for instance, narrated his love for his children in tandem with his desire, and responsibility, to bring those children sincerely to Christ.[79] For Philip Gosse, his son's rejection of his Christianity was tantamount to rebuffing paternal love and duty as Philip understood it. The Gosse family were rooted in a different social milieu to the working-class families under discussion here but the memoir illuminates the potential for paternal efforts to guide and protect to be freighted with affective significance in positive and negative terms.

In reconstructing his childhood, T. A. Westwater paid effusive tribute to his father. The solitary source of discord between them was religion. Westwater's father, a Christian, harboured ambitions for his son to enter the ministry. An atheist, Westwater struggled even to discuss religion with his father, a marked contrast to the harmony that characterised every other aspect of their dynamic. This was no mere trifle. For years, the son's departure from his father's beliefs made both men 'miserable', causing them 'mental agony'. This clearly had a power dimension: his father wanted his son to share his beliefs and he was confounded by what amounted, in a secular sense, to obstinate disobedience. Yet, the meanings Westwater invested in this antagonism refuse to be understood in an affective vacuum. For Westwater, his father's bid for his soul was rooted in the profound and sincere belief that salvation was 'most vital' to his son's future, and their reunion in the afterlife; it was a sign of his father's devotion.

---

[76] Doolittle, 'The protection of children'.
[77] Edmund Gosse, *Father and son: a study in two temperaments* (London: William Heinemann, 1907).
[78] Ann Thwaite, *Edmund Gosse: a literary landscape* (Stroud: Tempus, 2007); Ann Thwaite, *Glimpses of the wonderful: the life of Philip Henry Gosse* (London: Faber, 2002).
[79] Smith, *Gispy Smith*, 221–38.

That Westwater gave so much emphasis to this in a narrative penned in old age suggested its ongoing significance for Westwater's adult self, his memory of his father and their relationship. In spite of his claim that their variance over religion 'never made a scrap of difference to our love for each other, a love born of perfect understanding', Westwater's memoir was suffused with self-recrimination and sadness for having disappointed his father.[80] Hopes and desires for an offspring's salvation represented the gifts a father could bestow. Paternal politics or the promotion of particular cultural pursuits within the home could operate in much the same way. Children's acceptance, comprehension or rejection of those efforts was, almost invariably, emotionally charged. Chester Armstrong was acutely sensitive to the 'pressure of heavy obligation' that sat upon him as head of a family of eight. Simultaneously, he recoiled from the 'repressive discipline' of imposing his beliefs on the 'plastic' minds of children. Somewhat naively, perhaps, he believed he had resisted any attempt to direct his children's thought in favour of setting an example and facilitating their philosophical and cultural curiosity. Stating his 'genuine satisfaction' in his children, allowing for individual preference and admitting that he had not anticipated competing attractions such as cinema, the seventy-year-old Armstrong conceded that the results of his childrearing experiment 'lagged behind' the aspirations of his youthful fathering. This was fair enough: he had 'no right' to expect his children to fulfil his desires. Despite favouring 'persuasion' and 'guidance' over the imposition of paternal belief, Armstrong clearly invested his identity as a father in cultivating children who were mirrors of himself. His assertion that 'much that I hoped for may emerge in later years' hinted at Armstrong's mild disappointment in his middle-aged children and his effort to be reconciled with their seeming ambivalence to his 'great experiment'.[81]

Protection could prove a source of recrimination and regret when men appeared to fail in fulfilling obligations too. The anti-vaccination movement is generally associated with working-class radical politics but it is also worth noting that some fathers refused to vaccinate children simply because older children (or friends' children) had died following vaccination and they became fearful of losing other offspring.[82] Edward Purkiss (born 1881) recounted the pride he felt when his 'bonny' son, Leonard,

---

[80] Westwater, *The early life*, 20.
[81] Armstrong, *Pilgrimage to Nenthead*, 278–283.
[82] See for example, Slater, *Think on!*, 5; and, Watkin, *From Hulme*, 3. See also Nadja Durbach, *Bodily matters: the anti-vaccination movement in England, 1853–1907* (Durham, N.C.: Duke University Press, 2005).

was born in 1909; he took the babe for walks as soon as his wife allowed. This offset Purkiss's distress when his son had a mental health breakdown in his late teens. By the time Purkiss composed his life story, his son had been in an asylum for twenty-eight years. The note that Leonard had not recognized him during Purkiss's most recent visits suggested the pain and 'loneliness' of paternal helplessness.[83] For some authors, fathers were not authoritative enough or enacted their authority in ineffective or misguided ways. John Eldred regretted his father's lack of 'positive manliness' which manifested in peevishness or 'gusts of rage'. Worse, his father's shame and misery after an outburst of temper amplified his shortcomings and strengthened his wife's supremacy.[84]

Louise Jermy's stepmother physically abused her. Acknowledging that he 'shielded' her from the worst, Jermy nevertheless held her father responsible: too often, he turned a blind eye to his wife's everyday 'brutality'. In the direct reverse of Dayus's connection between her father's protection and love, Jermy asserted that, if her father had any love for her, he 'certainly didn't show it'. Jermy expected her father to protect her: it was his duty as head of household and would have demonstrated his attachment to her. Instead, he used his authority to stifle her freedom. Although a tender nurse and, as Jermy matured, a pleasurable companion, her father's ultimate failure to marshal his authority in her defence cut their ties asunder. Indeed, he only realised his authority after Jermy left home, docking his wife's housekeeping in retaliation for driving his daughter away. 'From that time', he 'hardened' towards his wife, becoming a 'different man'. This came too late for Jermy, who relates with bitter triumph his subsequent efforts to make amends and her rejection of them.[85]

Valerie Sanders's analysis of literary Victorian fathers records their manifold failures: failure to provide, failure to live up to one's own father's achievements, failure to cultivate interesting and motivated children (mostly sons) and failure to live long enough. In particular, child death delivered a resounding blow to notions of paternal protection, encompassing as it did, myriad failings. Although a child's death rocked the foundations of maternity (after all, motherhood was grounded in caring for children) fathers, too, felt the blow of bereavement. When working-class fathers expressed their grief, they did so in specifically

---

[83] Edward Purkiss, *The memories of a London orphan boy* (Bexley: The Author, 1957), 812.
[84] Eldred, *I love the brooks*, 22–5.
[85] Jermy, *The memories of a working woman*. See also Jane McDermid, 'The making of a 'domestic' life: memories of a working woman', *Labour History Review*, 73:3 (2008), 253–268.

'paternal' manifestations: through provision of a funeral, via workplace rites of condolence or by being 'strong' for other family members.[86] Nevertheless, the triumph of Death over Daddy struck at men's pride and confidence. As Sanders notes of Archibald Tait, Bishop of Carlisle, later Archbishop of Canterbury, the failure of his faith to save five daughters from death or to offer adequate consolation for his immediate emotional suffering was, in many ways, a failure of Tait.[87] For working-class fathers, frustration at child death and the struggle to reconcile spiritual beliefs with bereavement could be compounded by suspicion that hunger or environment, however little understood, had contributed to the loss.

James Turner, an unskilled Halifax labourer, went to chapel, attended classes at the YMCA and prayed for God's help in finding better paid work that his family 'should not be so poor'. At the start of 1882, he and his heavily pregnant wife lived in a one-roomed cellar with their three small children, Emily, Tom and Annice. On 21 January, his diary recorded that his family were gripped by 'coughing mania'. Annice, the middle child, was particularly poorly. Turner consulted a doctor who diagnosed acute bronchitis. By 31 January, Tom and Emily were improving but Annice remained ill. Turner went to work but helped nurse his child in the evenings and at weekends. By Saturday 11 February, it was clear she was dying. He, his wife and his mother watched over the child, 'cuddled' her and held her hand as she died. On 16/17 February, Turner reflected that 'We do miss her.' She was buried in her grandfather's grave but, as the Turners had never been able to afford burial insurance, they borrowed three pounds to pay for the coffin and interment.

Turner's reflections on his daughter's death were hardly profound. Annice had always been delicate. He wished God had spared her but resigned himself to the idea that He deemed it 'better' to 'take her away'. He fell back on clichés that Annice had gone to a 'better' world. He noted his other children's response to the death, emphasising that the family 'loved [Annice] very much'. He did not wrestle with scripture or appear to undergo any theological crisis. Still, in the weeks following Annice's death, Turner prayed that God forgive his sins so that he could be reunited with her in Heaven, bought an assortment of religious texts and commended the expulsion of atheist MP, Charles Bradlaugh, from the House of Commons. Turner stopped going to his chapel and turned to the Salvation Army. He liked the Army's hymns and thought them a

---

[86] Julie-Marie Strange, 'Speechless with grief: bereavement and the working-class father' in Broughton and Rogers, *Gender and fatherhood*, 138–52.
[87] Sanders, *The tragic-comedy*, 41–50.

force for social good, but his shifting allegiance had more to do with resentment at the Methodist pastor who had promised to baptise Annice before she died but failed to arrive until two days later. Turner intended 'to let him know about it sometime'. He did not appear, however, to think that the omission would prevent Annice's entry to the afterlife. In March, Turner was still making entries about 'my little girl', a 'good child' as his wife gave birth to another daughter. They considered calling the babe Annice, as Turner's siblings thought proper, but decided the name was simply too painful: they feared thinking only of 'our [dead] darling'.

There was another strand to Turner's grief. After Turner reported the death, a 'gentleman' from the town council had called on the family. He commended Turner on his children's 'good heads' and 'plenty of brains', but drew attention to their 'poor delicate bodies', want of nourishment and the woeful conditions in which the family lived. Turner resolved to move to a better part of town with a 'suitable' house. On 25 February, his resolve hardened when the family that lived above them also lost a child to bronchitis. Turner's new job promised an upturn in family fortunes as he earned 'the most money I ever drew in my life'. Although still massively in debt, he hoped his family could get on 'very nicely' now, although he continued to pray for God's assistance in improving the family's lot. By 1 April, Turner secured a new house to rent. Although filthy, the landlord made an allowance to help clean it. Turner spent a week, painting, scrubbing and papering the house with the assistance of two friends. The family moved to their new home on 10 April. All that summer, Turner tended his daughter's grave.[88] At no point did Turner's diary explicitly suggest self-recrimination for his daughter's death. But his desire to clear household debt, to work harder and improve the family's accommodation, powerfully suggest a sense of responsibility, if not for the death just passed, then for the future wellbeing of his (growing) family. This is not to say that Turner became a paragon of self-sacrifice and protection. Rather, the bitter bereavement sharpened his awareness of his family's dependency upon him and focused, most of the time, his resolve on trying to better fulfil his obligations to them.

What might represent a burden of obligation to men could provide comfort to children. Patrick MacGill's (born 1890) mother and siblings were superstitious and afraid of shadows; his father was 'afraid of nothing'.[89] When strong fathers did show weakness, then, the shock to

---

[88] Turner, *Halifax labourer*, 31–47.
[89] Patrick MacGill, *Children of the dead end: the autobiography of an Irish navvy* (Berkshire, [1914] 1980), 3.

children was profound. MacGill was astonished when his fearless father wept so freely over the death of his young son.[90] Elizabeth Flint portrayed her father as a jovial family man, resourceful and committed to spending time with his children. When his eldest son, Ted, volunteered for war in 1914, her father was forlorn. When Ted died, Father took the news worst, sobbing and shaking uncontrollably in 'real, dark, bitter grief'. His children were appalled at the 'never-to-be-forgotten' sight of their strong father weeping: 'It was not possible to have imagined that Dad could be touched like this by anything.' As Flint reflected, there was something 'wrong' about his children witnessing father's distress. The indignity of bearing witness to father's impotence was compounded when Flint's mother ventured the revelation that Ted was not her spouse's son. In the overall narrative of family life, however, the exposure of paternal weakness offset the father's solidity and confirmed his deep attachment to his children. Paradoxically, he grew closer to his wife after the 'dreadful' night, continued to speak of 'my Ted', and when the son's widow gave birth to a son, the little boy and his grandfather became the best of friends.[91]

Jack Jones contrasted his father's broken-heartedness over the death of a younger son at the front in the Great War with the miner's previous vitality: father's return from the pit was no longer marked by washing and tea, but by his tearful repetition of his dead son's name. Jones was at a loss what to do with this weeping man. All the usual 'man' things his father desired, like beer and the pub, walks and work talk, made no incursion into his grief. The older man's diminished masculinity reminded Jones of other tender facets of the miner's fathering, notably singing to his small son. In terms of narrative structure, it made sense to synthesise stories of paternal gentleness around this emotional moment as a point of climax in a family story that for the most part, had played upon the miner's brooding vigour. Indeed, Jones's father never recovered his masculinity in the memoir after this point: his grief made Jones alive to how 'very old' and, by implication, how frail, his father looked.[92] In a similar vein, Joseph Stamper's father became a shadow of his former self after the death of his wife. Stamper recalled surprising his father who stood, eyes blinking, holding his wife's hat against his chest, or heart if Stamper were being 'sentimental'. In declaiming sentiment, Stamper offset the implicit truth of his observation against an assertion of manly reticence. As Stamper sought to comfort his father, their roles were

---

[90] *Ibid*, 11.
[91] Elizabeth Flint, *Hot bread and chips* (London: Museum Press, 1963), 70, 100–108.
[92] Jones, *Unfinished journey*, 172–7.

irrevocably reversed. As with Jones, this moment of paternal weakness prompted narrative organisation of other moments of father-son tenderness. Notably, the recollection of his grief-stricken father provided a prelude to the story of father and son's holiday in Wales in Stamper's youth (Chapter 4) that he recalled with such warmth.[93]

Authority, autonomy and reconciliation

As the stories above illustrate, relationships with fathers were far from static. In autobiographical contexts particularly, authors needed to give characters and plots coherence. As with other elements of the family story, authors rehearsed paternal authority to explain the formation of authorial identity and outcome. This is not to say that conflicts or criticisms concerning paternal authority were necessarily resolved: for some authors, like Louise Jermy, the oppressive authority of fathers continued to cause pain and disappointment long into adult life. For others, like Pat O'Mara and Vero Garrett, the tyranny of fathers could become in hindsight the motor to strive for a different kind of life and to adopt the mantle of 'protection' to mothers and siblings. Sam Shaw's autobiography suggested acceptance of his father's shortcomings, although that did not signify reconciliation with the man.

Shaw measured his father against an ideal of fatherhood, culled from childhood observation of his friends' fathers 'quite happily' scooping offspring into their brawny arms. To have a father, in Shaw's model, was to experience the 'joy of hero worship': 'every child' venerated their father, looking up to them as a 'big, big father supreme over all other fathers'.[94] If some authors pointed to the generic qualities of fatherhood to emphasise the particular merits of *my* father, Shaw put this into reverse: fathers were supposed to be devoted, but his father's diffidence 'robbed' Shaw of affection. Shaw's reference to theft suggests a model of paternal attachment whereby love and devotion are the rightful property of the child. Having cheated his son of this, Shaw concluded that his father must have disliked him.[95] It is notable that throughout his story, Shaw veered between referring to 'father' and the more irreverent 'Joe'. The shortcomings of the older man culminated in his responsibility for curtailing Shaw's childhood at the age of ten. On his father's instructions, Shaw went selling matches without a license; he was arrested and sent to borstal.

---

[93] Stamper, *So long ago*, 108–9.
[94] Shaw, *Guttersnipe*, 5.
[95] Other authors also looked to friends' fathers to emphasise the failure of their father. See Eldred, *I love the brooks*, 60; Roberts, *A classic slum*, 117.

Shaw never saw his parents again. His mother died when he was sixteen. Living in Wales, his lack of funds prohibited attendance at her funeral. Sixteen years later, his father died. By this time, Shaw was married, had children and was working as a miner. One of the very few references to any of his children in Shaw's autobiography occurred in relation to his father's funeral. Shaw took his six-year-old daughter with him, from South Wales to Birmingham, for the interment: 'As I stood by the graveside I paid him all I ever owed, the tribute of a passing sigh.' There was a lot in that sigh. That Shaw's debt to his father amounted to a 'passing' sigh posed a damning evaluation on a parental relationship, especially when set against Shaw's searing grief at the death of his mother and, for that matter, at the demise of a fellow borstal boy. If most funerals demanded respect for the dead, Shaw's attendance here was suffused with resentment and contempt, set in a context of acute (comprehensible) self-pity and regret.

Despite the affected nonchalance of the 'passing sigh', Shaw went to extraordinary trouble to attend this funeral. In the midst of the First World War, with limited passenger services, he and his daughter travelled one hundred miles by rail. The decision to take his child, and his inclusion of the detail here, suggests the significance of father-child companionship in this moment, not least to contrast Shaw's cognisance of affective dynamics as a father with the detachment of his father. Shaw's sentiment for the older man, a sigh, was an exhalation. It could denote sadness for what was not; weariness for what was; or, possibly, yearning for something else. Perhaps Shaw's sigh encompassed all those things but, in reference to paying what was owed, he also implied that the sigh, lacking effort, letting go, was an act that released him from the thrall of disappointment to settle the old account with Joe. In doing so, Shaw left the bitter struggle of his past to focus on his struggle for a better future. The inclusion of his child in this story referenced Shaw's efforts to fulfil his paternal obligations; he would be a hero. Indeed, shortly after this, Shaw was widowed with five children, aged between fifteen months and eight years.[96] It also signalled his political commitment. Notably, within the genre of working-class autobiography, Shaw's experience ought to have made him a socialist. Instead, he was a Tory and worked actively to promote anti-socialist propaganda (his autobiography was an extension of this). For Shaw, his father's failure was all the more acute because it was not ameliorated by rage against the system; it was personal. Shaw's politics were, in part, an extension of this: to appeal to individualistic aspirations in working men to do better for their children.

[96] Many years ago, Sam Shaw's granddaughter contacted me to tell me of the esteem and affection his children and grandchildren held towards Shaw.

If some autobiographers were unequivocal in their damnation of paternal failure, others took a more conciliatory line. The death of Alice Foley's deadweight father in her youth freed his family from the tyranny of his authority. Yet her relief at his passing was shot through with 'profound pity' and, as she gazed upon his corpse, recognition of dignity in the man (if not the father) that moved her deeply.[97] Recalling his rendition of Othello's anguished 'the pity of it', Foley mused that this could have been her father's epitaph. Certainly, it summarised her reflections on him. Her first loyalties were with her mother whom she 'loved passionately'.[98] Her feelings for her father veered between fear, frustration, and compassion. Embracing her on his knee, her father would present a scenario, such as both parents drowning, and ask Foley whom she would save. Had she replied instinctively, she would have chosen mother, of course; but 'pity' for her father precluded this. Sensing a 'secret yearning' in the man, the child sought to resolve the dilemma with tactile assurances that she would save both, a compromise that never satisfied him. So traumatic was his pestering for a definitive choice that these exchanges morphed into a recurring nightmare where all effort to rescue her drowning mother was thwarted by 'father's frantic arms closing around me'.[99] This is powerful stuff. The abominable position her father placed Foley in with his 'tragic dilemma' mirrored the tragedy of her family story. The textual conflict between pity and frustration simultaneously distanced and embedded her father within Foley's adult identity.

Other authors regretted their part in clashes of the past. D. R. Davies's story recounted the depth of his youthful resentment toward his father. The older man, a miner, had broken his back just before Davies was born, an accident that severely affected the family's long-term prospects. Throughout his youth, Davies had to sacrifice his ambition to support his parents. He had 'resented' this obligation 'like hell': it was 'my father's fault, or somebody's fault'. With hindsight, Davies reconfigured his 'grudge' as a 'basic weakness' in character that made him careless of his parents' feelings and vulnerable to the lure of radical politics. His autobiography paid tribute to the 'purgatory' of suffering his father endured and the 'martyrdom' of his mother; both his parents extolled the virtues of Christian humility and faith. Davies the author was a father, had experienced one failed marriage and knew the struggle of providing for a family. He was also an Anglican minister. His account of 'growing up' was literal and metaphorical: Davies's adult reconciliation with his

---

[97] Foley, *A Bolton childhood*, 67.   [98] *Ibid*, 3.   [99] *Ibid*, 9–10.

parents was inextricable from his criticism of socialism as immature and self-indulgent and his decision to embrace their establishment Christianity.[100]

Other memoirs, written in less self-consciously intellectual registers, or for less philosophical reasons, nevertheless advanced complex conceptions of the shifting nature of relationships. T. A. Westwater paid tribute to a father's devotion and attempted to balance, posthumously, the account of filial gratitude towards his father against his rejection of the older man's beliefs. In Westwater's case, grief for his father fused with a whiff of disappointment in his relationship to his children; they were so independent, they made him feel superfluous.[101] Jack Jones's motive for writing his first autobiography (he later wrote other volumes) was prosaic. His income as a writer was shaky. His autobiography revisited the themes of his most successful novels, *Rhondda Roundabout* (1934) and *Black Parade* (1935), books that drew material from Jones's experience and presented his mother as a key sympathetic figure. Jones's autobiography extended the tribute to his father, who was still alive when he composed it and had expressed disgruntlement that the novels sidelined him.[102] The autobiography reimagined the conflicts of Jones's youth, especially his defiance of his father to join the army and his rejection of his father's trade, to pay homage to his father's reason, sacrifice and devotion, and to effect reflective reconciliation.

As many authors explained, their parents were of a different generation, embedded in the working practices and ideas of the mid-nineteenth century. The world of autobiographers was radically different to that of their parents. The last quarter of the nineteenth century and first decade of the twentieth witnessed increasing national wealth, the growth of pluralistic, mass politics, the formation of the Trades Union Congress (1868) and the introduction of universal education. Many authors noted the generational differences between their and their father's politics. Highlighting individual battles against paternal authority could amplify an authors' success: the struggle to pursue individual dreams was achieved against all the odds. Authors frequently deployed stories of conflict with fathers, who were the mouthpieces of a worldview in many homes, to demonstrate that, as harbingers of a new generation and different world, their youthful self had been 'right'. After all, the

---

[100] Davies, *In search of myself*, 16–22; 33; 49; 56–7; 188–92.
[101] Indeed, one daughter had emigrated. A curious autobiographer, Westwater ends with a series of regrets for the decisions he made and the wish that he had listened to his father more. Westwater, *The early life*, 63–4.
[102] Jones, *Unfinished journey*, 288.

sheer act of publishing autobiography vindicated some authors' decisions to eschew the trade or politics of fathers. Few autobiographers went so far as George Ratcliffe (born 1863) in recreating a scene of father-son dialogue where Father was forced to admit 'Well, lad, perhaps you knew best.'[103]

Few fathers (or mothers) had the necessary experience or knowledge to give useful advice to sons and daughters who wanted to pursue paths that were different, unthinkably so in some cases, to their own. For parents caught up in the economic pressures of family life, children's ambitions or preoccupations could appear selfish and unrealistic. This was the source of the antagonism between Sidney Campion and his father, with whom we started this chapter. Campion recalled his indignation when his father, 'regardless of my feelings and wishes', arranged an apprenticeship for his son. Campion signed the apprenticeship agreement but before his indenture was complete, absconded to London. After two days on the road (and only making it as far as Northampton), relatives dispatched Campion back to his parents where his employer sacked him for breaking the terms of his apprenticeship. His father was mortified, for this was his workplace, too. Although the ultimate outcome of Campion's story vindicated his youthful instincts, his retrospective view made concessions towards his father's anxiety. Had MacDonald not taken him up, there was every possibility that his father's prophecy would have been realised: he could well have ended up a 'waster'. Had he completed his apprenticeship, his wages would have been double those of his father. Acknowledging the 'impetuosity' of youth, Campion also noted that his period as an apprentice was marked by the development of his ideas, partly because of the friendship of two slightly older men he worked alongside.[104] Campion may have been proved right in the long run, but his father was not necessarily wrong, either.

Even where adult children continued to reject the beliefs of paterfamilias, reflection could generate recognition of an affective dynamic underpinning youthful debate and disagreement. Tom Tremewan's (born 1888) grandfather was a fond student of the Bible who liked to sit by the fire quoting passages or 'remarkable' hymns in an 'absent-minded' way. As a boy, Tremewan took little heed of these 'mutterings'. As a young man, he grew more critical of his grandfather's seemingly slavish beliefs. Tremewan used the dreamily reverent grandfather to expound on religious free thought and the differences between doctrine and action, religion and belief. An older Tremewan continued to find his

[103] Ratcliffe, *Sixty years of it*, 5, 35.
[104] Campion, *Sunlight on the foothills*, 29–38.

grandfather's 'dogma' oppressive. Nevertheless, he paid tribute to the multifaceted dimensions of the older man's religious life: his grandfather's beliefs identified his brand of respectable conformity, his willingness to discuss an angry youth's diatribes signalled his generosity of spirit and his sincere perplexity for his grandson's soul acknowledged scope for interpersonal tenderness in disagreement.[105]

Rehearsing youthful conflicts with fathers enabled authors to establish the (usually successful) outcome of their choices and, from a position of reflective benevolence, rehabilitate paternal authority. Herbert Morrison described his father as a Conservative monarchist, a 'stolid, reliable' police constable who worshipped at the altar of respectability. In a biography that charted a socialist life (Morrison's note that 1888, his birth year, was a significant date for socialism implied a kind of political predestination), such loyalties were the deadly hallmarks of working-class oppression. His occupational duty to control strikes and riots placed Morrison's father firmly in antipathy to the strike-supporting son. In memoir, Morrison diluted the remembered antagonism to 'misunderstanding' and sought to explain his father's choices. His father was a product of a well-established and pervasive class system that lulled the population into unthinking conformity with the 'divine order of things'. Little wonder his son's embrace of the new-fangled socialism alarmed Pater-policeman. His father knew that police attempts to control strikes and protests frequently backfired. Morrison even sought to reclaim his father as a comrade to the cause. Small trade unions sometimes requested police assistance to encourage crowds to remain 'orderly' yet ordinary constables were powerless to determine how to do this. In following the instructions of inept police commissioners, constables inevitably mismanaged pickets and demonstrations. The men working in the name of oppression were just as oppressed as the people were.

In hindsight, father's 'disquiet' at his son's involvement in protests was legitimate: he had merely been seeking to protect him. Shortly after birth, Morrison lost the sight of his right eye. He took his mother's concern for granted: 'naturally' mothers worried about their children. It was only 'looking back' that Morrison 'realized' his father must have 'been deeply worried', too. Here, then, paternal antagonism towards his son's politics was rooted in his 'ever-present' fear that blindness would leave the boy 'helpless'. Again, this enabled Morrison to reposition his father from adversary to comrade. His father knew that the son, ranged on the side of social and political rebellion, would need 'all my strength and

---

[105] Tom Tremewan, *Cornish youth: memories of a Perran boy, 1895–1910* (Truro: Oscar Blackford, 1968), 113.

faculties' to survive industrial capitalism. When his father chastised him for reading socialist texts ('dangerous rubbish'), Morrison reclaimed his criticism as concern: it stemmed from his fear that reading was detrimental to Morrison's sound eye. The conflict that characterised his youth stood, in Morrison's seventies, for his father's desire to shield a disadvantaged boy from life's knocks. Similarly, his father's refusal to allow Morrison to become a compositor at fourteen because the job would cause undue strain to his eye could be construed retrospectively as fatherly tenderness.[106]

Morrison's career with the Labour party took him to the highest levels of government (among his posts were Minister for Transport, Home Secretary, Secretary of State for Foreign Affairs, Deputy Prime Minister and Leader of the House of Commons). By the time he published his autobiography in 1960, Morrison was a life peer. The socialist son with poor eyesight could well afford to be benevolent toward the conservative policeman. As a public figure of reason and authority with a specific political agenda (Morrison advocated a more conciliatory, consensual labour politics), Morrison was also alive to the importance of reputation: there was, perhaps, something unseemly in denigrating a well-meaning man who, in all probability, had much in common with other fathers of his generation and class, and who could not dispute his son's interpretation of events from beyond the grave. Morrison might even have thanked his father for refusing him that compositing apprenticeship, for where would Lord Morrison be in a print shop. Less pessimistically, it is possible to read this reconciliation as an extraordinary, albeit brief, personal moment in a biography focused overwhelmingly on public politics. In this context, the political provided a vehicle for illuminating the shifting interplay of family relationships and power; equally, Morrison demonstrated that family life did not exist in a vacuum but rather provided a space for rehearsing public-political conflicts, in real time and reflection.

Emanuel Shinwell's (another Labour MP) arguments with his father over occupation, and his desire to join the navy, drove an eighteen-year-old Shinwell to strike out for independence, leaving his father's home and tailoring workshop for the bright lights of Glasgow. Once there, Shinwell got married, against the wishes of both sets of parents. His downfall, Shinwell suggested, was almost inevitable. After a month of marriage, he was unemployed. After three months without work, he 'had to admit defeat' and return to his father in South Shields. Shinwell cast

---

[106] Morrison, *An autobiography*, 12, 20–27.

his father as a 'relic of the Victorian age' where even workers with radical inclinations grew complacent because conditions had improved since the 'hungry forties'. Nevertheless, the similarities between Shinwell and his father were sufficient for Shinwell to place their conflicts in a broader context of overall sympathy.

Although their politics were different, Shinwell and his father were both politically motivated in youth. Indeed, his father had taken an infant Shinwell to a meeting about workers' rights where the labour leader, John Burns (then in the Social Democratic Federation), bounced the babe on his knee. Shinwell could claim, therefore, to have been 'cradled in the Labour movement'. This was his father's anecdote. Shinwell's inclusion of it in his life story referenced the son's fulfilment of a political destiny and made space for his father within it. As Shinwell's title to his autobiography intimated, his story was one of *Conflict without malice*. With hindsight, his youthful rebellion against his father's authority was intrinsic to learning independence. Indeed, his father also left home after clashing with his father. The ructions of youth, described as 'the old disputes', acquired a veneer of banality while enabling Shinwell to acknowledge his father's constancy; he got the prodigal son a job on his return.[107]

Differences with fathers in youth paradoxically could forge bonds in memory. Walter Southgate was a member of the Social Democratic Foundation, a conscientious objector and activist for the Labour Party. His father's armchair liberalism looked tame in comparison. Father and son's political heroes and solutions were, in many ways, radically different. Nevertheless, Southgate's reproduction of his father's caustic political commentary highlighted basic, shared 'truths'. Southgate recalled his father's sneering contempt for his ornate School Merit Certificate: a 'pinchpenny bit of council cardboard' worth 'the price of a toffee apple when it came to getting a job'.[108] Southgate's narrative replaced youthful indignation with validation of his father's opinion. Having attended a 'ragged School', his father had also received an ornate certificate, which he kept as a symbol of outrage: the word 'ragged' was offensive, fancy scrolls were no substitute for education and patronage was nauseating.[109] The tale of two certificates entwined father and son in a shared critique of the education system. Although Southgate exercised considerable license

---

[107] Shinwell, *Conflict without malice*, 16 and 21–28.
[108] Other examples include reference to the Boer War, religion, funeral custom, patriotism and the thievery of landlords. Southgate, *That's the way it was*, 20; 32; 39; 53; 56; 73.
[109] *Ibid*, 54–5.

in ventriloquising his father's voice, the story identified the Liberal father as a vital cog in the socialist son's political awakening.

Southgate recollected his youthful exasperation with his father's constant interruption of his homework to impart his opinion on assorted issues. Despite best efforts to ignore the older man, Southgate recalled the irresistible pull of debate, a dynamic his mother referred to as 'polishsticks'.[110] Southgate's jaunty tone reflected father and son's shared passion for politics alongside a friendly antagonism that, in all probability, irritated the beleaguered Mrs. Southgate: the playful swipe of that mispronunciation ('polishticks') makes clear the triviality of such talk to a woman trying to juggle domestic management with limited resources. In excluding his mother from debate, Southgate drew a specifically masculine dynamic that paid tribute to his father's fulfilment of an obligation to socialise his son (women, of course, did not have the vote) in the rights and wrongs of Man, even when father and son diverged over ideological responses. Indeed, Southgate's father was repeating the schooling he received from his father as a boy. That Southgate learned this family history from his father perpetuated a radical pedigree, although each heir fashioned his politics to the time. Southgate's memoir interwove the personal and political to demonstrate the family, particularly the father, as the kernel of political conscience.[111] Even where this created conflict in youth, it could be incorporated retrospectively into an elastic conception of fatherly protection to signal reevaluation of a relationship.

Conclusion

Paternal obligations to protect and guide children devolved the privilege of authority on fathers. This was a source of power that some men abused. It exposes the dark side of family life and troubles us because it is a potent reminder of how children seek to manage everyday unhappiness and incorporate the inequalities of family into a normative worldview. For other fathers and children, paternal protection was the well of affection. In the absence of idealised models of 'involved' fathers, that is, fathers who shared childrearing tasks, in late-Victorian and Edwardian contexts, autobiographers could transform men's mundane commitments and obligations into transcendental acts of devotion. The dutiful father was sometimes a feeling father, especially when duty caused men anxiety or discomfort. The degrees to which authors accepted or rejected paternal authority and protection also served as proxy for the

[110] *Ibid*, 102–3.   [111] *Ibid*.

interpersonal acceptance, reconciliation or rejection of the man. Like breadwinning, authors' appropriation of paternal authority and protection as attachment complicates the polarisation between caring *about* (fathers) and caring *for* (mothers) children. To some authors here, fathers who sought to assert authority, influence and protect children could cross the divide from caring *about* them to actively caring *for* them in a moral, affective or disciplinary context, especially when authority and protection had tangible or measurable outcomes.

Conclusion: discovering fatherhood

This book has sought to correct and complicate the liminal presence of working-class men as fathers in historical scholarship on late Victorian and Edwardian Britain. If key components of paternity were fixed in legal and socioeconomic structures, fatherhood as a process, identity and interpersonal relationship was far more fluid. Dynamics between fathers and children were situational, dependent on personalities and changed over the life course. In focusing on autobiography, this book has demonstrated how far adult children located late Victorian and Edwardian fathers in shared, public notions of paternal identity and obligation to articulate the intimate dimensions of interpersonal relationships. Fathers did spend much of their time in work but this did not render them absent from, or even peripheral to, family life. In paying attention to everyday responsibilities and practices, the 'small' things of family life, and the reevaluation of childhood experience and intersubjectivity from the vantage point of maturity, it is possible to firmly embed fathers in domestic childhood contexts and to recognise the importance of fathers in constituting the adult self.

The marginalisation of men in family life is false: on a pragmatic level, most fathers were in the home for at least some of the day, every day, and most had specific paternal spaces within it. On an imaginative level, fathers played a crucial role within family life whereby their obligations to dependents could embed them, in real time and reflection, in children's development and identity. This further suggests that scholars' bifurcation between parenting tasks into caring *for* and caring *about* children may be overstated. Certainly, in recollection, many children interpreted men's waged labour, protection and guidance as caring 'for' them. Likewise, the assumption that 'togetherness' demands special space and/or time in physical proximity excludes many of the abstract associations children drew between fathers, men's interests and attachment. This also raises questions over historians' tendency to correlate family with home, and home with mothers. Family and home were material and imaginative spaces. This research suggests that men were embedded in these spaces. This does not mean that men at home and in family somehow were feminised but rather suggests the bounded nature of historical (and contemporary) understandings of plebeian masculinity, family and domesticity.

Men's material obligations may have removed them from the home on a daily basis but, paradoxically, this could enhance the affective importance of fathers in memory, especially when labour alienated men or placed them in danger. Certainly, children could invest the paternal duty to provide with beautiful properties. This is, perhaps, reassuring for today's parents. For fathers and mothers who are 'absent' through working patterns, children's recollections suggest that work performed *for* children could be freighted with extra economic significance while some adults clearly expressed personal pride in parental work-based skills. There is a danger, however, in continuing to privilege material provision as the key component of fathering. As Lynn Abrams observed in 1999, this has typically meant that fathers are pursued for their money, not their fathering skills. Indeed, family courts in the late-twentieth century perpetuated the late-Victorian assumption that children needed mothers and, beyond financial provision, fathers' input into child development was negligible.[1] While acknowledging the importance of provision as an affective medium for father-child attachment, this book challenges the dominant view of fathers as financial providers and little else.

For most of the autobiographers studied here, men's time in work meant time spent with children adopted particular importance. Even the banal practices of everyday life, such as teatime and men's evening occupation of their chair, became times and spaces for father-child intimacy. In a similar vein, children utilised an elastic conception of fathering to identify men's values, ideals and experiences as intrinsic to paternal identity and to give meaning to interpersonal relations. What men did in their spare time, whether it included children or not, could be appropriated by adult authors to signify authenticity of paternal character, to place fathers on a public scale of esteem to intimate personal feeling and to highlight how fathers might 'matter' in ways that blurred boundaries between public and private; work and home; leisure and childcare.

The book also calls for a reconsideration of working-class memoir. The so-called shortcomings of working-class memoir, as outlined in the introduction, are well documented. But perspectives on working-class writing

---

[1] Abrams, 'There was Nobody like my Daddy', 242.

as limited or clichéd take for granted the 'rightness' of middle-class models of authorship and selfhood. Inevitably, viewed from this perspective, working-class autobiographies can lack literary sophistication and demonstrate limited authorial skill in conveying the complexities of feeling. Yet instead of scholarly focus on what is not there, or the ways in which self-expression might be clumsy, why not read working-class memoir on its own terms? Let's embrace what *is* there, analyse the ways in which these authors *do* give meaning to experience and the forms in which selfhood and affect *are* expressed. As this book demonstrates, even the least 'literary' authors had an internal logic to their memories and could intimate the profundity of relationships through relatively banal expression. The book calls for a rethinking of working-class forms of expression that, instead of patronising assumed triviality and distraction, takes them seriously. One of the most imaginative forms of talking about affective alliances was seemingly through unsophisticated comedy and laughter, supposedly the antithesis of profound feeling and, too often, taken literally to stereotype working-class culture.

As noted above, polarisations between mothers and children on the one hand, and fathers on the other, may provide the framework for many of the stories told, but they were far from rigid. Children often were caught in the power play between spouses, but affinities with mothers, especially over time, cannot be taken for granted. Undoubtedly, some men negatively affected family life, but this book suggests that the conflation of children's experience of oppression and inequality with that of mothers is unsatisfactory. While the majority of authors aligned their child self's interests with those of mothers, sympathised with maternal suffering and understood their father first and foremost through the lens of their mothers' perspective, these views were neither fixed nor straightforward. Moreover, scholars' tendency to collapse children's experience into that of mothers does not convey the conflicted loyalties of family life or children's attempts to give meaning to family intersubjectivities over the life course and in relation to other factors, such as sibling conflict, the different experiences of friends and adult's repetition and recognition of personal and parental (mother and father) flaws.

For children who did not necessarily articulate attachment to fathers in childhood, reflective evaluations that took a 'strengths-based' perspective of fatherhood enabled authors to consider what father did as pivotal to understanding who he was, rather than focusing on his flaws, failures and absences. This could facilitate a retrospective acknowledgement of the complexity of family life, conflicts and loyalties, and, in some cases, germinate new sympathies and insights into men as fathers rather than men as mothers' husbands. When Loane asked if working-class men were any 'less self-sacrificing, less solicitous, less devoted' than their bourgeois counterparts, the answer in this book is not for most children, not for most of the time. This is not because working-class fathers were 'less affectionate' than middle-class men were but because few father-child relationships (or mother-child for that matter), regardless of class, were fixed.

The perpetuation of historical models of 'family' that privilege mothers and children supports the lazy assumption that histories of family are of interest mostly to women and that fatherhood is, somehow, not a feminist issue. Yet, as Adrienne Burgess of contemporary lobby group The Fatherhood Institute observes, feminists generate much of the contemporary research on fathers and children.[2] In order to comprehend the family, including women and children's experiences of oppression and inequality, we need to address and understand men's place within it and different family members' experience. For some scholars, the study of family relationships and interpersonal, affective relations threatens to be inward looking and fragmented, and distracts from 'big' issues of class, power and politics.[3] As this book demonstrates, family is where individuals learn about power and structural inequities. Narratives of affective family relationships could be saturated with political significance, for feminists certainly, but for trade union, education and political activists, too. In many of the autobiographies cited here, the family story provided a public-private interface for explaining the development, character and expression of ideological subjectivities. Autobiography was a deliberate exercise in charting, defending and justifying a present self in light of past choices and experiences; personal histories were inextricable from the formation of beliefs and values. The overwhelming majority of authors here depicted childhood as the first locus of class-consciousness (that is, consciousness of class and, for others, a less politically defined sense of 'otherness'). Adult memories of parents and grandparents who experienced hardship and slaved for their offspring were powerful motors, in literary and experiential terms, to varying degrees of dissatisfaction with socioeconomic, age and gendered (that is, for both genders) inequalities. Intimate histories are not the antithesis of 'big' politics; they are the very things that underpin those politics.

As the autobiographies studied in this book demonstrate, fathers (biological or otherwise; present and absent) were no less important to

---

[2] Burgess, *The fatherhood institute*, 9–15.
[3] Selina Todd, 'History from below: modern British scholarship' in 'The future of history from below', www.manyheadedmonster.wordpress.com/2013/08/23/selina-todd-history-from-below-modern-british-scholarship/.

creating a coherent story of personal development than mothers. This is not to suggest that fathers and mothers were the same but rather to urge that for most adults, fathers in their many forms really did, and do, matter. Authors depicted relationships with fathers as characterised by conflicting, changeable, manifold feelings: pity, pride, gratitude, appreciation, frustration, disappointment, loathing, resentment, jealousy, enchantment, anger, empathy, fear, compassion, devotion and pleasure. These sensations were not mutually exclusive; they highlight the kaleidoscopic, situational ambivalences of human relationships. The working-class family, of course, depended on women's exploitation under patriarchy. Many adult authors giving meaning to their childhood and constructing adult subjectivities paid tribute to their mothers for the many sacrifices women made on behalf of offspring. But the majority of authors also said so much more. Working-class families were complex formations; they involved members in multiple, shifting and specific inter-personal relationships. They could be places of frustration, fear, affection and comfort. More to the point, fathers were deeply embedded in the multifaceted adult understandings of that family.

Bibliography

FILM

North of England Film Bureau, *Durham Miner's Gala*, black and white silent film, 35mm, North West Film Archive, Manchester Metropolitan University.
A day in the life of a coal miner (1910), Kineto Films. 35mm, black and white, silent film. North West Film Archive, Manchester Metropolitan University
Screening the poor, 1888–1914, curated by Martin Loiperdinger and Ludwig Vogl-Bienek (Edition Filmmuseum, 2011)

MANUSCRIPT SOURCES

John Rylands Deansgate Library. Manchester City Mission, 'Look on the Fields', 1910. Wood Street Mission Archive, WSM 14/1
Liverpool City Archives, League of Welldoers, M364 LWD 7/1 LWD Publications, 1893–1936

NEWSPAPERS

Daily Mirror
Illustrated Police News
Lloyds Weekly Newspaper
Penny Illustrated Paper
Reynolds Weekly Newspaper

ORAL HISTORY COLLECTIONS

Elizabeth Roberts Oral History Collection, University of Lancaster
Bolton Archives and Local Studies Oral History Collection, Bolton Archives and Local Studies

AUTOBIOGRAPHIES

George Acorn, *One of the multitude* (London: William Heinemann, 1911)
Guy Aldred, *No traitor's gait! The autobiography of Guy A. Aldred* (London: The Strickland Press, 1956)
Ernest Ambrose *Melford memories: recollections of 94 years* (Melford: Long Melford History and Archaeology Society, 1972)

Elizabeth Andrews, *A woman's work is never done* (ed. Ursula Masson; Place: Honno Classics, [1967] 2006)
Francis Anthony, *A man's a man* (London, 1932)
Chester Armstrong, *Pilgrimage from Nenthead: an autobiography* (London: Methuen and Co Ltd., 1938)
George Baldry, *The rabbit skin cap: a tale of a Norfolk countryman's youth*. Ed. By Lilias Rider Haggard (Ipswich: Boydell Press, 1974).
Phillip Ballard, *Things I cannot forget* (London: University of London Press, 1937)
George Barber, *From workhouse to Lord Mayor: an autobiography* (Tunstall: The Author, 1937)
Tom Barclay, *Memoirs and medleys: the autobiography of a bottle washer* (Leicester: Edgar Backus, 1934)
Joseph Barlow Brooks, *Lancashire bred: an autobiography* (Oxford: Church Army Press, 1951)
Thomas Bell, *Pioneering days* (London: Laurence and Wishart, 1941)
Silvester Gordon Boswell, *The book of Boswell: autobiography of a gypsy* (London: Victor Gollancz, 1970)
George Bourne, *Change in the village* (London: Gerald Duckworth & Co., 1955)
Fred Bower, *Rolling stonemason: an autobiography* (London: Jonathon Cape, 1936)
William Bowyer, *Brought out in evidence: an autobiographical summing up* (London: Faber and Faber, 1941)
Barnabas Britten, *Woodyard to palace: reminiscences* (Bradford: Broadacre Books, 1958)
Percy Brown, *Round the corner* (London: Faber and Faber, 1934)
William J. Brown, *So Far* (London: George Allen and Unwin Ltd., 1943)
Elizabeth Bryson, *Look back in wonder* (Dundee: David Winter and Son Ltd., 1966)
Reader Bullard, *The camels must go* (London: Faber and Faber, 1961)
Thomas Burke, *The wind and the rain: a book of confessions* (London: Thornton Butterworth, 1924).
Mick Burke, *Ancoats lad: the recollections of Mick Burke* (Manchester: Neil Richardson, 1985)
H. M. Burton, *There was a young man* (London, 1958)
Sidney Campion, *Sunlight on the foothills* (London: Rich and Cowan, 1941)
Neville Cardus, *Autobiography* (London: Collins, 1947)
Centreprise, *The Island: the life and death of an East London community, 1870–1970* (London, 1979)
Charles Chaplin, *My early years* (London: Bodley Had, 1979)
A. V. Christie, *Brass tacks and a fiddle* (Kilmarnock: Author, 1943)
Walter Citrine, *Men and work: an autobiography* (London: Hutchinson, 1964)
J. R. Clynes, *Memoirs 1869–1924* (London: Hutchinson and Co., 1937).
A. E. Coppard, *It's me, O Lord! An abstract and brief chronicle of some of the life with some of the opinions of A. E. Coppard* (London: Methuen & Co., 1957)
J. H. Crawford, *The autobiography of a tramp* (London: Longmans Green and co, 1900)
Aubrey Darby, *A view from the alley* (Cornwall: Judith Darby, 2012)

David Davies, *In search of myself: the autobiography of D. R. Davies* (London: Geoffrey Bles, 1961)
Fred Davies, *My father's eyes: episodes in the life of a Hulme man* (Manchester: Neil Richardson, 1985)
Kathleen Dayus, *Her people* (London: Virago, 1982)
Wil Edwards, *From the valley I came: reminiscences of the author's life up to 1926, with special reference to his mother* (London: Angus and Robertson, 1956)
John Eldred, *I love the brooks: reminiscences* (London: Skeffington, 1955)
Ralph Finn, *Time remembered: the tale of an East End Jewish boy* (London: Hale, 1963)
Elizabeth Flint, *Hot bread and chips* (London: Museum Press, 1963)
Grace Foakes, *Four meals for fourpence: a heart-warming tale of family life in London's old East End* (London: Virago, 2011)
Alice Foley, *A Bolton childhood* (Manchester University Press and WEA, 1973)
V. W. Garratt, *A man in the street* (London: J. M. Dent and Sons, 1939)
Arthur Gair, *Copt Hill to Ryhope: a colliery engineer's life* (Cheter-le-Street: Crichton Publishing Co., 1982)
Rose Gibbs, *In service: Rose Gibbs remembers* (Royston: Archives for Bassingbourn and Comberton Village Colleges, 1981)
Harry Gosling, *Up and down stream* (London: Methurn and Co., 1927)
Edmund Gosse, *Father and son: a study in two temperaments* (London: William Heinemann, 1907)
Fred Gresswell, *Bright boots* (London: Robert Hale Ltd., 1956)
James Griffiths, *Pages from memory* (London: J.M. Dent and Sons, 1969)
Mark Grossek, *First movement* (London: Geoffrey Bles, 1937)
Anthony George Grundy, *My fifty years in transport* (Buckingham: Adam Gordon, [1944] 1997)
George Hardy, *Those stormy years: memories of the fight for freedom on five continents* (London: Lawrence and Wishart, 1956)
Harry Harris, *Under oars: reminiscences of a Thames lighterman, 1894–1909* (London: Centreprise Trust, 1978)
Henry Hawker, *Notes of my life, 1870–1918* (Stonehouse: W. G. Davis, 1919)
Percy A. Heard, *An octogenarian's memoirs* (Ilfracombe: Stockwell, 1974)
Richard Hillyer, *Country boy: the autobiography of Richard Hillyer* (London: Hodder and Stoughton, 1966)
T. J. Hunt, *The life story of T. J. Hunt: an autobiography* ((London: T. J. Hunt, 1936)
Philip Inman, *No going back* (London: Williams and Norgate, 1952)
T. A. Jackson, *Solo trumpet: some memories of socialist agitation and propaganda* (London: Lawrence and Wishart, 1953)
Albert S. Jasper, *A Hoxton childhood* (Slough: Barrie & Rockliff, 1971)
Henry Jones, *Old memories: autobiography of Sir Henry Jones*, edited by Thomas Jones (London: Hodder & Stoughton Ltd., 1924)
Jack Jones, *Unfinished journey* (New York: Oxford University Press, 1937)
Lewis Jones, *Cwmardy: the story of a Welsh mining valley* (Cardigan: Pathian, [1937] 2006)
Joseph Keating, *My struggle for life* (London: Simpkin, Marshall, Hamilton, Kent and Co., 1916)

Charles Kightly (ed.), *Country voices: life and love in farm and village* (London: Thames and Hudson, 1984)
David Kirkwood, *My life of revolt* (London: G.G. Harrap & Co., 1935)
Henry Lauder, *Roamin' in the gloamin'* (London: Hutchinson and Co., 1928)
Jack Lawson, *A man's life* (London: Hodder and Stoughton, 1932)
W. M. Lax, *His book. The autobiography of Lax of Poplar* (London: The Epworth Press, 1937)
Michael Llewellyn, *Sand in the glass* (London: John Murray, 1943)
John McGovern, *Neither fear nor favour* (London: Blandford Press, 1960)
Patrick Macgill, *Children of the dead end: the autobiography of a navvy* (Ascot: Caliban, [1914] 1980)
Albert Mainsbridge, *The trodden road: experience, inspiration and belief* (London: J.M. Dent and Sons, 1940)
Jack Martin, *Ups and downs: the life story of a working man* (Bolton: Stephenson, 1973)
Betty May, *Tiger woman: my story* (London: Duckworth, 1929)
George Meek, *Bath chair man; by himself* (London: Constable, 1910)
Herbert Morrison, *An autobiography* (London: Oldhams Press Ltd., 1960)
Edwin Muir, *An autobiography* (London: The Hogarth Press, 1954)
Pat O'Mara, *Liverpool Irish slummy* (Liverpool: Bluecoat Press, 2007)
John Paton, *Proletarian pilgrimage: the autobiography of John Paton* (London: Routledge & Sons, 1935)
Margaret Penn, *Manchester fourteen miles* (Firle: Caliban, 1979)
Elsie Pettigrew, *Time to remember: growing up in Liverpool from 1912* (Liverpool: Toulouse, 1989)
Florence Petty, *The pudding lady. A new departure in social work* (London: Stead's Publishing House, 1912)
Margaret Powell, *Below stairs* (London: Pan, 1970)
Edward Purkiss, *The memories of a London orphan boy* (Bexley: The Author, 1957)
George Ratcliffe, *Sixty years of it: being the story of my life and public career* (London: A. Brown and Sons Ltd., 1935)
George Reakes, *Man of the Mersey* (London: Christopher Johnson, 1956)
George Reilly, *I walk with the king* ed. by Sarah Reilly (London: Epworth Press, 1931)
Jean Rennie, *Every other Sunday: the autobiography of a kitchen maid* (London: Arthur Barker, 1955)
Robert Roberts, *A classic slum: Salford life in the first quarter of the century* (London: Harmondsworth, 1971)
James Royce, *I stand nude* (London: Hutchinson and Co., 1937)
Dolly Scannell, *Mother knew best: an East End childhood* (London: Macmillan, 1974)
Sam Shaw, *Guttersnipe* (London: Sampson Low, 1946)
Emanuel Shinwell, *Conflict without malice* (London: Odhams Press, 1955)
Lilian Slater, *'Think on!' said Mam: a childhood in Bradford, Manchester 1911–1919* (Manchester: Neil Richardson, 1984)
Emma Smith, *A Cornish waif's story: true tale of a workhouse child* (London: Odhams Press Ltd., [1954] 2010)

Rodney Smith, *Gipsy Smith: his life and work* (London: National Council for the Evangelical Free Churches, [1911] 1998)
Lord Snell, *Men, movements and myself* (London: J.M. Dent and Son, 1936)
Bob Stewart, *Breaking the fetters* (London: Laurence and Wishart, 1967)
Walter Southgate, *That's the way it was* (Oxted: New Clarion Press, 1982)
Joseph Stamper, *So long ago* (London: Hutchinson, 1960)
   Less than dust: the memoirs of a tramp (London: Hutchinson & Co., 1938)
Allan Taylor, *From a Glasgow slum to Fleet Street* (London: Alvin Redman Ltd., 1949)
Lord Taylor, *Uphill all the way: a miner's struggle* (London: Sidgwick and Jackson, 1972)
John Birch Thomas, *Shop boy: an autobiography* (London: Routledge and Kegan Paul, 1983)
Joseph Toole, *Fighting through life* (London: Rich and Crown, 1935)
Tom Tremewan, *Cornish youth: memories of a Perran boy, 1895–1910* (Truro: Oscar Blackford, 1968)
Ben Turner, *About myself, 1863–1930* (London: Humphrey Toulmin, 1930)
James Turner, *Hard-up husband: James Turner's Halifax diary, 1881/2* (Cambridge: Ellisons editions, 1981)
Edgar Wallace, *People: a short autobiography* (London: Hodder and Stoughton, 1926)
Thomas Warr, *Fogs lifted: a slum child's story* (London: Simpkin, Marshall and Co., 1909)
Henry Watkin, *From Hulme all blessings flow* (Manchester: Neil Richardson, 1985)
T. A. Westwater, *The early life of T. A. Westwater: railway signalman, trade unionist and town councillor in County Durham* (Oxford: Ruskin College, 1979)
Kathleen Woodward, *Jipping Street* (London: Virago, 1983)

OTHER PRINTED SOURCES

Lynn Abrams, 'There was nobody like my Daddy: fathers, the family and the marginalisation of men in modern Scotland', *Scottish Historical Review* 78:2 (1999), 219–42
Robert Ainslie, *The rod and its uses, or Thomas Dodd and Bill Collins* (London: S. W. Partridge, 1865)
Anonymous, 'Review: Mrs. S. A. Barnett, *The making of the home*', *Academy*, 716 (Jan, 1886), 57
Neil Armstrong, 'Father(ing) Christmas: fatherhood, gender and modernity in Victorian and Edwardian England' in Trev Lynn Broughton and Helen Rogers (eds.), *Gender and fatherhood in the nineteenth century* (Basingstoke: Palgrave, 2006), 96–110
Andrew August, *Poor Women's Lives: gender, work and poverty in late-Victorian London* (London and Cranbury: Associated University Presses, 1999)
   'A culture of consolation? Rethinking politics in working-class London, 1870–1914', *Historical Research*, 74:184 (2001), 193–219.
Victor Bailey, *This rash act: suicide across the life cycle* (Stanford University Press, 1998)

Joanne Bailey, *Unquiet lives: marriage and marriage breakdown in England, 1660–1800* (Cambridge: Cambridge University Press, 2003)
  Parenting in England, 1760–1830: emotion, identity, and generation (Oxford University Press, 2012)
Peter Bailey, *Leisure and class in Victorian England: rational recreation and the contest for control, 1830–85* (London: Methuen, 1978)
  'Will the real Bill Banks please stand up? Towards a role analysis of mid-Victorian working-class respectability', *Journal of Social History*, 12 (1979) 336–53
  Popular culture and performance in the Victorian city (Cambridge University Press, 1998)
Mikhail Bakhtin, *Rabelais and his world* trans. Helene Iswolsky; (Bloomington: Indiana University Press, 1984)
Henrietta Barnett, *The making of the home: a reading book of domestic economy for school and home use* (London: Cassell and Co., Ltd, 1885).
Brad Beaven, *Leisure, citizenship and working-class men in Britain, 1850–1945* (Manchester University Press, 2005)
William Beveridge, *Unemployment: a problem of industry* (London: Longman and Co., 1909)
Alison Blunt and Robyn Dowling, *Home* (London: Routledge, 2006)
Helen Dendy Bosanquet, *The family* (London: Macmillan and Co., 1906)
J. Bourke, *Working-class cultures in Britain, 1890–1960: gender, class and ethnicity* (London: Routledge, 1993)
A. L. Bowley and A. R. Burnett-Hurst, *Livelihood and poverty: a study of the economic conditions of working-class households in Northampton, Warrington, Stanley and Reading* (London: Bell, 1915)
Gary Boyd-Hope and Andrew Sargent, *Railways and rural life: SWA Newton and the Great Central Railway* (Swindon: English Heritage, 2007)
George Boyer, 'The evolution of unemployment relief in Great Britain', *Journal of Interdisciplinary History*, 34:3 (2003), 393–434
Nelsie Brooks, *Never give up: a Christmas story for working men and their wives* (London: S. W. Partridge, 1862)
  Nothing like example and George Ranford's happy Christmas Eve, or, facts for young working men (London: S. W. Partridge, 1874)
Trev Lynn Broughton and Helen Rogers, 'Introduction: the empire of the father' in Broughton and Rogers, *Gender and fatherhood* (2006), 1–30
Inga Bryden and Janet Floyd (eds.), *Domestic space: reading the nineteenth-century interior* (Manchester University Press, 1999)
Elizabeth Buettner, 'Fatherhood real, imagined, denied: British men in Imperial India' in Broughton and Rogers (eds.), *Gender and fatherhood*, (2006) 178–189
Carolyn Burdett, Introduction to New Agenda: sentimentalities', *Journal of Victorian Culture*, 16:2 (2011), 187–194
Adrienne Burgess, *The Fatherhood Institute: advocating for involved fatherhood in the UK, 1999–2012* (London: The Fatherhood Institute, 2012)
John Burnett, *Idle hands: the experience of unemployment, 1790–1990* (London: Routledge, 1994)

Edward Cadbury, Cecile Matheson and George Shann, *Women's work and wages: a phase in an industrial city* (London: T. Fisher Unwin, 1908)
Julia Chandler, *A night with baby* (Stourbridge: J Thomas Ford, 1873)
Carl Chinn, *They worked all their lives: women of the urban poor, 1880–1939* (Manchester University Press, 1988)
Anna Clark, *The struggle for the breeches: gender and the making of the British working class* (London: Rovers Oram, 1995)
  'The New Poor Law and the breadwinner wage: contrasting assumptions', *Journal of Social History*, 34:2 (2000), 261–82
  "Domesticity and the problem of wife beating in nineteenth-century Britain: working-class culture, law and politics' in Shani D'Cruze (ed.), *Everyday violence in Britain, 1850–1950: Gender and class*, (Harlow: Longman, 2000), 27–40
Candace Clark, 'Emotions and micro-politics in everyday life: some patterns and paradoxes of "place"' in T. Kemper(ed.), *Research agendas in the sociology of emotions* (Albany: State University of New York Press, 1990), 305–334
  Misery and company: sympathy in everyday life (Chicago and London: University of Chicago Press, 1997)
Thomas Legh Claughton, *The duty of fathers concerning the education of their children. A [short, plain] sermon addressed to the working classes* (Oxford: J. Henry and J. Parker, 1864)
Deborah Cohen, *Household gods: the British and their possessions* (New Haven and London: Yale University Press, 2006)
Anne Collins, *Attachment* (London: Fostering Network, 2008)
Colin Creighton, 'The rise of the male breadwinner family: a reappraisal', *Comparative Studies in Society and History*, 38 (1996), 310–337
  'The rise and decline of the "Male Breadwinner Family" in Britain', *Cambridge Journal of Economics* 23:5 (1999), pp. 519–41
Andy Croll, *Civilizing the urban: popular culture and public space in Merthyr, 1870–1914* (Cardiff: University of Wales Press, 2000)
  'Starving strikers and the limits of the "humanitarian discovery of hunger" in late-Victorian Britain', *International Review of Social History*, 56: 1 (2011), 103–131
Shani D'Cruze 'Unguarded passions: violence, history and the everyday' in *Everyday violence in Britain, 1850–1950: Gender and class*, (Harlow: Longman, 2000), 1–26
  'The eloquent corpse: gender, probity and bodily integrity in Victorian domestic murder' in Judith Rowbotham and Kim Stevenson (eds.), *Criminal conversations: Victorian crimes, social panic and moral outrage* (Columbus: Ohio State University Press, 2005), 181–197
Kerry Daly, 'Deconstructing family time: from ideology to lived experience', *Journal of Marriage and Family* 63:2 (2001), 283–94
Leonore Davidoff, Megan Doolittle, Janet Fink and Katherine Holden, *The family story: blood, contract and intimacy, 1830–1960* (London and New York: Longman, 1999)
Andrew Davies, *Leisure, gender and poverty: working-class culture in Salford and Manchester, 1900–1939* (Buckingham: Open University Press, 1992)

Jessica Milner Davis, *Farce* (London: Methuen and co., 1978)
Lucy Delap, 'Kitchen sink laughter: domestic service humour in twentieth century Britain', *Journal of British Studies*, 49:3 (2010), 623–54
Esther Dermott, *Intimate fatherhood: a sociological analysis* (London: Routledge, 2008)
Thomas Dixon, *From passions to emotions: the creation of a secular psychological category* (Cambridge University Press, 2003)
Robert Dolling, *Ten years in a Portsmouth slum* (London: Swan Sonneschein & Co., 1896)
Megan Doolittle, 'Fatherhood and family shame: masculinity, welfare and the workhouse in late-nineteenth-century England' in Lucy Delap, Ben Griffin and Abigail Wills (eds.), *The politics of domestic authority in Britain since 1800* (Basingstoke: Palgrave Macmillan, 2009), 84–109
  'Time, space and memories: the father's chair and grandfather clocks in Victorian working-class domestic lives', *Home Cultures*, 8:3 (2011), 245–264
  'Fatherhood, religious belief and the protection of children in nineteenth-century English families' in Broughton and Rogers (eds.), *Gender and Fatherhood*, (2006), 31–42
Nadja Durbach, *Bodily matters: the anti-vaccination movement in England, 1853–1907* (Durham, N.C.: Duke University Press, 2005)
T. Eagleton, *Walter Benjamin, or towards a revolutionary criticism* (London: NLB/Verso, 1981)
The Economic Club, *Family Budgets, being the income and expenses of twenty-eight British Households, 1891–1894* (London: P.S. King and Son, 1896)
Tim Fisher, 'Fatherhood and the British Fathercraft Movement, 1919–1939', *Gender and History* 17:2 (2005), 441–62
Martin Francis, 'The domestication of the male? Recent research on nineteenth and twentieth-century British masculinity', *Historical Journal*, 45:3, (2002), 637–52
  'Tears, tantrums, and bared teeth: the emotional economy of three Conservative Prime Ministers, 1951–1963', *Journal of British Studies*, 41:3 (2002), 354–87
Elaine Freedgood, *The ideas in things: fugitive meaning in the Victorian novel* (Chicago and London: University of Chicago Press, 2006)
Sam Friedman and Giselinde Kuipers, 'The divisive power of humour: comedy, taste and symbolic boundaries', *Cultural Sociology*, 7:2 (2013), 179–195
Ginger Frost, *Living in sin: co-habiting as husband and wife in the nineteenth century* (Manchester University Press, 2008)
Reginia Gagnier, *Subjectivities: a history of self-representation, 1832–1920* (Oxford University Press, 1991)
Vic Gatrell, *City of laughter: sex and satire in eighteenth-century London* (London: Atlantic Books, 2006)
John Gillis, 'Making time for family: the invention of family time(s) and the reinvention of family history', *Journal of Family History*, 21 (1996), 4–21
  World of their own making: myth, ritual and the question for family values (Oxford University press, 1997)
George Gissing, *The nether world* (London: J.M. Dent and Sons, [1889] 1976)
Erving Goffman, *The presentation of self in everyday life* (London: Penguin, 1990)

Susan Goldberg, *Attachment and development* (London: Arnold, 2000)
Donna Goldstein, *Laughter out of place: race, class, violence, and sexuality in a Rio shantytown* (Berkeley, CA; London: University of California Press, 2003)
Eleanor Gordon and Gwyneth Nair, 'Fathers and the Victorian Parental Role', *Women's History Review* 15:4 (2006), 551–9
Nina Gorst, *The thief on the cross* (London: Evelegh Nash, 1908)
Philip Greven, *Spare the child: the religious roots of physical punishment and the psychological impact of physical abuse* (New York: Alfred Knopf, 1990).
Nan Hackett, 'A different form of self: narrative style in British nineteenth-century working-class autobiography', *Biography* 12:3 (1989), 208–26
Frederick Hastings, *Back streets and London slums* (London: Religious Tract Society, 1888)
Elizabeth Hallam and Jenny Hockey, *Death, memory and material culture* (Oxford: Berg, 2001)
Thomas Hamer, *Nellie Barton or her father's ransom* (London & New York: Frederick Warne, 1885)
Jane Hamlett, *Material relations: domestic interiors and middle-class families in England, 1850–1910* (Manchester University Press, 2010)
James A. Hammerton, *Cruelty and companionship: conflict in nineteenth-century married life* (London and New York: Routledge, 1992)
José Harris, *Unemployment and politics: a study in English social policy, 1886–1914* (Oxford: Clarendon, 1972)
Karen Harvey and Alexandra Sherpard, 'What have historians done with masculinity? Reflections on five centuries of British history, 1500–1950', *Journal of British Studies* 44 (2005), 274–80
Karen Harvey, 'Barbarity in a teacup? Punch, domesticity and gender in the Eighteenth Century, *Journal of Design History*, 21:3 (2008), 205–21
  'Men making home: masculinity and domesticity in eighteenth-century England', *Gender and History*, 21:3 (2009), 520–40
Ernest Hennock, *The origin of the welfare state in England and Germany, 1850–1914: social polices compared* (Cambridge University Press, 2007)
Martin Hewitt, *The emergence of stability in the industrial city: Manchester 1832–67* (Aldershot: Scolar Press, 1996)
  'District visiting and the constitution of domestic space in the mid-nineteenth century' in Bryden and Floyd, *Domestic space* (1999), 121–41
Octavia Hill, 'Blocks of model dwellings: influence on character', in Charles Booth (ed.), *Life and labour of the people in London* Volume 2 (1891)
John Hobson, *Problems of poverty: an inquiry into the industrial conditions of the poor* (London: Methuen and Co., 1891)
Eric Hobsbawm, 'The tramping artisan', *Economic History Review*, New Series, 3:3 (1951), 299–320
Silas Hocking, *Her Benny* (Liverpool: Gallery Press, [1879] 1968)
Richard Hoggart, *The uses of literacy: aspects of working-class life* (London: Penguin, 2009)
Katrina Honeyman and Jordan Goodman, 'Women's work, gender conflict and labour markets in Europe 1500–1900', *Economic History Review*, 44 (1991), 608–628

S. Horrell and J. Humphries, 'The origins and expansion of the male breadwinner family: the case of nineteenth-century Britain', *International Review of Social History* 42 (1997), 25–64

S. Horrell and D. Oxley, 'Crust or crumb? Intra-household resource allocation and male breadwinning in late-Victorian Britain', *Economic History Review* 52:3 (1999), 494–521

Howard & Co.'s comic annual (London: Howard & Co., 1892–1903)

Matt Houlbrook, 'A pin to see the peepshow: culture, fiction and selfhood in Edith Thompson's letters, 1921–22', *Past and present*, 207 (2010), 215–49

Mike Huggins and J. A. Mangan (eds.), *Disreputable pleasures: less virtuous Victorians at play* London: Cass, 2004)

Mike Huggins, *The Victorians and sport* (London: Hambledon, 2007)

Jane Humphries, *Childhood and child labour in the British Industrial Revolution* (Cambridge University Press, 2010)

H. Hunter and Walter Redmond, *The beautiful baby, or Dr. Ridge's food* (London: Unknown, 1876)

Karl Ittmann, *Work, gender and family in Victorian England* (London: Macmillan, 1994)

Louise Jackson, *Child sexual abuse in Victorian England* (London: Routledge, 2000)

Louise Jermy, *The Memories of a working woman* (Norwich: Goose and Son Ltd., 1934)

Martin Johnes, 'Pigeon racing and working-class culture in Britain, c. 1870–1950', *Cultural and Social History*, 4:3 (2007), 361–83

Paul Johnson, *Saving and spending: the working-class economy in Britain, 1870–1939* (Oxford: Clarendon, 1985)

Ben Jones, 'The uses of nostalgia: autobiography, community publishing and working-class neighbourhoods in post-war England', *Cultural and Social History*, 7:3 (2010) 355–74

Joseph Kestner, *Masculinities in Victorian painting* (Aldershot: Scolar Press, 1995)

Dagmar Kift, *The Victorian music hall: culture, class and conflict* (Cambridge University Press, 1996)

Laura King, 'Hidden Fathers? The significance of fatherhood in mid-twentieth-century Britain', *Contemporary British History* 26:1 (2012), 25–46

'"Now you see a great many men pushing their pram proudly": family-orientated masculinity represented and experienced in mid-twentieth-century Britain', *Cultural and Social History* 10:4 (2013), 599–617

Family men: fatherhood and masculinity in Britain, c.1914–1960 (Oxford University Press, 2014)

Neville Kirk, *Change, continuity and class: labour in British society, 1850–1920* (Manchester University Press, 1998)

Seth Koven, *Sexual and social politics in Victorian London* (University of Princeton Press, 2004)

Tamar Kremer-Sadlik, Marilena Fatigante and Alessandra Fasulo, 'Discourses on family time: the cultural interpretation of family togetherness in Los Angeles and Rome', *Ethos*, 36:3 (2008), 283–309

Clare Langhamer, *Women's leisure in England, 1920–1960* (Manchester University Press, 2000)

'The meanings of home in post-war Britain', *Journal of Contemporary History* 40:2 (2005), 341–62

'Love, selfhood and authenticity in post-war Britain', *Cultural and social history*, 9:2 (2012), 277–97.

The English in love: the intimate story of an emotional revolution (Oxford: Oxford University Press, 2013)

Jon Lawrence, 'Class, 'affluence' and the study of everyday life in Britain, c. 1930–64', *Cultural and social history*, 10:2 (2013) 273–299

Lynn Hollen Lees, *The solidarities of strangers: the English poor laws, 1700–1948* (Cambridge University Press, 1998)

Henri Lefebvre, *Critique of everyday life*, trans. John Moore (London: Verso, 2008)

Marjorie Levine-Clark, 'The politics of preference: masculinity, marital status and unemployment relief in post-First World War Britain', *Cultural and social history*, 7:2 (2010), 233–52

Jane Lewis, 'Gender and the development of welfare regimes', *Journal of European Policy*, 2 (1992), 159–173

J. Lewis, 'The decline of the male breadwinner model: the implications for work and care', *Social Politics* 8:2 (2001), 152–70

Jane Lewis, *The politics of motherhood: child and maternal welfare in England, 1900–1939* (London: Croom Helm, 1980)

Jane Lewis, (ed.), *Labour and love: women's experiences of home and family, 1850–1940* (Oxford: Blackwell, 1986)

M. Loane, *The Queen's poor: life as they find it in town and country* (London: Edward Arnold, 1906)

M. Loane, *The next street but one* (London: Edward Arnold, 1908a)

From their point of view (London: Edward Arnold, 1908b)

An Englishman's castle (London: Edward Arnold, 1909)

Thad Logan, *The Victorian parlour* (Cambridge University Press, 2001)

Thomas S. Lonsdale, *A night with the baby* (London: C. Sheard, 1884)

Matthew McCormack, 'Married men and the fathers of families: fatherhood and franchise reform in Britain' in Broughton and Rogers, *Gender and fatherhood*, (2006), 43–54

Jane McDermid, 'The making of a 'domestic' life: memories of a working woman', *Labour History Review*, 73:3 (2008), 253–268

Michael McKeon, *The secret history of domesticity: public, private and the division of knowledge* (Baltimore: John Hopkins University Press, 2006)

Donald MacDonald, *Will o' the wisp flashes: a selection of stories, sketches, poems and c.* (Dundee: J. Leng & Co., 1890)

Albert Mainsbridge, *Margaret McMillan, prophet and pioneer* (1932)

Anna Martin, 'The irresponsibility of the father' in Ellen Ross (ed.), *Slum travellers: ladies and London poverty, 1880–1920* (Berkley, London: University of California Press, 2007), 148–60

Andy Medhurst, *A national joke: popular comedy and English cultural identities* (London: Routledge, 2007)

Jacob Middleton, 'The experience of corporal punishment in schools, 1890–1940', *History of Education* 37:2 (2008), 253–75

'The cock of the school: a cultural history of playground violence in Britain, 1880–1940', *Journal of British Studies*, 52 (2013), 1–21

Daniel Miller, *A theory of shopping* (London: Polity, 1998)

The comfort of things (Cambridge: Polity Press, 2008)

Stuff (Cambridge: Polity Press, 2009)

Claudia Nelson *Invisible men: fatherhood in Victorian periodicals, 1850–1910* (1995)

Alastair Owens, Nigel Jeffries, Karen Wehner and Rupert Featherby, 'Fragments of the modern city: material culture and the rhythm of everyday life in Victorian London', *Journal of Victorian Culture* (2010), 15:2, 212–225

Susan Pederson, *Family, dependence and the origins of the British welfare state* (Cambridge University Press, 1993)

Anna Pertierra, 'Creating order through struggle in revolutionary Cuba' in Daniel Miller (ed.), *Anthropology and the individual* (Oxford: Berg, 2009), 145–58

Linda Pollock, *Forgotten children: parent-child relations from 1500–1900* (Cambridge University Press, 1983)

'Anger and the negotiation of relationships in early modern England', *Historical Journal*, 47:3 (2004), 567–90

Leonard Potts, *Comedy* (London: Hutchinson's University Library, 1949)

Edwin Pugh, *The Cockney at home: stories and studies of London life and character* (London: Chapman & Hall Ltd., 1914)

Ellen Ranyard, 'Dinner for the bread-winner' in Ross, *Slum Travellers* (2007), 198–207.

Eleanor Rathbone, *Report on the results of a special inquiry into the conditions of labour at the Liverpool Docks* (Liverpool Economic and Statistical Society, 1903-4)

William Reddy, *The navigation of feeling: a framework for the history of emotions* (Cambridge University Press, 2001)

Maud Pember Reeves, *Family life on a pound a week* (London: Fabian Society, 1912)

Helen Rogers, 'In the name of the father: political biographies by radical daughters' in David Amigoni (ed.), *Life writing and Victorian culture* (Aldershot: Ashgate, 2006), 145–164

Helen Rogers, 'First in the house: daughters on working-class fathers and fatherhood' in Broughton and Rogers, *Gender and fatherhood*, (2006), 126–37

Michael Roper, 'Splitting in unsent letters: writing as a social practice and a psychological activity', *Social History*, 26:3 (2001), 318–39

'Slipping out of view: subjectivity and emotion in gender history', *History workshop journal*, 59 (2005), 57–72

The secret battle: emotional survival in the Great War (Manchester University Press, 2011)

Jonathan Rose, *The intellectual life of the British working classes* (New Haven and London: Yale University Press, 2001)

Lionel Rose, *Rogues and vagabonds: vagrant underworld in Britain 1815–1985* (London: Routledge, 1988)

Sonya O. Rose, *Limited livelihoods: gender and class in nineteenth-century England* (Berkeley: University of California Press, 1992)

Barbara Rosenwein, *Emotional communities in the early Middle Ages* (Ithaca, N.Y.; London: Cornell University Press, 2006)
Elizabeth Roberts, *A woman's place: an oral history of working-class women, 1890–1940* (Oxford: Blackwell, 1984)
Ellen Ross, *Love and toil: motherhood in outcast London, 1870–1918* (Oxford University Press, 1993)
  'Introduction', *Slum travellers: ladies and London poverty, 1860–1920* (Berkeley, London: University of California Press, 2007), 1–39
B. Seebohm Rowntree and Bruno Lasker, *Unemployment: a social study* (London: Macmillan and Co, 1911)
Terri Sabatos, 'Father as mother: the image of the widower with children in Victorian art' in Broughton and Rogers, *Gender and fatherhood* (2006), 71–84
Valerie Sanders, 'What do you want to know about next? Charles Kingsley's model of educational fatherhood' in Broughton and Rogers, *Gender and fatherhood* (2006), 55–70
  The tragi-comedy of Victorian fatherhood (Cambridge University Press, 2009)
W. Seccombe, 'Patriarchy stabilized: the construction of the male breadwinner wage norm in nineteenth-century Britain', *Social History*, 11 (1986), 53–76
  Weathering the storm: working-class families from the industrial revolution to the fertility decline (London: Verso, 1993)
Robert Browning Settlement [Francis Herbert Stead], *Eighteen years in the Central City Swarm, an account of the Robert Browning Settlement at Walworth* (London: W. A. Hammond, 1912)
  To the workers of the world: an appeal for personal religion by eight members of parliament (London: W. A. Hammond, 1913)
Jade Shepherd, 'One of the best fathers until he went out of his mind: paternal child-murder, 1864–1900', *Journal of Victorian culture*, 18:1 (2013), 17–35
Carol Smart, *Personal life: new directions in sociological thinking* (Cambridge: Polity Press, 2007)
Peter Stearns, *Be a man! Males in modern society* (New York: Holmes and Meier, 1979)
  and Carol Zisowitz Stearns, *Anger: the struggle for emotional control in America's history* (Chicago; London: University of Chicago Press, 1986)
Gareth Stedman Jones, Working-class culture and working-class politics in London 1870–1900, *Journal of Social History*, 7: 4 (1974), 460–508
Carolyn Steedman, *Landscape for a good woman* (London: Virago, 1986)
  Past tenses: chapters on writing, autobiography and history (London: Rivers Oram, 1992)
Julie-Marie Strange, *Death, grief and poverty, 1870–1914* (Cambridge University Press, 2005)
Julie-Marie Strange, 'Speechless with grief: bereavement and the working-class father' in Rogers and Broughton, *Gender and fatherhood* (2006), 138–52
  "Tramp: sentiment and the homeless man in the Late-Victorian and Edwardian City." *Journal of Victorian Culture* 16:2 (2011), 242–258

Naomi Tadmor, *Family and friends in Eighteenth Century England: household, kinship and patronage* (Cambridge University Press, 2001)
Melanie Tebbutt, *Women's talk? A social history of 'gossip' in working-class neighbourhoods, 1880–1960* (Aldershot: Scolar, 1995)
  'Rambling and manly identity in Derbyshire's Dark Peak, 1880s–1920s', *Historical Journal*, 49:4 (2006), 1125–153
Ann Thwaite, *Glimpses of the wonderful: the life of Philip Henry Gosse* (London: Faber, 2002).
  Edmund Gosse: a literary landscape (Stroud: Tempus, 2007)
John Tosh, *A man's place: masculinity and the middle-class home in Victorian England* (New Haven: Yale University Press, [1999] 2007)
Robert Tressell, *The ragged trousered philanthropists* (London: Flamingo, [1914] 1993)
James Vernon, *Hunger: a modern history* (Cambridge (MA) and London: Belknap Press of Harvard University Press, 2007)
David Vincent, *Bread, knowledge and freedom: a study of nineteenth-century working-class autobiography* (London and New York: Methuen, 1981).
  Poor citizens: the state and the poor in the twentieth century (London: Longman, 1991)
Andrew Walker, 'Father's pride? Fatherhood in industrialising communities' in Broughton and Rogers, *Gender and fatherhood* (2006), 113–125
Janet Walker, 'The traumatic paradox: documentary films, historical fictions, and cataclysmic past events', *Signs*, 22:4 (1997), 803–825
Diana di Zerega Wall, 'Sacred dinners and secular teas: constructing domesticity in mid-nineteenth century New York', *Historical Archaeology* (1991), 69–81
Tracey Warren, 'Conceptualising breadwinning work', *Work, Employment and Society*, 21 (2007), 317–36
John Welshman, *Underclass: a history of the excluded, 1880–2000* (London: Hambledon Continuum, 2006)
Martin Wiener, 'Alice Arden to Bill Sikes: changing nightmares of intimate violence in England, 1558–1869', *Journal of British Studies*, 40:2 (2001), 184–212
Deborah Wynne, *Women and personal property in the Victorian novel* (Aldershot: Ashgate, 2010)
Peter Wilmott and Michael Young, *Family and kinship in East London* (Harmondsworth: Penguin, 1962)
  The symmetrical family a study of work and leisure in the London region (Harmondsworth: Penguin, 1980)

UNPUBLISHED DOCTORAL THESES

Megan Doolittle, 'Missing fathers: assembling a history of fatherhood in Mid-Nineteenth Century England', PhD Thesis (University of Essex, 1996)
Tim Fisher, 'Fatherhood and the experience of working-class fathers in Britain, 1900–1939', Unpublished PhD thesis (University of Edinburgh, 2004)
Laura King, 'Fatherhood and masculinity in Britain, c.1918–1960', PhD thesis (University of Sheffield, 2011)

WEBSITES

Selina Todd, 'History from below: modern British scholarship' in 'The future of history from below', www.manyheadedmonster.wordpresscom/2013/08/23/selina-todd-history-from-below-modern-british-scholarship/.

Luke Fildes, *The Widower* (1874) www.victorianweb.org/painting/fildes/paintings/2.html

Thomas Faed, *Worn out* (1868) www.christies.com/LotFinder/lot_details.aspx?intObjectID=4051698

Arthur Stocks, *Motherless* (1883) www.lookandlearn.com/history-images/P000108/Motherless?img=2&search=yew%20trees&cat=all&bool=phrase

Index

Abrams, Lynn 1, 2, 3n.5, 6, 181, 212
Acorn, George 29, 162–3, 179
Ainslie, Robert 181n.17
Aldred, Guy 26n.17, 27–8, 45, 84n.9, 129–30, 134, 138, 142, 181
Ambrose, Ernest 174–5
Andrews, Elizabeth 35–6, 109n.99
Anthony, Francis 190n.62
Armstrong, Chester 124–5, 196; Neil 116n.14
August, Andrew 3n.8, 114n.10

Bailey, Joanne 65n.56; Peter 113n.10, 134–5, 147n.5; Victor 60
Bakhtin, Mikhail 147n.5
Baldry, George 39n.61, 185–6, 188
Barber, George 13n.39
Barclay, Thomas 52n.15, 84n.9, 133–4, 156
Barlow Brooks, Joseph 105–6
Barnett, Henrietta 93
Beaven, Brad 113n.10, 120n.28
Bell, Thomas 33n.44, 83n.8, 126
Beveridge, William 49n.3
Blunt, Alison 83n.4
Bosanquet, Helen Dendy 85
Boswell, Silvester Gordon 24n.12, 31, 43, 107
Bourke, Joanna 3n.8, 23, 56n.27, 108, 112n.5, 182
Bourne, George 114n.12, 137n.79, 162
Bower, Fred 33, 106–7, 155
Bowley, A. L. 49n.3
Bowyer, William 14, 151–2, 154, 186
Boyer, George 50n.5
Britten, Barnabas 40, 188, 191
Brooks, Nelsie 95n.56
Brown, Percy 20n.55, 123n.33; Roy Chubby 176; William J. 16, 159, 189
Broughton, Trev Lynn 6–7

Bryden, Inga 83n.4
Bryson, Elizabeth 24n.12, 76–7, 87–8, 97–8, 109n.99, 116–17, 129–31, 137, 189–90
Buettner, Elizabeth 5n.13
Bullard, Reader 75–6, 168
Burdett, Carolyn 15n.48
Burgess, Adrienne 2–3, 214
Burke, Thomas 166–7; Mick 128
Burnett, John 50n.7
Burton, H. M. 27n.22, 89–90, 134

Cadbury, Edward 87
Campion, Sidney 33n.44, 41–2, 168–9, 172, 173–4, 177–8, 188–9, 205
Cardus, Neville 94, 181
Centreprise, 39n.61, 110n.22, 183n.30
Chandler, Julia 170–1
Chaplin, Charles 149–50
Chinn, Carl 3n.8, 112n.6
Christie, A. V. 14, 34, 160, 181
Citrine, Walter 7–14, 33n.44, 39n.61, 90
Clark, Anna 5n.17, 22n.4, 153n.21; Candace, 28n.28, 30n.33
Claughton, Thomas Legh 181n.17
Clynes, J. R. 103n.79
Cohen, Deborah 102n.77
Collins, Anne 16n.49
Coppard, A. E. 41–2, 64–5, 139
Crawford, J. H. 31–2
Creighton, Colin 22n.2
Croll, Andy 38n.58, 72n.74, 114n.10
D'Cruze, Shani 51n.8, 153n.21

Daly, Kerry 82n.3
Darby, Aubrey 26n.17
Davidoff, Leonore et al. 7n.21, 178n.5
Davies, Andrew 23n.6, 112n.6; David R. 13, 123, 203–4; Fred 68–9

231

Index

Davis, Jessica Milner 152n.17, 153
Dayus, Kathleen 44–5, 119–20, 164–5, 181n.18, 192, 197
Delap, Lucy 6n.20, 145, 146–7, 150, 163
Dermott, Esther 51–2
Dixon, Thomas 16n.51
Dolling, Robert 111, 144
Don't go down the Mine Dad, 36
Doolittle, Megan 6, 17, 22n.5, 23n.9, 51, 53n.19, 62n.42, 84–5, 92n.44, 93, 95, 124, 178, 195
Dr. Ridge's food 169
Durbach, Nadja 196n.82

Eagleton, Terry 33n.41 b
The Economic Club, 57, 66, 72–3, 86n.17, 88n.26, 97n.62, 138n.81
Edwards, Wil 37
Eldred, John 42–3, 45–7, 136, 187, 197, 201n.95

Faed, Thomas 92, 101–2
Fildes, Luke 101
Film, *A Day in the Life of a Coal Miner* 82, 85; *Durham Miner's Gala* 25
Finn, Ralph 20n.54
Fisher, Tim 5n.15, 182n.27, 193n.73
Flint, Elizabeth 200
Foakes, Grace 14, 24n.17, 26, 87n.23, 103, 142–3, 157–8
Foley, Alice 93, 115–16, 140–1, 158, 179, 185, 203
Francis, Martin 16n.51
Freedgood, Elaine 103n.82
Friedman, Sam 160n.40
Frost, Ginger 5n.17

Gagnier, Reginia 11n.31, 12n.34, 25n.16, 29, 32
Garratt, Vero W. 43n.73, 52n.16, 103n.78, 179, 182–3
Gatrell, Vic 158n.31
Gair, Arthur 83n.8
Gibbs, Rose 64n.50, 67–8, 71
Gillis, John 3–4, 24, 47n.81, 85n.16, 114–15
Gissing, George 96
Goffman, Erving 125
Goldberg, Susan 16n.49
Goldstein, Donna 147–8, 176
Gordon, Eleanor 5n.13, 83
Gorst, Nina 91–2
Gosling, Harry 34, 99n.79, 175
Gosse, Edmund 195

Gresswell, Fred 34–5, 99n.79, 123, 180
Greven, Philip 180n.14
Griffiths, James 126–7, 173
Grossek, Mark 34, 117–18, 173
Grundy, Anthony George 67

Hackett, Nan 12n.34, 25n.16
Hallam, Elizabeth 105n.86
Hamer, Thomas 95n.56
Hamlett, Jane 102n.77
Hammerton, James A 51n.8
Hardy, George 89, 112n.5
Harris, Harry 39n.61, 40, 118–19, 168–9, 172, 173–4; José 50n.7
Harvey, Karen 83, 10
Hastings, Frederick 58–9, 71
Hawker, Henry 132
Heard, Percy A. 27n.22
Hennock, Ernest 50n.5
Hewitt, Martin 85n.14, 114n.10, 123n.34
Hill, Octavia 108
Hillyer, Richard 143, 180, 188n.55
Hobsbawm, Eric 63n.48
Hocking, Silas 95
Hoggart, Richard 103
Honeyman, Katrina 23n.8
Horrell, S. 22n.2, 23n.9
Howard & Co.'s comic annual 169n.64
Houlbrook, Matt 14
Huggins, Mike 112n.4
Humphries, Jane 22n.2, 52n.13
Hunt, T. J. 83n.8, 119

Inman, Philip 20n.54
Ittmann, Karl 23n.6

Jackson, Louise 149n.12; Thomas A. 33, 107, 128, 132
Jasper, Albert S. 155–7, 175
Jermy, Louise 131, 149, 197, 201
Johnes, Martin 112n.4
Johnson, Paul 84n.10
Jones, Ben 142n.94; Gareth Stedman, 113n.10, 147n.5; Henry 95n.58, 123–4; Jack 36–9, 43–4, 70, 99n.70, 108–9, 161–2, 167–8, 174, 191–2, 193–4, 200, 204; Lewis 39–40

Keating, Joseph 52n.15, 133–4, 163
Kestner, Joseph 100n.72
Kift, Dagmar 147n.5
Kightly, Charles 36n.55, 188n.51

Index

King, Laura 5n.15, 14n.44, 47n.81, 113n.7, 138n.81, 167n.56, 178n.5, 182, 183n.32
Kirk, Neville 113n.10
Kirkwood, David 30–1, 41, 139–40, 190–1
Koven, Seth 6n.19
Kremer-Sadlik, Tamar 82n.3

Langhamer, Clare 14, 83n.4, 112n.6
Lauder, Henry 179–80
Lawrence, Jon 143n.97
Lawson, Jack 28–9, 90, 127–8, 138
Lax, W. M. 33n.44, 34, 41, 63, 99n.79, 123n.36, 125–6, 168, 184
Lees, Lynn Hollen 50n.5
Lefebvre, Henri 139n.87
Levine-Clark, Marjorie 22n.4, 50
Lewis, Jane 3n.8, 22n.2, 50n.7
Llewelyn, Michael 67, 105, 136–7
Loane, M. E. 1–2, 39, 99, 167n.57, 100, 111, 115n.12, 131, 132, 138, 171–2, 183–4, 188, 213–14
Lonsdale, Thomas S. 169

McCormack, Matthew 5n.17
McDermid, Jane 197n.85
McGovern, John 181n.18
McKeon, Michael 83n.4
MacDonald, Donald 129n.52
MacDonald, Ramsay 25n.14, 177–8, 205
Macgill, Patrick 199
Mainsbridge, Albert 33n.44, 121–2
Martin, Anna 27n.21; Jack 91, 103n.78, 122n.32, 135, 179
May, Betty 26n.17, 52, 84n.9, 122n.32, 179
Medhurst, Andy 146–7, 160, 176
Meek, George 189
Middleton Jacob 151n.16, 181n.18
Miller, Daniel 26, 30, 85
Morrison, Herbert 26, 42n.71, 117, 206–7
Muir, Edwin 13, 35, 78–9, 109, 134, 138, 148–9, 181, 187–8

Nelson, Claudia 3–4, 180

O'Mara, Pat 26n.17, 52n.14, 103n.78, 152–4, 185, 201
Owens, Alastair et al. 84n.11

Paton, John 162
Pederson, Susan 50n.7
Penn, Margaret 90–1, 190
Pertierra, Anna 45n.75
Pettigrew, Elsie 98

Petty, Florence 57, 105
Pollock, Linda 16n.51, 180n.14
Potts, Leonard 151n.17
Powell, Margaret 27n.22
Pugh, Edwin 170–1
Purkiss, Edward 196–7

Ratcliffe, George 42n.71, 205
Rathbone, Eleanor 72
Reakes, George 182n.24
Reddy, William 16n.51
Reeves, Maud Pember 70n.65, 72
Reilly, George 20n.54
Rennie, Jean 163–4
Robert Browning Settlement 25
Roberts, Elizabeth 3n.8, 23n.6, 98n.65; Robert 43n.73, 87n.22, 88–9, 103–4, 106n.89, 155, 156, 201n.95
Rogers, Helen 6–7, 10, 99n.68, 178n.5
Roper, Michael 13n.38, 15, 25n.12, 28
Rose, Jonathan 123n.34, 125n.40, 130n.53, 163; Lionel 68n.63; Sonya O. 23n.8, 50n.7
Rosenwein, Barbara 16n.51, 30n.36
Ross, Ellen 2–3, 6n.19, 23n.7, 24, 27n.21, 46, 52n.16, 56n.27, 70–2, 86n.18, 128n.49, 132n.63
Rowntree, B. Seebohm 19, 49–50, 51, 53passim, 62, 65–6, 70n.66, 71, 72, 73–6, 87n.21, 94, 97
Royce, James 43n.73, 83n.8, 165–6

Sabatos, Terri 101–2
Sanders, Valerie 5, 51, 63, 83, 113, 138n.83, 169n.64, 197–8
Scannell, Dolly 94, 159, 182, 192
Seccombe, Wally 22n.2, 23n.6, 81
Shaw, Sam 43n.73, 58, 71, 84n.9, 91, 183, 201–2
Shepherd, Jade 60
Shinwell, Emanuel 42, 63–4, 207–8
Slater, Lilian 36n.54, 65n.56, 89, 92, 112n.5, 119, 120, 138n.84, 141–2, 158–9, 196n.82
Smart, Carol 3n.9, 16
Smith, Emma 26n.17, 79–80, 99, 149–50; Rodney, 126, 172, 184–5, 191, 195
Snell, Henry 148
Stearns, Peter 16n.51
Stewart, Bob 128n.49
Stocks, Arthur 102
Southgate, Walter 27n.22, 32, 95–6, 107, 138, 159–61, 167–9, 172–4, 182, 208–9

Stamper, Joseph 39n.61, 52–3, 64, 75, 77–8, 99n.70, 118, 120–1, 123, 135–6, 138, 161, 173, 191, 200–1
Steedman, Carolyn 3, 5, 13, 46
Strange, Julie-Marie 63n.48, 198n.86, 23n.7

Taylor, Allan 61–2;
  Bernard Taylor, 27–9, 35n.51
Tebbutt, Melanie 112n.6, 120n.28
Thwaite, Ann 195n.78
Todd, Selina 214n.3
Toole, Joseph 59, 120
Tosh, John 4, 83, 112–13, 138n.83, 180, 187, 188
Tremewan, Tom 205–6
Tressell, Robert 21, 59–61, 88
Turner, Ben 66–7;
  James 118, 125, 137, 198–9

Vernon, James 71n.71
Vincent, David 10, 15n.46, 25n.13, 33n.43, 50n.5, 123n.34, 125n.40

Walker, Andrew 5n.17;
  Janet, 149n.13
Wall, Diana di Zerega 103n.81
Wallace, Edgar 20n54
Warr, Thomas 27n.22
Warren, Tracey 22n.3
Watkin, Henry 89, 92n.45, 112n.5, 116, 141, 166, 173, 192–3, 196n.82
Welshman, John 49n.3
Westwater, Thomas A. 112n.5, 135, 168, 195–6, 204
Wiener, Martin 51n.8
Woodward, Kathleen 77
Wynne, Deborah 103n.82

Printed in Great Britain
by Amazon